Client Care for Lawyers

an Analysis and Guide

Client Care for Lawyers

an Analysis and Guide

Second Edition

by

Avrom Sherr

Woolf Professor of Legal Education,
Institute of Advanced Legal Studies,
University of London

SWEET & MAXWELL

Published in 1999 by Thomson Reuters (Legal) Limited
(Registered in England & Wales, Company No 1679046. Registered Office
and address for service: 100 Avenue Road, London, NW3 3PF)
trading as Sweet & Maxwell

Reprinted 2010 by TJI Digital Ltd, Padstow, Cornwall.

For further information on our products and services, visit
www.sweetandmaxwell.co.uk

ISBN 978 0 421 57 470 0

No natural forests were destroyed to make this product;
only farmed timber was used and replanted

A CIP catalogue record for this book
is available from the British Library.

TO

MY MOTHER AND FATHER

Charlotte and Louis Sherr

AND

TO

Claire Montgomery, Jill Evans

Neil O'May, Judy Kemish

and

Geoffrey Bindman

who exemplify care for their clients

PREFACE TO THIS SECOND EDITION

The world of legal education has changed since the first edition of this book was published 13 years ago. The teaching of legal skills, such as client interviewing, client handling and the process of the lawyer client relationship, is now the norm within practical and professional legal education courses. The direct teaching of other legal skills such as legal writing, case and statute method and legal research are also now to be found more often in undergraduate legal education curricula. Most teachers agree that a more direct approach to the teaching of all such skills is necessary—although there is still much discussion on the appropriate amount of such teaching and the level at which it should be studied. For a summary of the current position as well as a vision of the possible future see the "Report on Legal Education" from the Lord Chancellor's Advisory Committee on Legal Education and Conduct, May 1996.

Interestingly, what has not changed is the amount of reported research into the operation of legal skills, that is into the actual subject matter which is being taught. There is burgeoning interest in literature about teaching skills and the beginnings of some theoretical material on this, but the mystical quality that surrounds the exact nature of legal work has still somehow prevented the opening up of professional portals to rigorous enquiry. So, although there is much more *teaching* about legal skills, there is still much too little known about what they are *in practice*, how they are best undertaken, and therefore how best to develop them in new lawyers.

The first edition of this book was based on the results of some early research on client interviewing carried out both in the laboratory, looking in particular at methodology, and empirically inside lawyers' offices to discover the practical reality and deficiencies of then current practice. The sub-title of the book *"Client Interviewing for Lawyers; an Analysis and Guide"*, reflected the attempt that the book made to provide practical teaching advice—just like any other of the skills teaching materials which followed in the succeeding 10 years. The book was based not on personal intuition alone, but more firmly within a structure informed by the literature concerning interviewing generally within the helping professions and the laboratory and empirical studies mentioned. The publishers were more keen to stress the teaching nature of the work, whilst the author wanted very much to report the research in order to provide more effective teaching material. In publishing terms the compromise seems to have worked and it is not intended therefore to change that mix in the Second Edition. But the difference in this approach needs to be noted, especially by those who may be seeking a deeper, or more academic, or more real base to their teaching or study of this particular set of legal skills. For this reason the book may well be important now in some undergraduate legal programmes, as it has been in practice and at the vocational stage until now. In continuing the particular compromise reached, this book also provides a little further research background in the areas covered to reflect the author's own work and other research which has taken place since. Although the basic techniques of client interviewing have not changed enormously over the last 13 years, what we know about teaching them has definitely grown, as has the wealth of teaching material which has since appeared covering nearly all areas of legal skills.

What has also changed in the intervening period is the atmosphere and culture concerning such issues. This is not only a factor within the legal profession and legal education. Medical education (sometimes sooner to change than law) has undergone a considerable movement with regard to training in communication skills which is now the orthodoxy rather than a strange and revolutionary alternative. Ley summarises these in his excellent work *Communicating with Patients* (London Chapman and Hall 1993), p. xv. In addition, many medical schools and teaching hospitals have moved over to a system of "problem based learning" which enhances the context of the issues to be considered in relation to each patient and therefore emphasises the importance of good patient handling in order to achieve an understanding of the wider "problem" and the patient's "needs". Within law, although professional legal education has entirely moved over to a skills based approach, and there is now at least an acceptance that some elements of legal skills can be taught directly, there is still a nagging reluctance to let go of the "rigour" of previous systems of training for the "softer" option of skills. I suspect that these are teething problems only and the correct balance will be achieved in time. An approach to skills study which involves a more academic base would, naturally, provide rather more intellectual rigour—but not necessarily within the discipline acceptable to the practising profession. The approach of this book may therefore not necessarily, for some skills critics, answer this particular problem. The "lack of rigour" may of course only be the dinosaurs reacting to innovation, but it could also be that the quality of skills training (rushed, as the teachers had suddenly to become expert in this new field) has not yet reached an optimum level. Each of these would seem to be curable simply through the progression of time.

Noting the journey ahead, it is important to see how far we have gone. The climate has changed considerably so that innovation has become norm and the norm is now under further reform. And more importantly, the professional bodies themselves (which were the barriers to such change in England and Wales), have now placed themselves at the forefront of change with the new Bar Vocational Course and the Legal Practice Course for solicitors.

Other new elements within this edition, and the environment within which it is being published, are indicative of other changes within the profession and professionalism. Both the Bar and Solicitors' ethical codes have grown, and the Solicitors' Book of Conduct has grown exponentially during the period. This is due to a number of factors. A more heterogenous profession, coping with the commercialisation of its work may need a clearer and more comprehensive set of rules. Specialisation spawns its own ethical needs and the deregulation which has followed the advent of Licensed Conveyancers, and the implementation of the Courts and Legal Services Act 1990 had engendered an increase in regulations for the legal profession and its competitors. The standardisation of practice necessitated by low fees for legal aid work and the industrialisation of legal services in some subject areas has produced the need for rules which are concerned far more with competence of the work than the previous system of rules which was largely about etiquette between lawyers and the court. These competence rules are perhaps those most important for the purposes of this book. The effect of Rule 15, the written standards of guidance under it and its repetition within the new Practice Management Standards cannot be minimised. And the Appendices to the book now detail all of these new rules and aspects of guidance for the profession.

The combined effects of the skills movement and of rules of conduct incorporating rules of competence in legal work, has been the creation of an articulated framework for certain parts of legal work for the first time. The production of such a framework has involved professional bodies, practitioners, academics and legal writers in accomplishing an, at least partially, agreed approach. Previously the approach to legal work was passed on through the medium of apprenticeship by word of mouth from generation to generation. Hence its message was diffuse, intense, individualistic, personal and variable. The new regime and orthodoxy provides the opposite of this—a standardised, almost agreed, unvarying, step-like checklist formation, sanitised of personality, credo and culture but intended to accomplish a strong basic standard of work response. What deficiencies there may be in the new system of teaching and "formation" will need to be addressed: its advantages cannot be seen in insolation.

I have argued elsewhere (see Sherr, "The Warwick Clinical Legal Programme Twenty Five years On", *Frontiers of Legal Scholarship* (Wilson ed., 1995)) that skills teaching should be thought of, and if possible taught, in the context of the legal work which was its seedbed both here and in the United States. Part of the reason for this is the necessity to provide the richness of personality and humanity, and the reality of practice to the otherwise rote conditioning of behaviour. The passing on of the mantle of legal professional practice through the traditional method had the great benefit of the richness of personality of those who imparted it. The intensity of personal beliefs wrought in the fire of experience would transmit to an apprentice, articled to the skilled artisan. These would have proved an attractive teacher where they were successful, and something of this element must now be found elsewhere. It would be a highly-skilled legal skills teacher who could transmit that level of fire, belief and personality three times a day on so many days a year. But the strength of personal clients' needs might sometimes have the same effect through the medium of a clinical programme, which might provide something of the same intensity and practical reality.

Another result of a standardised framework for professional legal practice is that, for the first time, there will be wide ranging and grand discussion of these issues between practitioners, if only in order to attack the new orthodoxy. This is perhaps the most important result of all. By articulating one approach, a full discussion of all possible appoaches can occur. Such discussions lead to further demystification of legal work which is of interest to researchers for its descriptive capacity, and to teachers for the production of good training material. But standardising legal work could fossilise it and over-protect it from review and innovation— another effect which the future will need to guard against.

Avrom Sherr
Russell Square,
London
July 1998

ACKNOWLEDGMENTS

I would like to thank the copyright holders for permission to reprint material from the following publications:

Bellow, G., and Moulton, B., *The Lawyering Process—Materials for Clinical Instruction in Advocacy* (The Foundation Press, Inc., 1978)

Berlin, Sir Isaiah, "Two Concepts of Liberty" in *Four Essays on Liberty* (Oxford University Press, 1969)

Byrne, P.S. and Long, B.E., *Doctors Talking to Patients* (DHSS, HMSO 1976)

Goodpaster, G.S., "The Human Arts of Lawyering" (1975) 27 *Journal of Legal Education* 33

Greenebaum, E., *Understanding Clinical Experience* (unpublished 1986)

Kennedy, I., *The Unmasking of Medicine* (Allen & Unwin, 1981)

The Expense of Time (Law Society, 3rd ed. 1981)

Law Society, *The Guide to the Professional Conduct of Solicitors* (7th ed., 1996)

Ley, P., "Psychological Studies of Doctor—Patient Communication", in Contributions to Medical Psychology (Rachman S.J., ed.) (Pergamon Press, 1977)

Morley, I.E. and Hosking, D.M., "Decision-making and Negotiation: Leadership and Social Skills" in *Social Psychology and Organizational Behaviour* (Gruneberg, M. and Wall, T., ed.) (John Wiley & Sons, 1984)

Nizer, J., *The Implosion Conspiracy* (Doubleday & Company, Inc., 1973)

Shaffer, T.L. and Redmount, R.S., *Legal Interviewing and Counselling* (Matthew Bender, 1980)

There are many other people to thank. Lorraine Sherr gave constant help and advice from initial ideas through to completion. On the other hand Ari Refael Sherr and Ilan Gavriel Sherr by day did their best to prevent the appearance of this book and Yonatan Dan Sherr did his best by night. The Law School of UCLA (special thanks to Paul Bergman) gave me time to write, a place to think and people to talk to. Funding came from the Nuffield Foundation and the (then) Social Science Research Council. Blessings came from the Law Society who gave permission for solicitors' involvement in the research.

Carol Chapman, Phil Trull and Margaret Wright unerringly typed and word processed their way through tapes and drafts and tables. Paul, Tom, Lo, Philip Britton and Dad read drafts of chapters. Alan Paterson gave encouragement by way of shuttle tickets to Scotland and meals at Hendersons.

Thinking back on its inception, "Ben", Mr. D.W. Benjamin (who died tragically earlier this year) was the only person I met in practice who was interested in teaching, and introduced me to the idea of teaching the practice of law. William Twining helped by understanding the importance, and some of the difficulty, of what I was doing and encouraging me with it. Tom Hervey, of course, gave the simulated Karate kick that began it all. Peter and Marjorie Smith provided a home from home and confidence boosting throughout. Lou Brown patronised a "Milky Way" to my understanding his child—"Preventive Law." Roger Burridge was a good listener and did not let too many of my ideas run away with me. Julian Eule gets the prize for Succa building and photography. David Lewi's incredulity kept me going.

I would like especially to mention "Cas" Silvester (who died in 1980) and Jennifer Andrew (who died in 1982), two Legal Practice students in whose memory and honour this book was conceived; and all other Legal Practice students from Warwick and UCLA who suffered and assisted in the formulation of the ideas and their practical trial. The cartoons were also drawn by an ex-student, Jerry Glover, who has pointed the suggested ideas with some humour.

My sincerest thanks go to the numbers of lawyers and clients who had the interest and courage to let us film them, but whose names must be preserved in confidentiality. Without them much of what has been written here would have been intuitive only. I am indebted to Professor David Metcalfe for providing some analogous material from the area of medicine in a talk to Legal Practice students in 1976.

Lastly, if faults there be, as I am sure there are, they can all be blamed on Paul Bergman who has bigger shoulders than me, and should learn not always to beat me at squash.

CONTENTS

		Page
Preface		vii
Acknowledgments		xi
Introduction		xv
1	The Lawyer-Client Interview	1
2	Listening	12
3	Questioning	29
4	Advising	50
5	Some Specific Interviewing Problems	80
6	The Continuing Relationship	92
7	Getting Going: the Beginning, not the End	117
8	Client and Case Management Techniques	138
9	Regulation and Guidance for Lawyer Communications with Clients	148
Appendix 1		158
Appendix 2		169
Appendix 3		180
Bibliography		181
Index		183

INTRODUCTION

This is a book about effective interviewing techniques for lawyers. It sets out a step-by-step approach to what should occur in a consultation between lawyer and client. Whilst it is primarily intended for less experienced lawyers and legal advisers it may also serve as a reminder for the more experienced practitioner of how to get the best out of a client. Based on empirical research carried out at the University of Warwick, the book also provides a description of the legal interview which is intended to be useful to law students and researchers generally.

This book is therefore both a learning book on how to interview, as well as an analysis of what occurs when lawyers interview clients. It can be used for private reading, as set material for legal course work, or as informal material for discussion between new lawyers and their principals. Its self-teaching aspects includes self-training exercises and self-monitoring checklists.

Objectives

This book is aimed at introducing lawyers to what is involved in the process of interviewing clients. It intends to build up the confidence of new lawyers by giving information about what is involved in interviewing which could otherwise only be gained by experience on the job. The book also includes a large amount of information gathered from research on lawyers' and other professionals' interviewing practices, which no amount of experience could teach.

Why do lawyers need a book on interviewing clients?

The first interview between lawyer and client is the foundation of a legal case. A lawyer's good interviewing technique is the crucial factor in a correct and full understanding of the facts of the case and the client's wants and needs. Better interviewing techniques save time and effort throughout the handling of a case. The relationship of mutual trust and confidence between the lawyer and client also relies on an effective interview.

This is obviously why interviewing is important but why is it necessary for lawyers to read a book about it? Isn't it possible just to pick it up by the experience of carrying out interviews like all the other skills of practice? There is certainly no substitute for actually doing interviewing. But, just having the experience does not necessarily mean that a lawyer will become a good or efficient interviewer. This book aims to help lawyers and legal advisers to learn *more* from the experience they will gain on the job. It aims to use that experience to accelerate the learning that will naturally occur from interviews which are carried out.

The faults of the examination question approach

By the time young lawyers sit down for their first interview with a client they will usually have been through some four or five years of legal training for university examinations and for the professional qualification. The tenor of those years of legal training will have been to train those students how "to think like a lawyer" but not how to act like one. The application of legal principles, comparing and distinguishing cases and looking up the relevant law will be almost second nature. It is therefore a little frightening to realise how small a part this sort of work plays in a normal practitioner's life.

Whilst law students have been taught largely only to manage legal issues, handling clients' cases often involves immense, complex factual issues and personal emotional issues as well. Young lawyers who have been trained for years to answer legal questions in an examination problem setting with facts laid out neatly within the framework of a 20-minute answer, feel great unease at the uncertainty of real life problems where the facts have not been sifted for legal relevance.

What mistakes are most often made?

The mistakes which lawyers make in interviewing can be divided into two groups. Some more subtle errors are considered later on in the book. But a number of more basic errors seem to occur frequently not just among lawyers but among other professionals such as doctors and business managers who have not had time to think about the interviewing process:

(a) *Legal peg holes.* The most common error is that of rushing to a preliminary view of what is important and concentrating all efforts on a very narrow view of what seems to the lawyer to be legally relevant.

(b) *Meeting and greeting.* Many young lawyers seem to forget ordinary social skills such as getting up out of their desk and chair when the client enters or leaves, or introducing themselves to the client.

(c) *What the client wants.* Lawyers generally complain that they are not always able to find out what the client really wants, and of being pestered by telephone calls from uncertain and unsatisfied clients.

(d) *Legalese.* Lawyers sometimes use jargon without realising it.

(e) *Client's agreement.* They do not check properly that the client agrees with a proposed plan of action or even with the lawyer's idea of the facts.

(f) *Own reactions.* Many lawyers do not trust sufficiently their own reactions to a client, preferring the strictly rational process of deciding a case "on the merits" of its facts.

(g) *Questioning.* Some cross-examine a client as though they were in the witness box, testing the story before it has begun to be told.

(h) *Effective listening.* Every lawyer's nightmare is hearing for the first time from the witness box a completely new side of the case. But few lawyers are prepared to spend the necessary time in the beginning to listen effectively to a client and build that client's confidence, thereby saving time later in answering frustrating phone calls and making late demands for detailed information.

What types of lawyer is it for?

This book is intended to be useful to all lawyers whatever the subject matter they deal with and whatever their types of client. Good communication is an essential item for all areas of legal work.

Some would suggest that the sort of material to be covered in a book on interviewing is really only applicable, or more applicable, to the "general practice" lawyer or the lawyer covering "legal aid work" or the lawyer who deals mainly in "crime" or "matrimonial" matters. This is not so. One or two examples may help to explain why.

Conveyancing matters are often given as a prime example of an area where good communication skills are not of great importance. All one needs, it is said, is a set of forms, a book on practical conveyancing and the clients' full names and present and putative addresses. But buying and selling a house is a harrowing business, as anybody who has done so knows (a recent study says it is one of the most traumatic life experiences). People usually buy or sell houses at critical stages in their lives, such as getting married/divorced, moving job, having children or entering retirement. For many people, a residential property transaction is the first contact they have ever had with a lawyer. All of these factors mean that a lawyer needs to take special care and understanding with such clients and find out more about their reasons for moving, in order to provide proper advice and a good conveyancing service, than would appear necessary from a strict, legalistic view of the operation. Lawyers who feel this might be a waste of time should consider.

(i) whether more of their time might not be wasted by continuous client telephone calls resulting from the lawyer's lack of understanding of the client's anxiety and therefore the lawyer's inability to alleviate it;

(ii) whether some of the other critical events consequent upon moving house might not be susceptible to legal help which that lawyer could provide and be paid for, *e.g.* drafting wills for prospective parents and retiring couples, advising on new job contracts or cases of unfair dismissal for people moving job; and

(iii) since the average family moves home once every seven years, the benefits that might accrue in the future by retaining the clients for their next conveyance. The collapse of the statutory ban on non-solicitor conveyancing has exaggerated the need for solicitors to provide a better and wider service than their competitors. Unless clients really feel they are better served by solicitors, conveyancing, which represents over 50 per cent of solicitors' work, will be lost.

A second example, which seems more difficult an argument to refute, concerns "commercial" work. The larger firms, who specialise, so the argument goes, in the affairs of big business do not deal with personal matters or matters affected by emotions. Lawyers in these firms, when they meet their clients, are dealing with people from the same social background as themselves and often with other professionals and "in-house" lawyers. Their clients are articulate and have experience of legal terminology, procedure and manners. All that remains, we are told, is for the lawyer to do a business lawyer's job. "No need to play the amateur psychologist."

This view is also quite wrong. Large companies and big businesses, as all good lawyers are aware, also operate on the personalities of those involved. In-house lawyers and individual directors have a particular relationship with the other people they advise, serve or manage. Often a seemingly ideal "legal" solution will be rejected as totally impractical in the real world of business. In other instances there may be problems for a lawyer to balance the needs of the client company (which is, after all, the solicitor's actual client) against the needs of individuals within the management of the company (including the representative who instructs the solicitor), which may be different. In such cases, for example where a solicitor may feel that an individual has made a bad error, or where a piece of litigation is unlikely to be successful, this information may somehow not get through beyond the instructing representative to the chairman of the board. This is often a result of an inadequate understanding on the part of the "commercial" lawyer of what was involved. The human element was not taken into account. Not enough attention perhaps was paid to the client contact's unease about the whole issue, so that not enough questions were asked by the lawyer about the instructing contact's personal involvement in the situation. The good "commercial" lawyer knows all this without having to be told, but it is so much a part of unconscious attitudes that it is difficult to recognise its effects openly. This book aims to encourage more awareness among less experienced lawyers of such issues.

The network of referral

We now know quite a lot from research about how clients find their way to particular lawyers and other professionals. Unlike the search for plumbers or television engineers, which usually occurs through lists like the Yellow Pages, clients rarely find their lawyers in this mannner. Lawyers, and doctors, are found mainly by the personal recommendation of a previous client or patient. This means that every client, however small in terms of the amount of money which that client brings in, is a possible passport to many more. Treating even the most insignificant client properly becomes increasingly important in the fight to retain legal work.

An understanding relationship with each client, and confidence in the work the solicitor is performing have become necessities for the future of the profession. The growth in "consumerism" generally has not left lawyers with the best of public images. We must take note of the major criticisms of the profession. Poor communication in relation to work on cases, delay, and cost, heads the list. We have to increase our understanding of what goes wrong in interviews and how to become more effective communicators with our clients. This book is aimed at taking the first major step in that direction.

Chapter One

THE LAWYER-CLIENT INTERVIEW

An interview as described in this book is a meeting between a lawyer or legal adviser and a client for the purpose of dealing with a client's work, needs or problems. This chapter begins by exploring the importance of the interview in the context of legal work. It then goes on to discuss how a lawyer might prepare for the interview. The chapter concludes by presenting an outline of what should occur in an interview and explains how succeeding chapters will go in more detail through the specific tasks involved in a lawyer's first meeting with a client.

(1) *Centrality of the interview in legal work*
An interview is usually the first step taken by a lawyer in handling any legal matter. It has two main functions. It is the first and most important fact-finding exercise which enables the lawyer to ascertain a good overview of the facts and issues of the client's problem or requirements. It is also the beginning of a working relationship between lawyer and client in which both parties need to develop confidence and trust in each other if the lawyer's work is to be carried out effectively.

Clients are especially concerned about such good communication. The figures from the Royal Commission on the Provision of Legal Services headed by (now Lord) Benson show that poor communication is the largest reason for dissatisfaction with their solicitor and good communication one of the most important reasons for satisfaction. Similar findings appear in the research carried out by the Consumers' Association and many of the complaints that arrive at the Law Society and the Lay Observer share similar concerns. Where clients are satisfied with their relationship with their lawyers it also appears that their legal cases are run more effectively.

Such consumerism, in terms of complaints about professionals generally, has grown in recent years. Lawyers are by no means the only profession to have received criticism, for example, much criticism has also been levelled at the medial profession. There appear to be a number of possible reasons for this. The professional disciplines have become more specialised, more fragmented and more complex and detailed in the last few decades. There is more medical knowledge and more law which it is necessary for the professional to learn. As the disciplines grow so does the new terminology develop in order to cope with its intricacies. This often causes further barriers between professionals and lay people.

The market economy generally both encourages and enables consumers to compare and criticise the goods and services they are offered. People are less likely to simply accept without question the treatment they are given. The large growth in home ownership since the war has also brought a greater number of people in contact with lawyers. The legal intricacies of the Welfare State have also involved lawyers in issues to do with the less financially privileged. Lawyers have therefore come into contact in their working lives with people with whom they may not otherwise have mixed socially. The law, rather than being merely the preserve of the propertied elite, has come to be used by wider groups in society. It has therefore become more important to understand the preconceptions and feelings of such clients.

(2)   *Analogy–A visit to the doctor*

> "I've set as my task the unmasking of medicine. It isn't that I think there's something sinister behind the mask. But I do detect a sense of curiosity, of concern, if not disquiet. The practice of medicine has changed. There's a feeling abroad that all may not be well. This feeling grows out of a sense of distance, out of a sense that medicine is in the hands of experts and sets its own path."
>
> Ian Kennedy, Q.C.,
> *The Reith Lectures: Unmasking Medicine*

It is sometimes difficult to understand specifically what is meant by complaints about poor communication. Most young lawyers will not have been to a solicitor's office as a client and may know little of the inside of such an office before they start work there. It is therefore useful to envisage and compare a more familiar situation of which most have some experience—a visit to the doctor. Both situations involve a professional and a lay person coming to that professional for advice or work. It will be easier to discuss the difficulties of other professionals before attempting to be objective about the lawyer's own work.

Intuitively, one can recall a visit to the doctor, or at least the popular image of such a visit. Most people have sat as a prospective patient with some anxiety in a waiting room at a doctor's surgery, having been "screened" in some fashion by a receptionist. The patient glances at the table of magazines and a little furtively at the other patients wondering what their complaints might be, and whether they may be infectious. Finally, by some means or other the patient is called into the doctors surgery, often knowing little more about the doctor who will see them than the doctor's name, and sometimes not even that.

The doctor, burdened by along surgery list, looks up at the patient from a pile of notes and record cards, invites the patient to sit down and asks what the problem is. One can recall that feeling, as a patient, knowing that this is the important opportunity which should not be mishandled. All the partly rehearsed statement of symptoms that has been ging through the patient's mind since telephoning for the appointment begins to come out. The patient reacts as the doctor nods understandingly and listens to the speech sometimes looking through notes of previous consultations.

Then come the questions. How long has that pain been causing difficulty? Where exactly is it felt? How has the patient been sleeping? The doctor appears to be going through a rehearsed pattern of symptoms in order to fit the patient's particular problem into a diagnosis known to medical science, or at least to that doctor. Sometimes the questions seem a little off-beam, irrelevant to the patient's understanding of what is wrong. Sometimes they are directly to the point.

The questioning stops and perhaps a physical examination takes place. With some slight embarrassment the doctor asks the patient to remove or pull aside some article of clothing and the patient is asked to take some deep breaths or react to different pressures on different parts of the body. Very soon the patient is back in a sitting position and face to face with a doctor fast scribbling in the record card and dating a prescription.

With a little persuasion, the doctor tells the patient what is probably wrong, how often the medicine should be taken and perhaps when to return for further consultation. The patient receives the clear message that the consultation is at an end and leaves, thanking the doctor and gratefully clutching the magic prescription in one hand.

Afterwards, the patient may ponder over how he/she might have preferred the visit to the doctor to have gone. What things could the patient have done to make it a more successful visit? What might the doctor have done? What other factors are there that made it a worthwhile (or not so worthwhile) and pleasant (or not so pleasant) experience?

(3) *Back to the lawyer's office*
Later in this chapter the analogy of the visit to the doctor will be used as a scenario to which can be related the basic parts of a legal interview. For the present it may serve as a different lesson. Doctors and all helping professionals should perhaps be trained, or trained better, in how to conduct a consultation. Newer generations of doctors are receiving such training. Lawyers on the other hand, without the benefit of training, may use the experience of having been a patient going to a doctor, to understand what it might be like for a client coming to see a lawyer.

Preparation for the Interview

Mental preparation

> "The horrible thing about all officials, even the best, about all judges, magistrates, barristers, detectives and policemen, is not that they are wicked (some of them are good), not that they are stupid (some of them are quite intelligent), *it is simply that they have got used to it.*"
>
> Chesterton

For most lawyers in practice it is difficult to remember what it was like on the first day that they walked into the university or college to begin the study of law. It is easy to forget just how it felt to be a complete newcomer to all the heavily legal language, the different way of thinking and the books, people and paraphernalia of the law. Yet new clients have to enter the same portals and catch up with all those years of legal education every time they enter a solicitor's office.

Legal education is partly to blame. Like medical education it teaches its students to address themselves more to the professional problem than to the people behind it. With the doctor's surgery analogy still in mind it is worth remembering exactly what used to happen on the first day of medical education. The new entrant to the professional would attend, full of zeal, intent to cure illness, stop disease and help humanity and be met by the cold eeriness of a dead body. Traditionally, the first class of any medical training would be the anatomy lesson. It is difficult to expect doctors to see their patients as real people when their whole view of medicine starts with a dead body which the doctor cannot help any further, but can only learn from as an academic exercise.

Fortunately, medical schools are changing and many students now meet a live patient on their first day, in the company of their supervising teacher. The process of finding ou a live patient's problems is after all rather different from that used to discover what was wrong with a corpse.

How do lawyers fare on this score? On the first day of legal education students are faced usually with the legal equivalent of a dead body–something that the law has done all it can with and now cannot help those people involved any more: a reported case. All they can do with it is cut it up for analysis, criticise it and learn from it. Is it little wonder that lawyers see the people who bring their lives and their problems to them as "divorce cases", "unfair dismissals" and "conveyancing jobs"? What if on the first day of their legal studies law students were given the opportunity to experience law through the needs of a client rather than from reading a textbook or law report? There is probably only one law school in the world where anything like this occurs (Antioch School of Law in Washington). It is difficult even to contemplate such an idea, but the consumer research suggests that lawyers are often even worse than doctors in communicating with their clients.

It is therefore necessary to overcome the barriers that exist. The first step is obviously to recognise that these barriers cause problems to clients, and the task of interviewing clients must be approached with this in mind. Secondly, any of the unnecessary trappings of the legal world which could interfere in the lawyer-client relationship should be removed. A very good place to start with this is the simple physical surroundings of both the reception area and the room in which the interview will be conducted.

Physical preparation

(1) *The reception area*
Most lawyers will have noticed the reception area of their office on the first few days of working there, but soon have grown used to it. The older hands and more senior lawyers in the office, having passed through that area so many times will by now not even notice what is there. New clients, however, may have to spend much anxious waiting time there and it is well worthwhile taking stock of what it will look like to them, and consequently, what their first impression will be.

The problem is therefore how to develop a strategy which allows a lawyer who works in an office periodically to review what the reception looks like to an outsider. The results, though obvious to each newcomer tend to be forgotten quickly with accustomed usage. A few examples of such a "catalogue of the obvious" follow:

   (a) It would be a strange clientele that was *really* interested in two year old copies of *Punch* on the table, together with all the latest editions of the *Law Society's Gazette*.

   (b) Ways in which a dowdy reception are can be tidied up without breaking the office account are almost too obvious to mention but appear to be ignored in many offices. A little redecoration, a few posters or reproduction paintings and a couple of potted plants can work wonders. The provision of coffee or tea, even by machine if necessary, will also make a big difference to the atmosphere as it will in the interview room itself.

   (c) Where clients tend to bring their children with them a corner might be set aside for them with a few toys or children's books.

   (d) New rules permit forms to have available for existing clients a brochure about the firm or office and the sort of work it carries out, giving the names of all the staff and even pictures and short curricula vitae.

(e) When the client comes in, some system of indicting about how long they will have to wait reduces their anxiety and will help their relationship with their lawyer thereafter.

(f) Clear indication of the existence and direction of toilets also makes a substantial difference to a client's well-being.

On the one hand, a relative newcomer to work in the office will be in the best position to review its appearance. On the other hand, newcomers and more junior staff may have more difficulty putting these ideas across and getting them accepted. Whatever, such issues appear so obvious once they are pointed out that it is surprising how many offices suffer from the lack of them.

(2)   The interview room
The appearance of the lawyer's office or other interviewing room should also be assessed. In some offices interviews are conducted in a separate room set aside for the purpose. In others interviews will take place across a desk or table which is also used by the interviewing lawyer for general work. A major factor in the appearance of many lawyer's offices relates to the manner in which work is ordered and arranged. Many solicitors learn a particular way of working in which files are left out on a desk, on the floor or somewhere in the room when it is necessary to do some work on them. An alternative method is to make a list of such files or necessary work, but instead the files themselves are left out to act as a reminder that they need attention. Often cases which need daily attention are left out for long periods. Because of the importance of the papers and documents inside the files, cleaners are carefully instructed not to move anything which looks like it might be important. The result is that desks are piled high with waiting work, as well as telephones, cups of coffee, ash trays and other office paraphernalia, all gathering varying degrees of dust.

Many solicitors manage to keep an entirely empty desk and only bring out the papers they are actually working on at the moment. However the general ethos in the legal profession suggests that a busy lawyer needs a "busy" desk. Accepting this mode of work as fixed, it should be realised it may be somewhat difficult to communicate with a person across a table laden in such a manner.

(3)   Musical tables
Research into the conduct of interviews has shown that is more effective to communicate with someone without a table in-between. Doctors often try to do this by seating their patients at the corner of a table whilst they are at right angles to them, a little down one

side. Seating arrangements may well be very important to the conduct of interviews. Indeed, social psychologists agree that round tables, the shape favoured during negotiations at international summit meetings, are to be preferred. Each person must develop the seating situation and circumstances with which they are most happy. New lawyers tend to prefer placing themselves behind the formality of a table. It is probably more important to realise what the effect is of the choice one makes and to take this into account, than to change habits with which one feels comfortable. Young lawyers who have not yet developed their own style of seating arrangement may find it worthwhile experimenting with something different from the accepted norms to see what effects it has on them and their clients.

In other cultures, especially that of North America, it is common to "personalise" desks and offices with family photographs, degree certificates and prizes at high school. United Kingdom lawyers tend to be more formal and to keep their outside world to themselves whilst at work. Changing the physical surroundings, even just a little, to make them reflect the personal interests of the occupant does help them towards creating a more pleasant working environment for the lawyer. It may also help to tell clients more of what to expect from their lawyers than the conventional office surroundings.

(4) *Preparing for the particular client*
This book largely hypothesises the case of a new client on a new matter. Where the lawyer, or the office, have some prior knowledge of the client, full advantage should be taken of this in order to be as well prepared as possible. It is more advisable however to find out about the client and previous problems, than to try to jump to any conclusion about the nature and extent of the present matter.

Often reception personnel or secretaries will take a message from a new client with a short description of the issue when the client makes an appointment. Such descriptions are rarely helpful and often misleading. It would not usually be sensible to spend time researching an area of law, before hearing from the client's own mouth what the client regards as the details of the case.

(5) *Client collection procedure*
Some lawyer's offices have the luxury of a receptionist or secretary who can meet the client in the reception area and bring them along to the lawyer's office or interviewing room. It certainly adds to the lawyer's sense of importance and is clearly reminiscent of an age gone by, when household staff would show visitors into the receptions rooms of houses. Nowadays, it seems something of a discourtesy to allow clients to make a journey along poorly sign-

posted corridors in order to find a (usually unmarked) room. The defining rule of this process, as with the interview itself, should be for the lawyer to consider how best he or she would prefer to be met and brought in under similar circumstances, and to act accordingly with the client.

With these ideas in preparation for the interview in mind, the interview itself can be analysed.

The Three Stages

An interview may be divided into three parts or stages based upon the relative activities at each stage of the two participants. Returning to the scenario of the visit to the doctor these states, although perhaps not well well performed there, can be seen quite clearly.

In the first, "*Listening*", stage the client (like the patient above) tells the lawyer what the problem is and what the client feels is necessary. This stage is therefore characterised by much talking from the client who is often poised on the edge of the chair, and listening or note-taking by the lawyer.

At the second, "*Questioning*", stage the lawyer begins to take a more clearly active role, questioning the client on details, ironing out ambiguities and filling-in open gaps that have appeared from the client's telling of the story. The lawyer might even carry out a "physical examination" of a letter or other document. The lawyer, like the doctor above, is trying to sort out a view of the facts which falls as easily as possible within the framework of legal subject-matter. This stage may be rounded off by the lawyer's summary of the major facts and the client's wishes, to check with the client they have been properly understood. Lawyer and client generally participate about equally at this stage, with the lawyer gaining the edge on involvement.

In the final, "*Advising*", stage the lawyer either: (1) advises the client on the practical and legal effects of the client's problems and sets out a solution or some alternative solutions and their consequences; or (2) suggests a plan of action which may include carrying out legal research on the problem (if the lawyer is not well versed in that particular area) or finding out more facts before coming to a decision. The lawyer then sets the next contact before terminating the interview. In this stage the activity comes more from the lawyer and it is the client who does the listening.

Breaking down what happens in an interview into these three stages helps inform an understanding of the interview. The beginnings and ends of the different stages may be a little blurred in reality, but this is an adequate description for the purpose of an overview. It also conforms quite closely as a model to experiences at the doctor's surgery, or with any other helping professional. This is because the work involved in professional consultations naturally tends to fall into these sequential stages. This overview is presented as a helpful model through which one can begin to look with more detail at the legal interview.

One other point is worth noting here. The scenario of the visit to the doctor was presented largely from the point of view of a prospective patient, not from the professional's eye view of the doctor. From here onwards the text will be working from the lawyer's standpoint. But it should not be forgotten what it feels like to be a patient, and by analogy what it might feel like to be a client.

(i) *Working in the framework of the stages*

The three basic stages in an interview outlined above have evolved out of research both empirical and theoretical into the way lawyers and other helping professionals carry out their interviews or consultations (see Sherr, 1986), Goodpaster, Redmount, Binder and Price, and Byrne and Long). The full importance of this framework can best be appreciated by what occurs when the stages are either taken in the wrong sequence or stages are missed altogether.

The framework appears to conform to a common sense notion of what should take place in an interview. However, in practice, many professionals jumble the stages or do not give particular stages sufficient attention. For example, the listening stage is often very short in lawyers' interviews. Lawyers often jump to the questioning stage before a client has told their full story. The effect of this is that the area of enquiry is narrowed down too quickly to matters which appear to the lawyer immediately to be legally relevant, but which may not necessarily be the most relevant material, legal or otherwise, to the whole problem. Similarly, in some cases a short listening stage is followed by an advice stage without sufficient questioning in between. The result here is that the lawyer, or the professional, may jump to a conclusion not warranted by all the facts, but only by the facts which the client has so far told.

A last example is of a professional who misses out the final advising stage. This appears to happen quite often in doctor-patient consultations. A patient is sent away with very little hint of diagnosis, prognosis or explanation for any medication. This can sometimes occur in a legal interview as well, where a lawyer not fully conversant with a particular area of the law may send a client away unsatisfied as to what the case is about and what the lawyer is going to do to help.

The Thirteen Tasks

Whilst the three stages form the basic outline of the interview it is necessary to break down what happens in an interview into more detail in order to adapt this learning to practice.

Chapters Two, Three and Four will lay out in detail 13 basic tasks to be performed in a first interview with a client. Most of these tasks apply to subsequent interviews as well, but prime accent will be placed on the importance of the first interview in those chapters. These tasks provide a more detailed framework and therefore a more precise description of how the interview should be performed. In the table below the 13 tasks are set out showing their relationship to the listening, questioning and advising stages. The 13 tasks have evolved through experience from work in researching and training lawyers. They are useful as a training schedule because they are designed to underline for lawyers some of the aspects of interviewing which can most easily be missed. As headings they are not all immediately and understandable and a detailed explanation appears for each of them in succeeding chapters.

Table 1.1   First Interview: the Thirteen Tasks by Stages:

Listening	1. Greet, seat and introduce. 2. Elicit story with opening question etc. 3. Listen carefully to basic outline of personalities and case from client's own unhindered words.	
Questioning	4. Question on facts for gaps, depth, background, ambiguities and relevance. 5. Sum up and recount lawyer's view of facts, *and* check for client's agreement or amend. 7. State advice and/or plan of action and deal with question of funds. 8. Repeat advice/plan or action and check for client's agreement or amend.	6. Note taking
Advising	9. Recount follow-up work to be done by client. 10. Recount follow-up work to be done by lawyer. 11. State next contact between lawyer and client. 12. Ask if "Any Other Business" and deal with it. 13. Terminate, help out and goodbye.	

Conclusion

In this chapter it has been shown that interviewing is important because it is the first and often the most crucial fact-finding exercise in the handling of any client matter. It also forms the basis of the relationship between the lawyer and client. Consumer research and complaints about solicitors have also shown that clients place great store in the communication abilities of their lawyers.

It is helpful to try and see what coming to a lawyer's office for an interview might feel like to a prospective client. By analogy a visit to the doctor was considered, in which the visit was viewed from the perspective of the patient.

Some steps to be taken in both mental and physical preparation were then outlined which might help to overcome some of the barriers experienced by many clients. Lastly the legal interview was broken down into the three stages of listening, questioning and advising. These were then divided further into 13 tasks, to be examined in subsequent pages, which form the framework of a first meeting between lawyer and client.

Chapter Two

LISTENING

This chapter examines the first stage of the interview, the "Listening" stage. Although seemingly the least active stage of the interview for the lawyer it needs the utmost concentration on all the clues, both verbal and non-verbal, intended and unintended, which the client's presentation offers.

"Listening" as it is to be understood in the text, is used to include the skills of "active listening" in which the lawyer must use fine judgement in deciding how best to encourage different clients to explain their needs. The lawyer must take into account the work and time constraints of the law office without transmitting these to the client. The client must be given the immediate feeling of security in being able to tell a story without interruption and in the confidentiality of the relationship. These aims are not easily met, but working through the Stage One tasks will reveal some helpful methods.

Task 1: Greet, Seat and Introduce

One of the most startling results to come out of a study of new articled clerks/trainee solicitors carried out at Warwick University (Sherr, 1986) involved the lack of normal social skills shown within the interview setting. Few new lawyers got up out their chairs, moved from behind their desks and went across the room to greet their new clients at the door. Most appeared to feel so constrained by the formality of the office surroundings and worried about the importance of the task ahead that they completely forgot their ordinary social skills and either remained seated or stood uneasily behind their desks.

Table 2.1–Stage One Tasks

Stage One:	1. Greet, seat and introduce. 2. Elicit story with opening question, etc. 3. Listen carefully to basic outline of personalities and case from client's own unhindered words

From what we know of clients' feelings, judging from the Benson report and other research, individual clients generally only come to see lawyers when they are highly concerned about a particular problem or when they are involved in something which can be of great concern, such as buying or selling a house. Clients have two sets of reasons for anxiety: anxiety concerning the issue or problem itself and anxiety concerning the process for solving that problem. In other words, they are both anxious about their reasons for coming to the lawyer and anxious about whether the lawyer will help them and whether the relationship will be beneficial. Any hesitation on the part of the lawyer in confirming that the lawyer is ready and willing to try to help the client will only serve to further both those sets of anxiety. This heightens the importance of treating all clients with the normal social pleasantries. Clients should be helped with their coats, be shown where to sit and be introduced to the lawyer and any other people in the room and generally made to feel at ease.

"Responsibility for the Client's Case or Matter

1. The client should be told the name and the status of the person responsible for the conduct of the matter on a day-to-day basis and the partner responsible for the overall supervision of the matter.

2. If the conduct or the overall supervision of the whole or part of the client's matter is transferred to another person in the firm the client should be informed and the reasons should be explained.

3. The solicitor should advise the client when it is appropriate to instruct counsel. Whenever the client is to attend a hearing at which he is to be represented, he should be told the name of the solicitor or counsel who it is intended will represent him."

The Law Society's Professional Standards
Published June 1985

Introductions always appear to cause some difficulty. Unlike the normal social exchange, such as at an informal party, it is absolutely necessary for lawyers to know their clients' full names and it is also necessitates that the client be able to remember the lawyer's name. However, taking down a client's full name and address in writing as soon as they walk into the room may have a dampening effect on the first few minutes. It will also sound and feel to the client very much like the bureaucracy of a government office in which they may feel they are treated very much as "second class citizens." It may therefore be best to discover clients' surnames at the beginning and fill in the other details at a later stage when they have had a chance to disclose the story they came to tell.

For the client it may also be difficult to remember new details when anxious about something completely different. Clients therefore have a tendency to forget their lawyer's name very quickly and it is worthwhile trying to give them some help with this later in the interview, either by handing over a card or a compliment slip with the lawyer's name on it. Introduction in terms simply of a mutual exchange of name is probably not sufficient for a legal interview. A client almost certainly has the right to know not only who the lawyer is, but also the lawyer's position in the firm or office if this is material to the handling of the matter. Clients should therefore be told who is to handle the case and who is to supervise, if it is to be overseen by another lawyer or superior. Clients should also be told if someone else in the firm will be carrying out most of the work after the initial lawyer has conducted the first interview. This form of introduction can present some difficulty for a new lawyer such as a trainee solicitor/articled clerk or even for a junior solicitor. Many will find it difficult to explain their particular position or role to a client, and still retain the client's confidence. Full introduction does not need to take place whilst standing on foot in between the door and the office chair. However, it has to be faced at some point in the interview and some preparation should be made for it at the outset so that clients are not misled about the role or status of their interviewers.

Task 2:   *Elicit Story with Opening Question*

One of the major texts on interviews in psychiatry is entitled *The First Five Minutes* (Pittinger, Hackett and Danehy, 1960), it details what should occur during the early part of a psychiatric interview, placing the main importance of the interview on the first five minutes. There is little doubt that what occurs at the beginning of the legal interview also, and the first impression each side has of the other, will colour the relationship from then on.

Many lawyers, including some who have been in practice for some time, prefer to control very closely the form and content of the interview. They appear to do this right from the beginning by firing off sets of questions as soon as they have narrowed the issues down to what they consider to be a "legally relevant" topic.

(1)   *Open and closed*
A differentiation should be made between two types of question: "open" and "closed" questions. An open question is one which leaves it open to the client how it is to be answered. A closed question makes it much more clear what the lawyer wishes the client to answer. There is a continuum between open and closed questions and a question is only more "open" or more "closed" compared with another. In the following excerpt form a real interview (the names have been changed to preserve confidentiality) the lawyer is shown asking first an open question and subsequently much more closed questions on the same topic.

1. Lawyer:	Come on in and sit down.
2. Client:	Thank you very much.
3. Lawyer:	Right now, Mrs Jones what can I do to try and help you?
4. Client:	Er, its a long story.
5. Lawyer:	Alright, its a matrimonial problem is it?
6. Client:	Yes it is.
7. Lawyer:	How long have you been married?
8. Client:	Nearly eight years.
9. Lawyer:	Have you any children?
10. Client:	Yes one, this is the problem, now um, as I say I've been married for, I think its eight years, I'm not divorced yet by the way because my husband committed adultery and you know all what's involved with that.
11. Lawyer:	Yes, yes.
12. Client:	Well the divorce just hasn't sort of been started, to my knowledge anyway. Now, after we separated . . .

In this example the lawyer starts with an open question at no. 3 but narrows down immediately with nos. 5, 7 and 9 which were fired off in quick succession. In this particular interview the client takes over at no. 10, stops the flow of narrow or closed questions and begins to tell her story. Often, however, a client does not have the strength to overcome the lawyer's forcefulness. The interview just continues in the same pattern of a question followed by a one or two word answer, which is a very inefficient and potentially misleading schemer of approach. It is clear by nos. 10 and 12 that all the client really wanted at no. 4 was a few moments reflection, as well as perhaps to indicate that this was not a simple problem. It is much easier to divine such meanings afterwards watching a video-tape or reading a transcript. The skill is to be able to adapt in an interview itself to such differing client needs.

Some interviews begin with a particularly closed form of starting question. It is clear from some of these that the lawyer is working with certain expectations based upon a secretary's, or receptionist's, telephone note. Clients sometimes tell a secretary or receptionist that they have one problem (referred to in the psychological literature as "the presenting problem") when in fact they have a quite different problem which they are not necessarily prepared to divulge to anyone apart from a lawyer they can trust. It seems therefore to be best to ignore any such prior intimations of the nature of the problem and to encourage the client to tell the story anew. It is generally therefore most sensible just to sit down and allow clients to develop the story in their own unhindered words, without much directive prompting from the lawyer. Following introductory remarks, a helpful silence may be the most open question of all.

(2) *Silence*

It is rare for a lawyer to sit waiting patiently at this stage, without an almost immediate response from the client. Both parties know what is expected to happen next, and it is probable that a client who does not begin immediately is simply trying to find the best words. Silences such as this can actually be helpful during an interview, provided they are not being used by one party against the other. An inexperienced lawyer may find such a silence a little threatening. Many appear to start off with a very good general opening question such as "How can I help you?" They then tend to lose their nerve if there is no immediate answer and follow up to quickly with, "why don't you tell me about the divorce then?", very much like the lawyer in the Mrs Jones interview above. Having opened the gate wide with the first question, the next question effectively almost closes it so there is but one small opening for the client to get through.

The question of client reluctance to talk will be addressed later in this chapter. For the present, it is important to understand that, if necessary, further open questions should be attempted if the first does not elicit a full flow of the story. The lawyer's object under these circumstances is to find some manner of facilitating the client to talk. Unfortunately, many interviewers at this stage will immediately start asking a succession of closed questions which narrow down the subject area from the beginning. It is worth remembering that at Stage One the interviewer's job is to listen. The questioning does not start until the next stage.

(3) *The examination question syndrome.*

A major problem which faces a new lawyer, just out of university and professional training, relates to the manner in which all legal issues and problems are dealt with in legal education. Real life is rather more complicated and clients do not present themselves in the same way as the facts of a question in a law examination. Legal training concentrates on the handling of legal uncertainties in relation to a set of given facts. It is mostly the law which is uncertain, rather than the facts. The opposite is true for most cases in legal practice. Perhaps if clients entered the solicitor's office with the heading "Tort" or "Contract" stamped clearly on their foreheads and then immediately delivered themselves of a ten-line set of facts Including perhaps an intended "red herring") then the work of a lawyer would be closer to answering an examination question. Clients, however, are not so obvious in their approach and their problems transcend legal and social boundaries of categorisation. They are also not trained to deliver themselves of a few carefully chosen sentences describing their problem in outline before they go into detail.

For these reasons some lawyers prefer to encourage clients to outline the matter before they tell the whole story. However, for most clients, it is not the natural way of telling a story. Lawyers must therefore adapt to listening to a client, rather than needing to jump to a quick set of conclusions.

Task 3:   Listen Carefully to the Basic Outline of the Personalities and the Case from the Client's Own Unhindered Words

This task, which is the essence of this stage of the interview, appears to be difficult for many to perform. Listening, without interrupting the speaker, is a different process from that which takes place during normal social conversation. It appears to involve an extra set of skills which include certain memory skills and the exercising of patience and concentration.

Problems of listening
In theory, it would be simpler for one conversant not to need to formulate responses or questions in a conversation. It would seem to be easier to devote one's entire attention to another person including not only what they are saying but the manner in which it is said and their general demeanour. Indeed, a great deal can be learned about somebody just by listening to the way they have constructed their story, the issues which seem important to them, as well as noting which areas cause the most unease and which issues they seem reluctant to mention. The ability to do all this, however, appears to be an acquired skill which can only be learned with some practice.

A number of approaches can be helpful in working towards the proper performance of this task. One approach involves the jotting down of short notes of headings which the lawyer may use as a list of issues for attention in the questioning stage. Jotting down these notes, which should be in the shortest form possible so that they do not interfere with the client's flow, has the effect of enabling the lawyer to continue to listen to the rest of what the client is saying without worrying about the issues which need to be raised later. The lawyer's mind can be left clear to listen to what else the client has to say. In Chapter Three the question of note-taking will be considered in more detail. For the purposes of Stage One the lawyer should attempt to develop some method by which eye contact can be maintained with clients for most of their delivery, whistle writing a legible word or two which can be used as a prompt later in the interview.

Another approach for the lawyer is to confine all comments and reactions to simple encouragement for the client to continue to talk during this stage. This is what is meant by "active listening" referred to above. Each interview and each client will be different. Some clients will continue talking with just a nod or a "Hm Hm" to keep them going. Other clients may need a further open question or a reflection back to them of what they have just said in order for them to continue their story. A few examples of these methods can be found later on in the "Mrs Jones" interview, the beginning of which was excerpted above.

1. Client:	After a while I thought well I'd like to see Daniel. Just to see, you know, to put my mind at ease that everything is fine and doing well. And on the first occasion that I went to see Daniel, Daniel clearly remembered me and knew who I was and came away with me for the access because I went to court to actually get the access.
2. Lawyer:	Yes.
3. Client:	I got it and I went down, picked him up and this was the first time I'd seen him after eighteen months and he still remembered me and was quite happy to come away with me. And when we actually got to the bus stop I thought if there is going to be any sort of hassle about him coming away with me its going to be when he realises that he's actually going to get on the bus with me . . .
4. Lawyer:	Mm
5. Client:	. . . and come away with me and I was quite, I was quite um happy about, well not happy about, but I accepted that if he said "No" you know I won't have to push it.
6. Lawyer:	You might have to take him back.
7. Client:	Yes, well in actual fact the woman that my husband lives with, Gwen, came to the bus stop and made quite a big show of "Bye bye Daniel" and Daniel said "Bye bye" and off he walked . . .
8. Lawyer:	Yes.
9. Client:	. . . got on the bus and was fine. Now the order of the court at the time was every fourth Thursday in the month . . .

In the example one can see the lawyer encouraging the client to continue with such "active listening" responses as nos. 2 and 8 "Yes," no. 4 "Mm" and no 6. "You might have to take him back" is a good example of a reflection back to the client of what she has said. It shows more understanding than "Yes" and "Mm" but does not interfere with the client's flow. Any attempt by a lawyer to try to make it clear that the lawyer is attending to, and interested in, what is being said can usually be described as "active listening". The lawyer should be careful not to show any puzzlement or unease.

The aim of these approaches is to allow to develop an atmosphere in the interview that the client is important and will have an important part to play in helping the lawyer to resolve the matter, or in resolving thae matter together with the lawyer. We have said that many lawyers seem to feel the need for close control of the interview, and of the client. However, clients who feel involved in the resolution of their cases are more likely to bother their lawyers far less over the telephone and by letter, and to have a sense of control over their own destiny and therefore provide all the papers, information and witnesses necessary for the lawyer's proper handling of the case. They are less likely subsequently to complain if, and when, there is money to pay. They are more likely, as well, to give a good report to friends and acquaintances which may encourage them also to use the services of the lawyer concerned. Most people find their way to lawyers through the closed net of private recommendations and few simply pick up the Yellow Pages or a legal aid list. Treating all clients from the beginning as important individuals involved in the resolution of their matter may in this manner help the lawyer to beak into the complex network of social referrals which bring other clients to the practice.

There are other important effects of involving the client in this way from the outset. Some interesting research which was carried out with personal injury clients in New York in the 1970s shows that the group of clients involved there in personal injury litigation as plaintiffs were far more satisfied with the lawyers who allowed them some control, or equal control over their cases. Most surprising was the fact that the damages obtained, either through settlement or litigation, by the lawyers and clients who shared control of their cases, was significantly more than the amounts obtained by lawyers who showed more "control" over their clients as well as the case (Douglas Rosenthal, *Lawyer and Client: Who's in Charge?*).

Having looked at the problems of listening, it is now necessary to consider what problems exist in processing and understanding what the lawyer has heard and seen.

Problems in understanding

However careful a lawyer is in listening to a story and the way in which it is told, and however experienced a lawyer is in handling factual investigation, there are a number of difficulties which are endemic to the human processes of perception and information processing which will affect the lawyer obtaining an accurate picture of both what occurred and the client's needs. These difficulties can be divided into to those problems which are personal to the lawyer as information gatherer, and those problems which are personal to the client as information giver, as well as those problems which are a result of the information itself.

(1) *Problems of the information gatherer* /

(a) *Filling-in.* We learn form the psychological literature (Miller, 1956) that our minds are unable to process enormous amounts of information at one time. When we hear something new we therefore, unconsciously, set about placing the new factual information against the background of other things that we know. Even working on a minimum of information, we seem therefore prepared to make assessments and judgements without fully realising that we are making them. Apparently our minds "fill-in" the details of the extra information that we need, on the basis of things that we already know. So, for example, if we hear this short extract (taken once again from a real interview with "Mrs Smith") we might make certain assumptions.

Lawyer: O.K. Has he got another woman?
Client: He hadn't, but he has been seeing another girl yes. But he doesn't want to go for adultery like.

This particular exchange occurred in a first interview in a possible divorce matter. The lawyer was in fact posing questions on each of the five "grounds" for divorce. He did not return to the subject of the "other girl" until much later. Meanwhile, there are numerous unanswered questions which are raised by this little exchange. Some of those questions have direct legal relevance to the case, such as whether there has actually been adultery and whether the husband would admit it. Other questions, which are equally important to the lawyer's handling of the case and understanding other needs of the client would include how the client feels about her husband "seeing" another woman.

There will often be times in an interview where a lawyer cannot immediately ask questions along these lines but has to suspend curiosity in order to hear what else the client wishes to say. Without realising it, it is very easy for the mind to fill in a complete scenario of the husband's behaviour and the wife's reactions with very little foundation for these thoughts. Subsequently it may become more difficult to reopen such areas in the lawyer's own mind because many of the uncertainties will have been partially "filled in" without any active effort. This is why it is useful to make a one-, or two-word note of these issues as they occur in order to return to them later with further sequences of open questions to open up those areas.

(b) *Stereotyping.* Another familiar effect on information seekers with insufficient information is "stereotyping". Hearing a particular phrase, description or epithet or even seeing a particular form of dress or gesture can easily lead a fact-finder into conjuring up a stereotype image of the client or some other character in the story, or even a stereotype of the story itself. It is easy to jump to the conclusion that one case is similar to others, without sufficient evidence for this assumption. There is always so much evidence necessary and so much information available, even in the simplest of cases, that it is very easy during the earlier stages of the interview to gall into the trap of making unwarranted assumptions.

(c) *Identification.* A similar phenomenon is that the lawyer begins to identify either with the client's own predicament or with somebody else mentioned in the case. Such identification can also lead the lawyer to assume similarities in facts or feelings which are not necessarily present in the case in question and therefore mislead the lawyer's view of the case.

(d) *Perception.* There is a vast literature in the discipline of psychology relating to the human perception (see, *e.g.* Klatzky), much of which is helpful in appreciating how we understand each other. "Primacy" and "recency" effects are well noted. Items we hear or see at the beginning and at the end of an episode tend to be perceived better than items falling towards the middle.

Writings on perceptions also point out the difficulties of understanding the language of others. Each social class, trade, geographical area and educational grouping may have its own vernacular which is not always as precise or clear as necessary for legal manipulation. In the same way as lawyers use technical jargon so do clients, and any ambiguities or lack of clarity in terminology should be noted down and questioned later. A particular difficulty in relation to language and perception occurs where a client comes from a completely different social, or cultural, milieu such as somebody originating from a different country or perhaps someone who has spent most of their lives working on a factory floor. It may not simply be the terminology which they use by the subtle understanding and impressions intended to be conveyed by that terminology which will be difficult to understand. Rather like a visitor from "outer space" who has managed to master the English language but still does not understand how humans behave, lawyers sometimes find themselves without any background at all to help them in understanding the context from which their clients come. In these cases sometime must be spent with the client in obtaining the sort of background which is necessary for an understanding of the case. These items on perception will receive further treatment in Chapter Four when we look at the other side of the coin, the problems of the lawyer in advising the client.

(e) *Information processing.* This is another subject area which the psychologists have studied (see, *e.g.* Coltheart). One of the interesting findings is how limited the human brain actually is in processing units of information. Miller talks about the "magic" number seven and how the brain seems to have difficulty in processing more than seven units of the same type of information at the same time.

We also appear to suffer from "selective attention," not listening to everything that we hear but only things which catch our fancy or imagination, or things that we want to hear. This may be especially important for lawyers who are carefully listening for any item of special meaning or relevance to the law. Indeed, it is clear from transcripts and video tapes of legal interviews that lawyers do tend to pounce on words or phrases of obvious legal import and to screen out items which do not have immediate and obvious legal relevance. We can also learn from the information processing literature that the act of listening does in itself give cues to the speaker about what we are interested in. Hearing and listening should therefore, in this sense as well, be considered as active rather than passive tasks, and lawyers should be aware of the messages being sent back to the client.

Another interesting concept which comes out of this area of study is that it is difficult for us to listen to anything in an "open-minded" fashion. Our minds immediately begin to create hypotheses against which we test succeeding factual inputs. In the course of any listening episode we will probably be creating a number of hypotheses which are set up and then rejected by subsequent facts. It therefore seems important to remember how our minds are working in an effort to keep our vision as broad as possible.

(2) *Problems personal to the client as information giver* /
There are a whole plethora of reasons why a client may unintentionally miss out, cover up or gloss over certain facts. Some of these will be referred to in the next chapter, and in this section we will look more closely at possible reasons for client reluctance, both conscious and unconscious, to share information with the lawyer.

(a) *Uncertainty of relevance.* Perhaps most important of these, the client may be uncertain as to what particular issues are important for the lawyer's understanding of this particular type of case or area of law. The law is, after all, somewhat quirky and does not always accord entirely with intuition or common sense. An area of fact may simply be left out because the client does not realise it is important and does not wish to appear foolish or waste the lawyer's time, and the client 's money.

In addition, telling a story to a professional who needs to know certain facts for particular reasons is a very different exercise from the more normal social discourse of telling a story in a social gathering, or to a friend. Telling a story outside of the professional's office setting does not necessarily involve much detail; more a stringing together of representative facts. Strictly, chronological stories in social gatherings may also be considered boring, and stories are not always told in this way. Similarly, the proof of facts outside of the professional's office is accepted or rejected in the mind of a listener without the necessity for verbal feedback of that reaction. All of these differences can add to the difficulties of a lay person, whether or not sophisticated in the ways of lawyers, in deciding what to say and how to say it.

(b) *Guilt.* The client may not mention something out of a feeling of guilt in relation to those facts. This feeling of guilt, however, may not necessarily connote "guiltiness" or liability in a legal sense. It would therefore be wrong to come to the conclusion that a client's avoidance of a subject area, together with all the non-verbal signs of reluctance to discuss it, necessarily means that the clients guilty or blameworthy, or liable in the legal sense. Even where the factors surrounding legal liability or guilt would appear obvious to a lay client, the "moral" guilt relating to that subject may be sufficient for the client to be blind to the legal relevance and effect of what they have or have not said.

Clients may simply not be able to overcome these mental obstacles by themselves. An assumption by the lawyer that all of such lapses were intentional to cover up some fault of the client, would lead a lawyer into a harsher, "judgmental" attitude towards the client. It seems to be this form of reaction which leads to cross-examining of the client in order to confirm any assumption of guilt. It would not be surprising, under those circumstances, that clients withdraw even further into their shell and less progress is made on the subject areas and indeed on the whole of the rest of the interview. The lawyer must therefore, as stated above, suspend disbelief, and allow the client the same presumption as the courts would give, that of being perceived innocent until proved guilty.

(c) *Privacy.* Many clients will simply not wish to talk about everything with their lawyer. A lawyer may often ask a client more intimate details than a physical examination by a doctor could ever reveal. It is natural for clients to be wary of telling things about themselves which may be taken in the wrong way, or may lessen their importance in the view of the listener, or may simply be confidential to the client or someone else. A lawyer can usually ease this difficultly somewhat by pointing out the confidential nature of the lawyer-client relationship and how the lawyer is bound by the relationship not to repeat information given in the interview. A useful analogy for some people may be that a lawyer acts as if bound by the constraints of the priest's confessional.

(d) *Suffering.* A client will be reluctant to recall and discuss any events which have caused sufferings to the client or close family and friends. Very often cases which need a lawyer's help, such as family matter, criminal matters, probate and personal injury may all involve a certain degree of suffering. "Time being a great healer" is simply another way of noting that the mind tends to "forget" events which are not pleasant to remember. It may therefore be more difficult for the client to recall such events or to recall them with a sufficient degree of accuracy.

(e) *Professionalism and the lay person.* In the same way as the lawyer may have difficulty relating to the lay person because of differences in education, class and background so the client may have the same problem on the other side of the desk. The client's perceptions of what may be important, interesting or relevant to the professional may well be at odds with what the professional thinks. As stated above, the atmosphere of the meeting, of the room and general situation may in themselves cause difficulties for the client.

Such differences between the two will also be reflected in their different motivations in relation to the interview and the ensuing case. Whereas the lawyer may view the case as a matter of some intellectual interest or as a job of work, the client may see the issue as a matter of high principle or deep felt emotional need. What for the lawyer may be familiar in terms of the facts the client relates, may well be unique in the experience of the client. Their expectations of outcome may also be entirely different at this point in the interview. Before the lawyer has explained the legal position, the client may have unrealistic expectations of what is possible.

There may also be some conflict of direction or interest between the two. The client may well be rooted in the past facts of the case whereas the lawyer will be interest in those facts only to learn how to go forward from them. Often it will be necessary for a client to put aside feelings of unhappiness, suffering and revenge in order to come to a settlement which will be more in the client's interest than vengeful, but uncertain, litigation. All of these differences from the standpoint of the lawyer and client will have an effect on the interview and should therefore be taken into consideration by the lawyer.

(f) *Unitary view.* In many cases it may be difficult for clients in analysing their problems to separate themselves out from the facts of the case, since *they* themselves might be part of the problem or difficultly they face. In some cases the client may be the whole problem. Kuhn in *The Structure of Scientific Revolutions* shows how difficult it is for someone within a certain "mindset" to be able to see outside of it and to be able to see the same facts from a different point of view. This is why, according to Kuhn, changes in science often occur as a result of new researchers preparing hypotheses so directly opposite to previous theories.

Since the client has brought a particular concern to the lawyer, part of the lawyer's function may be to separate the client out from the problem (Fisher and Ury, *Getting to Yes*). The difficulty is in assessing the nature of the problem when all the information comes from the source of that problem itself.

(g) *Events v. Scenario.* In some types of cases, especially in family matters, a client may not have understood the whole chain of events which form the story which the lawyer wishes to hear in its entirety until the time of telling the story to the lawyer. Until now the incidents may each have been seen as separate, and it may be a shock to the client to be confronted with the whole story as a result of the layer's need to obtain an overview or full scenario of what has occurred. This may mean that the story is not told with a full appreciation of where all the facts fit in.

(3) *Problems of the information itself—facts, fiction and law facts*
Any approach to fact-gathering or information-gathering in an interview should take into account not only the factors mentioned above in terms of problems affecting the client and problems affecting the lawyer but also the nature of "facts," how facts are used in the legal process, the human memory and once gain human perception.

(a) *Facts.* Here we add a caveat to all that has been said up until now in relation to the nature of "facts" themselves. The legal philosophical school of "realists" included among them "fact skeptics" and perhaps the most famous of these are Jerome Frank and Karl Llewellyn. Their work has clearly shown that any attempt to retell a factual situation in court suffers from so many difficulties that it is unlikely that the "truth" will ever be heard. Since preparation for litigation serves as the model for most dispute-based legal work, what happens in court affects the preparation of all cases by lawyers and also affects the legal view of the "facts." Facts as known in the law are biased statements from one side or another of what they *say* occurred. Facts are given at different levels of generalisation depending upon the specific legal need.

Lawyers therefore seek factors presenting specific pictures in order to "prove" these ends. It is not easy to break out of this mould into a less constricted or unbiased view of what is necessary and therefore facts given by the client take on their own meaning within the context of a case irrespective of what the information-giver or information-gatherer would wish.

(b) *Perception and memory.* More recently the work of psychologists such as Elizabeth Loftus, who have looked into human ability in relation to witness testimony, have taught is a number of things that directly affect lawyer-client interviews. Apparently, a large number of people may see the same event but may all have a different perception of what occurred. Although people cannot remember an enormous amount of detail easily, it is possible to encourage recall in certain ways. Memory is fallible and the feeling that one remembers something clearly and definitely does not necessarily mean that this assumption is correct, or that one's memory is any better than somebody who appears less certain about what happened. In addition the mental functions of "filling in" and "stereotyping" mentioned above and others, all have the effect of polluting our memory pool regarding important events.

(c) *Questioning bias.* One special problem relating to legal cases is the factor of previous recitation of the events to others, sometimes in response to biased lines of questioning. Loftus' research seems to show that such recitation, where accompanied by the comments of listeners or where a questioner presents a specific line of questions, can affect what goes back into the memory pool of a witness or client. Therefore, for example, a client having being questioned by the police may start to think that the suggestions made by some of the policemen may actually have occurred when they do not have any real memory or knowledge of these facts. They become unable to discern which were facts perceived by them at the incident and which facts have been added by the questioning.

(d) *Outcome bias.* Similarly knowledge of the outcome of a particular situation has the effect of causing bias to the perception of the event. For example, where we know that an outcome was bad we tend to view previous events as if they were likely to have caused that outcome (Pennington, 1981). As it is impossible for us to wipe out from our memory what the outcome has been, the message of the factual information will always be tainted by the outcome.

All of these problems and issues must therefore be kept in mind in assessing the quality and quantity of information gathered from the client. Being aware of the difficulties is an important step forward. In succeeding chapter we look more closely at what can be done by the lawyer to help overcome these problems.

Conclusion ✓

The Listening Stage has been shown to a crucial first stage of the interview. It begins with fruitful attempt by the lawyer to place the client physically at ease by the normal social forms used in meeting and greeting new acquaintances. Introductions should be carried out with some care so that clients have some feeling of knowing who their lawyer is and how their cases will be handled.

It is important to allow clients to develop the story in their own way. This involves asking open questions and facilitating clients' delivery with active listening responses.

Listening and understanding are more difficult tasks than they appear. They need a great deal of concentration and some knowledge of traps which commonly exist leading to errors in understanding. Such mistakes can emanate from problems of the interviewer, problems of the person being interviewed and even from the factual information itself. It is therefore necessary to suspend belief or disbelief for a later sage of the relationship, and to encourage an atmosphere in which clients feel that their needs will be listened to and met. Lawyers should aim for a feeling of mutual co-operation in solving problems rather than unnecessary control of clients and interviews.

An interesting small piece of research was undertaken in a doctor's surgery where there were four partners, two upstairs and two downstairs. They found that their average consultation time for each patient was approximately five minutes. For experimental purposes over a period of a few months the two downstairs decided to spend on average ten minutes with each patient rather than five minutes. The other two doctors carried on as they had before.

After a few months the two groups of doctors totted up the number of occasions on which their patients had come to see them. They found that the group of patients who had been given double the time came to see their doctors on about half as many occasions as the patients who had been given the same amount of time as previously. There is very little similar research into the way the legal profession carries out its business. In research (mentioned in the Foreword) at Warwick University, video films were made of a range of lawyers interviewing new clients in their own office settings. It is interesting to see the effects of different techniques. It seems that those lawyers who give their clients the full opportunity of saying what they wish right at the beginning of an interview have far less interruptions from their clients in the third, Advising, Stage and have fewer problems having to go back over factual areas which they had covered in questions but had not given the clients a full opportunity to discuss.

The message is therefore strong and clear:

(a) More time spent on Stage One of the first interview may well *save* a great deal of *time* later handling the problems of anxious clients who are never quite satisfied that the lawyers know what they want.

(b) More time spent on Stage One can also *save* a great deal of time spent later *in the interview* when the client opens new areas or reopens areas not fully covered, as a result of advice inapplicable to the whole of the fact situation.

(c) Attention to clients at this stage and giving them the chance to speak gives the lawyer the opportunity to *take full stock* of clients, what they are saying and all those aspects of non-verbal communication we take for granted in normal conversation.

(d) Giving clients a chance to talk allows then to *get the problem "off their chest" and relate to the lawyer fully* as a person without having to answer series of questions.

(e) This form of communication *does not lessen the lawyer's control* since it is the lawyer's office and the client has come to see the lawyer for advice and help. The lawyer has the possibility of putting the brakes on at any time if any really irrelevant matter comes out.

(f) Most important of all, and an interesting and surprising factor that we did not expect to find our research, clients rarely, if ever, stray onto irrelevant material. It is simply that the things that they mention *do not seem relevant* at the point of the interview at which they are said. In other words, the client does not at that time explain their relevance and it is only later that this becomes obvious. Sometimes it is annoying that clients tell the whole story all at one go. It is not the case, however, that what they are saying is irrelevant. It is just that they are saying it in such a way that the lawyer is not able at this stage to make the necessary connections.

Chapter Three

QUESTIONING

This chapter explores the Second Stage of the interview. The Second Stage, as it appears from watching legal interviews, involves more active verbal involvement on the part of the lawyer, who begins by taking more explicit control over the interview.

By the end of the first stage, the lawyer should have a general comprehension of the client's story, and will already be trying hard to understand the story from a number of points of view. It is difficult from watching interviews and reading transcripts to sort out the lawyer's mental processes at this stage, but it seems that many lawyers will start questioning on the basis of some hypothesis or "hunch" which falls neatly into a well recognised legal subject area or category. It seems to be dangerous to press ahead too early, however, with one particular hypothesis of legal relevance; a "premature diagnosis" as Binder and Price refer to it. A helpful distinction here would be to differentiate the need first to understand the facts within their own context before beginning to fit those facts into some form of legal hypothesis. At the opening of the questioning stage, therefore, the lawyer's objective should still be to hear and understand the client's story as well as to begin sorting out what in particular might be of legal relevance.

Table 3.1–Stage Two Tasks

Stage Two:	4. Questioning on facts for gaps, depth, background, ambiguities and relevance 5. Sum up and recount lawyer's view of facts, *and* check for client's agreement or amend	6. Note taking

Task 4: Questioning on Facts for Gaps, Depth, Background, Ambiguities and Relevance

Developing a clear understanding of the story itself will involve some skills already mentioned in Chapter Two such as using one questions in order to develop particular factual areas, and will also involve skills of closer questioning which appear more naturally to form part of the public image of the lawyer.

The object is to make the story itself seem more real to the mind of the lawyer. It is therefore helpful to begin questioning on areas of fact where the client appears to have missed out sections of the story, or not to have given sufficient depth to explain fully what has occurred. The client may also have begun the story too far along, and the lawyer will need more background with which to understand the importance of what subsequently occurred.

Uncovering the client's story may be differentiated from the process of fashioning a sculptured form from a new block of wood or marble. A sculptor may be able to "see" within the square block the desired form of the finished product, and work the material, chipping away gradually towards that form, carefully using the existing grain in the wood or stone. The lawyer, however, should perceive no desired form within the mass. The story is in the client's mind and it is the lawyer's skill to help the client describe the facts and suggest to the client ways of separating material which may be important for understanding those facts, from that which is not. This stage should therefore be seen as a more of a joint effort between lawyer and client in fashioning the form of the story. The client, rather than being a passive answerer of "yes" or "no" questions, should still be doing most of the talking. But the form and detail of those answers will now be more controlled by the lawyer.

(1)   The list of "Issues for Attention"
Whilst the client is talking in Stage One either a mental or written note should be made of factual areas which need more scrutiny (see Chapter Two and more about note taking later in this chapter). This list should also include items with any particular factual ambiguity or strangeness as well as items mentioned by the client but which do not immediately appear to be relevant.

Picking up on all these verbal cues can also be a very helpful way of understanding the client and the client's needs. This is important here in trying to understand the story but especially important later for the fashioning of advice appropriate to the client. The text will first concentrate on the facts of the case and then turn to the needs of the client.

General Questioning

It may well be that a client will omit a whole area of fact or "forget" to explain reasons, or skim over an aspect because he or she has particular reason for avoiding the subject. As stated in Chapter Two, avoidance in itself need not be a conscious action, and neither is it necessary for avoidance to be covering up misdeeds, illegality, immorality or any form of guilt. A client may simply really forget to mention something or not realise its importance or relevance for a lawyer. This may sound trite and obvious but it is worth repeating because very often lawyers, trained to disbelief, jump to such conclusions. The psychological dimensions of such avoidance have already been discussed under "Problems in Understanding" in the previous chapter. For current purposes it will be assumed that such issues are not present in handling a factual situation and that the client is not reluctant to give the particular information.

It is essential for the lawyer to examine thoroughly with the client each heading in the list of "Issues for Attention". This exercise should be carried out by beginning, as before, with a relatively open question on the particular subject. For example, if a client accused of theft from a supermarket had told much of what happened from entering the store until leaving with a police officer, but missed out what had occurred after being approached by one of the store's staff, the lawyer might say:

Lawyer: Thank you for giving me that full account of what happened in the supermarket. Now, I think I would also find it helpful to hear a bit more about what happened after the member of the supermarket staff approached you at the cereals aisle. Can you tell ne about that?

If this does not begin a full outline of those facts from the client then a further open question should be attempted until the client has understood what the lawyer requires or it is clear that the client has unexpressed reasons for not wishing to discuss the matter.

More usually such open questions appear to elicit a fairly full response on the subject area. As in Stage One the lawyer should be most careful not to break in on the client or narrow down the area of inquiry whilst the client still has something to say. However, as the story becomes more detailed it will become necessary to ask more explicit, and more directed questions. As soon as this process beings it must be realised that the area of inquiry will naturally become narrower and narrower. The lawyer should therefore be aware that this phase has been reached.

(1) *Questioning in the funnel sequence*
A number of authors (see, *e.g.* Watson, p. 32 and Binder and Price, p. 92 *et seq.*) liken what should occur, to the opening up of a set of funnels. Each open question begins a new funnel and a new subject area. As the questioning becomes more closed and more precise, the area of inquiry becomes narrower and more constricted. It therefore becomes necessary to start the more general inquiry again by opening up another funnel with a new open question.

Figure 3.1—Questioning in the Funnel Sequence

Funnel No. 1

1. Now, I think I would also find it helpful to hear a bit more about what happened after the member of the supermarket staff approached you at the cereals aisle. Can you tell me about that?
2. What happened then?
3. How did she make it clear to you that you must accompany her?
4. Was this accompanied by any physical action?
5. Do you remember which hand of her's grabbed your arm?
6. Did this hurt?
7. Were there any bruises?
8. Did you see a doctor?
9. Did he make a full note of what he saw do you think?
10. Did you take any pictures of the arm?
11. Did anyone else see it bruised?

(and so on . . .)

Funnel No. 2

1. Now, could you tell me more generally how busy the supermarket was at that time?
2. How many people were in the cereals aisle?
3. How close were they to you?
4. Do you remember what this couple looked like?
5. Do you think they could overhear what the store detective said to you?
6. Can you remember whether she asked you any questions before telling you she suspected you of stealing?
7. Are you sure she said "stealing" and not "*attempted* stealing?"
8. What were the exact words used?
9. Do you think anyone else would have heard these?
10. Did the people at the checkout turn around to look?

(and so on . . .)

Funnel No. 3

1. You told me earlier that you were taken to the Manager's Office. How did all that happen?
2. (and so on . . .)

Unfortunately, many questioners do not see that the effect of this progressively narrower form of questioning is to push them and their own theories into straights from which it is difficult to move. Lines of questioning tend to become constricted and questioners do not think of reopening the subject area by starting a new funnel. The result is that the client is forced into going through certain particular paces, rather like a horse performing dressage at an equestrian show. It is very difficult for the client to state facts which appear to fall outside of the narrow constrictions allowed by the questions and the lawyer may therefore miss whole areas of factual material by not giving each subject heading more than one new open question or new "funnel". An illustration of the funnel sequence as it might occur in the shoplifting case appears below. Only the questions are shown.

The result of continuing along the same funnel within the narrow, confined area is that the interview turns into a continuous, detailed question and answer pattern, where the lawyer follows each new hunch or each new "hare" up to a point, sees another hunch then follows that and so forth. This method does not allow time for a full overall view of the case and develops the lawyer's understanding in a manner which gives great detail on a few small sections but insufficient grasp of the whole matter. Those sections will often be chosen by the lawyer for their legal importance and the facts will therefore be fashioned according to the law, rather than the other way around.

Where a lawyer attempts to attain an overall view using only this narrow form of questioning, interviews seem to take far longer than they would if clients had been allowed to develop a fuller account of each section in their own words.

Additionally, if a client learns the subservient behaviour of only answering narrow, closed questions when asked, it is more difficult to invite the client's collaboration later in the capacity of an equal. The learned style of client behaviour in the relationship will be important in deciding how the relationship will develop,

(2)   *The style of questioning*
For many lawyers, and indeed for most lay people whose visions of the law are gathered largely from film or television portrayals of lawyers in court, the lawyer's questioning activities at this stage are far closer to their image of the lawyer's work.

That image, so aptly portrayed in exciting film snippets of cross-examination in court, is still very unlike the questioning style which lawyers should adopt during this stage of the interview. It is perhaps doubtful whether such styles are even fruitful in cross-examination, but that is not a concern for this text. Inexperienced lawyers, who have never had any training in discovering facts, as opposed to discovering law, will very often model themselves on what they imagine a lawyer to be: the film version of the verbal duellist. Even more experienced practitioners easily fall into the habit or frequent question and response and often include direct interruption and interjection into clients' statements as a prominent part of their repertoire. This is sometimes excused with the argument that it is necessary to test out a client's story, to see whether the client would make a good witness under cross-examination by the other side's lawyer in court.

The need to test our the story is undoubtedly a major concern for lawyer contemplating litigation; and its importance in the process of preparing for trial, or even deciding whether to go to trial, cannot be understated. However, the occasion of the first interview may not be the most appropriate time to test out a client's answers under stress. The first interview should be viewed as the time for encouraging confidence between the lawyer and the client. It is an occasion for giving clients every possible opportunity to say what they want rather than what a lawyer would prefer to hear. Therefore, adopting a non-involved style and firing question after question is not likely to produce a happy client, confident that the lawyer understands what the client has said and what the client wants.

(3) *Lawyer uncertainty*
As stated above it appears to be necessary for the lawyer, at these stages of an interview, to continue to suspend for as long as possible uncertainty or disbelief in a story or in the client. It may well be that the common reaction of close cross-examination at an early stage is a result of such disbelief or uncertainty, on hearing the story for the first time.

Most lawyers seem to react intuitively to a story which appears to be strange or unusual. With minds trained to zoom in on inaccuracies and contradictions, it is far too easy to leap at a client with the questions which concern the lawyer most.

A number of results follow from this approach, as opposed to an approach utilising a more general set of open questions on a more general view of the issues involved as outlined above. Any client reluctance to talk about a topic is unlikely to be eased by a head-on collision with the lawyer on that subject, as has been seen above in "Problems in Understanding." Even if the client is not reluctant to discuss the matter, immediately proceeding on this sort of issue gives it undue prominence between the client and the lawyer. It presents the client with the idea that there is something special about this field, which may in turn colour the client's comments in relation to it.

(4) *Time constraints*
The table below shows what appears to be one traditional view of the time constraints of an interview. In this model its seems that

obtaining information by testing the story can be done with series of questions and answers and takes less time. Establishing mutual trust, however, would take more time and may therefore be an "inefficient" use of the lawyer's time.

Figure 3.2—Testing the Story: a Traditional View of Time

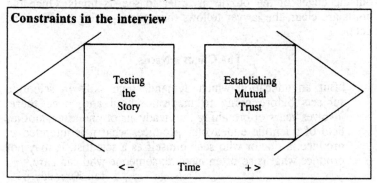

This model is not necessarily accurate. Most often the work of obtaining information is best handled by the same methods which will help in establishing mutual trust. Not only is that a more efficient way in which to obtain information, but it has the added supreme advantages, as noted above, that the client is more likely to give more information at the interview, further information later and to continue to be helpful and trusting throughout the case. This of course includes paying the lawyer's bill. Even if the "traditional" view were correct for the short-term aims of the first interview, it cannot be correct for the longer-term conduct of the whole case.

Summary
In summary, therefore, the lawyer should be attempting a continuation of the interview in line with what has already occurred in Stage One. The lawyer is still aiming at first for a general statement of the facts of the case, but this time triggered off by questions for the lawyer which begin to aim at more specific factual areas. Where more detail is necessary the lawyer should ask more closed questions. This should however be practised with the same caveat in mind. Moving into detail will make it difficult for the client to say what the client wishes to say, so much as what the lawyer wants to hear. It is therefore necessary to reopen general lines of questioning again, once the necessary detail has been acquired.

In this form of information gathering, the client spends a larger proportion of the interview speaking, than in a more closed question and answer approach. It allows the client to gain more confidence in the lawyer than if the client were being "cross-examined". None of this will affect the formation of the lawyer's mental draft of the story and its legal relevance. This will take place regardless. The lawyer is putting together the pieces of a jigsaw puzzle. Before finding exactly where each piece of "sky" in the "jigsaw puzzle" should fit it is first necessary to find the straight outside edges of the puzzle in order to see its limits. Once the limits are clear, the lawyer follows through in piecing together the detail.

The Client's Needs

"But an education which demands high skills in scientific subjects before going to medical school and, once there, involves years of breathing the heady air of one after another field of scientific endeavour, produces what it is intended to produce: a doctor who sees himself as a scientist. It may not produce what is so often needed: someone who can care."

Ian Kennedy Q.C.,
The Reith Lectures–Unmasking Medicine.

"Oh! Reasons not the need: Our basest beggars
Are in the poorest thing superfluous;
Allow not Nature nor than Nature needs,
Man's life is cheap as beast's."

William Shakespeare,
King Lear, Act II, scene IV.

"I'm being quite useful. This thing is a Thneed.
A Thneeds's a Fine-Something-That-All-People-Need!
It's a shirt. It's a sock. It's a glove. It's a hat.
But it has other uses. Yes, far beyond that."

Dr. Suess,
The Lorax.

Until now we have concentrated on the information to be gained from the interview as if it were a set of objective facts, sterile of their emotional importance in terms of client's needs. We now turn to the importance of discovering clearly at this stage of the interview what is the client's desired solution or what possible alternative solutions the client might prefer. Often clients attend an interview without any certainty about what they would like to happen simply because they do not know what possibilities are available. In such cases it is therefore necessary to discover what they need or what they would like generally, so that the lawyer can apply those needs to alternative solutions appropriate to the particular client.

Discovering desired outcomes and needs is not a simple process. Many lawyers feel that their responsibility is simply to match up a set of given facts to the apposite law. This is, after all, the basic craft which lawyers are taught. The skill, however, is to fashion the law, the practice if it and the practical implications of a knowledge of the law into a set of alternative solutions suited to the client from which the client may choose.

It is worth emphasising at this point, that the choice is the client's. In a later chapter we will discuss which choices are more properly those of the lawyer and which are those of the client. For the present discussion, it will be assumed that the overall direction and handling of the case is a decision or set of decisions to be made by the client on the advice of the lawyer. Since it is necessary for clients to make a choice consonant with their wishes, it is also necessary for the lawyer to know what those needs are in order to present to clients how best they can be fulfilled.

Some clients will of course have thought out exactly what they would like, or need, out of any given situation. A straightforward question along the lines of, "How would you like this whole thing to end up?" will usually elicit a full answer from such people. Others may be far more reticent to describe their true needs immediately. They may even be unaware of their real reasons for coming, or they may come to a lawyer in anger or upset and not be immediately capable of rational judgment.

Some hint can be obtained from an understanding of the "precipitating event" which finally made them come to the lawyer. There may often be a particular event which, in the client's mind, was the "straw that broke the camel's back," or something in particular which finally decided them to take action. A large number of events which have legal consequences occur to each of us every day. If we took legal action on all of them we would hardly have time to carry on the rest of our lives. There is usually, therefore, something special which makes us decide that one particular set of events is too much for us to bear. A client may well tell the whole background story without giving information on the precipitating event unless asked for it specifically. It might be, for example, a person whose spouse beat the child harder than ever before the previous night, or it might be someone whose superior at work shouted more harshly yesterday than ever before. The legal consequences of the situation will probably depend more on all the background factors than on just the precipitating event, but the nature of that event may in itself tell the lawyer a great deal about the client's immediate and short-term needs.

Where a client is reluctant to talk about needs or finds difficulty in expressing such ideas, a number of tactics may be adopted to facilitate their expression. These may also be useful where clients appear reluctant to talk about other issues as well.

(1) *Working with the Framework.*
By working within the framework of the stages outlined here, one should be providing clients with the utmost opportunity to say what they wish and what they feel. The atmosphere engendered by this process should make them feel more trusting towards the lawyer and confident in the lawyers's ability to handle such personal information.

(2) *Explanation.*
By explaining to the client the lawyer's reason for needing the particular information, especially about needs, the client may better understand its relevance for the lawyer. The client will then usually respond either with the information itself or an explanation in return for why it is difficult or not possible to give this information. An example of an explanation for needing to ask a question comes in the following extract from the "Mrs Smith" interview quoted in the last chapter.

1.	Lawyer:	Has he treated you badly?
2.	Client:	No not really so . . . um.
3.	Lawyer:	Well if he has not treated you . . . See, there are five ways you can get a divorce but most of them don't seem to apply to you. Either if you've been separated for five years you can get a divorce, whether he agrees or not. It you've been separated for two years you an get a divorce if he agreed. If he deserted you for two years you can get a divorce. But none of these apply. It's either because he's committed adultery or because he's treated you badly. It' got to be one or the other. I'm afraid, if you're to get a divorce now. Otherwise we could only just get you maintenance and custody and you'd have to wait . . .
4.	Client:	Um.
5.	Lawyer:	So. Has he ever hit you?
6.	Client:	Yes, but not for a long–quite a while like and it was ages ago.

Here at no. 3 the lawyer explains fully why he is asking a set of questions and why particularly he needs the answer for the question posed at no. 1. This full answer begins to be given at no. 6. One obvious problem with this form of questioning is that the client, becoming aware of the legal importance of a particular piece of information, will have the motivation to manufacture or embellish existing information in order to provide the lawyer with what appears to be necessary. There are therefore problems of ethical proprietary in giving such explanations. Any reaction which seems as if it may have been manufactured or embellished should therefore receive, at a later stage, some attention in order to ascertain its veracity.

Another way in which an explanation can help is that it will show clearly to the client that the client can receive a direct return in exchange for sharing this information. So, for example, in a negligence case against an employer an injured client may be reluctant to say how often a state of affairs was allowed to exist in the absence of injury, on the assumed basis that this might invoke the employer or other employees in legal liabilities which would not be relevant to the case in hand. However, an explanation from the lawyer that this would help to prove negligence or might even raise the level of damages in the particular case, might elicit more information from the loyal employee.

Similarly in (say) a case about local teenage vandalism the explanation that "if all right minded people were prepared to expose this conduct, the quicker such conduct could be eradicated from society," might appeal to some clients and make them feel better about expressing something that they would otherwise feel was confidential or unnecessary for the lawyer to hear.

(3) *Using client ideas.*
A more indirect method for approaching these areas of concern is to work with ideas that the client brings up in discussion. The lawyer can use these to follow through into finding out from clients what their needs might be. Once a client has raised a subject such as home life, or financial resources or physical or social well-being it is easier to take up the subject in further discussion. If the lawyer senses that these are difficult areas the subject matter can perhaps be taken forward at a different pace, and returned to when the conversation turns to that subject.

Information Categorisation

We can now bring the factual information gleaned from the client together with the context of the client's needs which provides the background to those facts. At this stage of the interview it is helpful for the lawyer to check this overview against a mental list of formal information likely to emerge. In carrying out research on information emerging in the legal interview some seven categories have been developed which may be helpful in checking mentally whether all subject areas have been covered (see Sherr, 1986). These categories appear, in tabular form in Chapter Six.

The first of these is *"personal information"* about the client. This includes the client's full name and address, telephone numbers at home and work, marital status, number of children and their ages, form of residence, job and work schedule among others. Formal information such as full name, address and telephone number is far better obtained right at the end of Task 4, the "questioning" task. As stated in Chapter Two, some questioners attempt to ask this information right at the beginning of an interview, and it can have a stultifying effect on what immediately proceeds thereafter. D. H. Lawrence's book *Sons and Lovers* contains a good example of the challenge involved in simply telling one's name to a stranger. The young Paul Morel is spoken to by a superior and asked who he is, on his first day as messenger boy in the artificial limb factory. Lawrence portrays his difficulty and embarrassment in saying his own name when challenged in those strange surroundings. The same may be true for many clients.

The second such informational heading is that of "*other parties*". It will usually be necessary to find out the full names and addresses of these other parties together with some personal information about them, so that the lawyer may be able to write directly to them (if they have not yet appointed legal representatives) or so that the lawyer can judge their responsiveness to any legal claims or proceedings, and their ability to pay. Once again such information may well come during he general part of the interview and formal details should be left until the end.

The existence, and names and addresses of, "*witnesses*" is a similar issue and one on which clients tend not to be able to give immediate details. The lawyer should retain a note to ascertain exact details about these in correspondence, or otherwise later from the clients.

"*Events*" was the fourth informational categorisation heading and applies generally to the course of events. It would be unusual for this to be entirely left out of an interview but it is worth reminding oneself of the necessity of obtaining as full a description as possible of what occurred.

The fifth heading, "*what the client wants*" is very similar to the heading above which dealt with client needs. It is a useful reminder always to think of this as a separate category.

When carrying out research on new lawyers and their abilities in obtaining information in interviewing new clients (Sherr, 1986) the two headings on which they fared worst in terms of actual information obtained were the last two, "*previous advice and assistance*" and the existence of "*legal proceedings*." These may well be items which an experienced lawyer would pick up more easily. However, clients are often uneasy about telling their lawyer immediately that they have been to another lawyer because they are worried about not obtaining legal aid, or in case lawyers decide to "club together". Similarly, they sometimes fail to mention that they have been to the Citizens Advice Bureau or other helping

Figure 3.3—Stage Two Flowchart

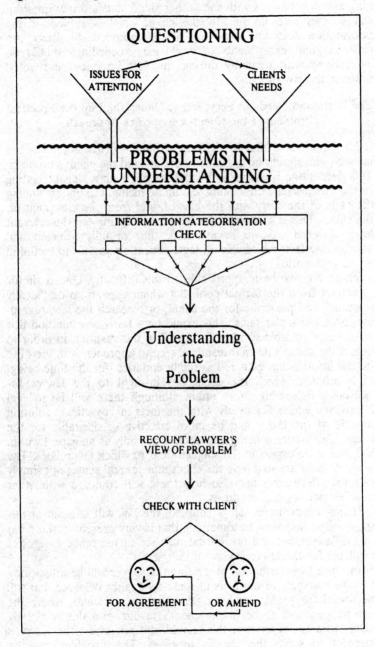

organisations. This information is exceptionally important in beginning any negotiations with the "other side"; and a direct question should therefore be put to the client on this subject if the information does not come out in the interview. Similarly, the existence and exact dates of any legal proceedings should be ascertained with certainty during the first interview and noted down in the lawyer's diary.

The Facts and Needs in Perspective: Understanding the Practical Problem of the Client—a Remedies Approach

It has been noted that by the end of Task 4 of the interview the lawyer's aim should be basically to understand the client's problem. This description is cast in a "factual" rather than a "legal " setting so that the lawyer's direct aims should be inclined to understanding the facts of the story with the bias of, and from the viewpoint of, the client. This is a different exercise from picking out the relevant legal material. As we have stated, the carefully selected and appropriate facts which exist in legal education are not to be found in the real world.

There are two basic approaches to this difficulty. One is simply to extract from the factual pool that which appears to be "legally relevant" and prescribe for the client, or research the law, regarding those particular facts. This would be a fairly safe method if it were easily possible to identify "facts" in this manner, in order to obtain the client's desired result. A second approach is to view the factual information gathered as the boundaries [for the time being] of a problem which the client has brought to the lawyer for assistance in solving. Very often, although there will be a legal alternative which fits neatly with the facts, a "practical" solution outside of the law would be more effective or desirable for the client. The lawyer is being approached not only as an expert within law, but as an expert in the subject areas to which law relates. The lawyer's skills are to advise the client in a general sense; not simply of legal alternatives but also how these will compare with other possible non-legal alternatives.

If the second approach is adopted, the law will be seen at this stage in the interview as something that is very present in the mind of the lawyer but will not be the only set of reference categories available for the lawyer's view of the facts.

In terms of information processing the lawyer will be attempting here to marshall all the facts in some semblance of order that will be useful for problem-solving generally. In particular, where the law happens not to be in the client's favour, and this is already clear from the interview, this should still not affect the lawyer's attempt to solve the client's problem. The problem may be amendable to a large number of other forms of solution, some of which would be in the capabilities of the lawyer; and other might need referral to another professional or a different type of institution.

A client, for example, who has a problem with a landlord who resides in the same house may have particular legal difficulties if relations with the landlord are not good. However, the social physical consequences may be worse than the legal implications and it may be that these social and physical consequences could be assisted by a non-legal approach such as an attempt by the client, with the lawyer's help, to understand the position from the point of view of the landlord. Many lawyers would not see this form of exercise as a part of their function, and indeed it could easily backfire unless carried out with some care.

Another example might be a case where a client has purchased a defective pair of shoes and on returning to the shop has been given a credit slip. It may be that at law the shop is entitled to treat this as a "settlement" of the dispute and therefore not capable of being reopened in court. Whatever the legal position, the shop may well be amenable to a different form of approach which reminded it of it's good name or even threatened public exposure in the media.

At this stage therefore the law should be taking something of a back seat and the case, should be viewed "backwards", entirely from the position of the client's required remedy. This will have a different effect from first analysing the factual material in terms of its legal categorisation and then seeing what remedies are available. Working backwards from the remedy to what it might be necessary to find in order to obtain that remedy imposes a different outlook on the case and on fact-gathering itself.

Task 5: Sum Up and Recount lawyer's view of Facts and Check for Client's Agreement or Amend

With a full view of the facts, an understanding of the client's problem and of the client's wishes obtained by the lawyer, it is now time to check with the client that the lawyer's understanding is correct and gives due weight to each aspect of the facts and client's feelings.

Being questioned, even in pleasant surroundings by a helpful and patient professional, can be harrowing for a client. Often it is not clear what the purpose of certain questions are and often recalling the events themselves will not be pleasant. It is therefore an appropriate point in the interview to be giving the client feedback on what the lawyer has understood and this time to allow the client to be placed in the "judging" position of deciding whether the lawyer has understood correctly.

It is essential in any event that the lawyer should check with the client the lawyer's perceptions of what the client has said or communicated. It would not be sensible to proceed with a legal analysis on a given factual situation, whilst being uncertain of all those facts. In addition, the lawyer may need to take immediate action, as a result of the interview, in contacting a third party. It is therefore essential to make sure that the lawyer has the correct facts whilst the client is still in the room. Here again life is very different from the educational experience. A legal examination question allows a lawyer to review the facts again and again, but a client can not be "reread" so easily.

The process of recounting the client's story also has a number of other effects. It gives lawyers the chance further to sort out the facts in their own minds. It gives clients a chance to add any additional facts that were forgotten, to correct misunderstandings and adjust the importance given to different items. It also allows clients, perhaps for the first time, to hear, from a relatively dispassionate observer, what the case is about.

Hearing a paraphrase of their words in this way can have the effect of allowing clients to feel that they are making a fuss about nothing or that their position was not quite as strong as they imagined. Because of the possibility of the latter effect the lawyer has to be especially careful to present the recounting of the story in an objective but sympathetic way (see Goodpaster, (175) *Journal of Legal Education* 40 *et seq.*).

Research has shown (Sherr, 1986) that many lawyers do not in fact check back with their clients that they have understood the facts and clients' wishes correctly. Some lawyers who do make an effort to ascertain that the client agrees with their understanding of the facts do so in such a powerful manner compared with the client's demeanour that the client is cowed into submission and feels weak in the face of a highly articulate and verbally powerful lawyer. The lawyer, whose job it is to represent such factual situations informal settings, may find it easy to summarise the client's problems and wishes into a legally relevant form which seems to the client to bear little resemblance to what they truly experienced and feel. In this situation it can be difficult for a client to suggest corrections or a complete change of outlook towards the case. A sign of the lawyer's skill in retelling the story would therefore be the client's ability to make any corrections that are necessary.

Here is an example of what a lawyer might recount to a client at Task 5 in an interview.

Lawyer: Let me just check with you Mr Kahn that I have understood all this correctly. About six months ago you bought a new car from Griffiths Motors on the High Street. You bought the car on hire-purchase through the Bardelow Finance Co,

After four months of making the payments on time you began to run low on your funds when you were made redundant. You contacted the Finance Company, in what seems to me to be a highly responsible manner, and you asked them what you should do. They immediately suggested that you hand over the car to them in order to avoid any extra costs. I think your feeling on thus is that they pushed you rather hard to do this quickly, before you had a chance to think about it properly.

You handed over the car to them about one month ago and then heard nothing for three weeks. You have now received this letter from the Finance Company which states that there is considerable damage to the car, both body work and mechanical, and that it will cost a further £500 for this to be fixed. They are asking you for this sum of money and you are annoyed and upset because you felt you had acted absolutely honourably and they represented to you that by handing the car back you would be saved further expense.

Is that a fair description?

Note that where facts exist on paper they do not need to be so clearly verified with a client in detail, unless of course the client has stated that the written communication is in itself defective. In some cases, however the facts which it is immediately necessary for the lawyer to rely on in giving both practical and legal advice are not so easily amenable but were entirely orally communicated to the lawyer in the interview. In this situation, such as a marital case where unreasonable behaviour is being alleged, more time has to be spent at this stage in repeating in full the most important factual statements on which the lawyer is going to rely. This summary will therefore need to be expanded or contracted in accordance with the lawyer's immediate requirements from this interview. These will not be clear until a general overview of the case has been developed.

It is helpful for clients to be given a slight pause at the end of the lawyer's summing up in order to allow them a real opportunity to comment. It would be very easy for the lawyer to jump straight from this point into giving advice and it is clear from our research that some lawyer do so. Clients should be given time to reflect and answer so that they can be committed in their own minds, with our pressure, to this view of the facts and so that they feel more jointly involved in the advice when it is communicated.

Task 6: Note-Taking

The taking of notes should; occur throughout the interview. It may well begin before the interview starts and will certainly go on after

'iew has been completed and the client has left the room.
this is an appropriate time to think of the subject of
g since at this stage the lawyer's understanding will be as
ιυιι, and as confirmed, as at any time during the interview. We will
look at note-taking by examining the effects, both positive and
negative, of note-taking during an interview, and end up with some
suggestions for dealing with the difficulties involved.

The effects of taking notes during an interview

(1) *Positive effects*

(a) *During the interview.* It will be seen from both this chapter and
Chapter Two that it is essential to make a list of "issues for
attention" during the interview. Such headings of issues need only
be short if they provide a sufficient reminder to the lawyer of the
questions that will be necessary to ask relating to those subject
headings. Some items have to be noted down in full, such as full
names, addresses, telephone numbers and any figures or amounts
that are important to the case. Some of these items will be helpful
during the interview itself in framing questions to the client and
subsequently framing advice for the client. It does not appear to be
possible to carry out a proper interview without making some notes
in this form.

(b) *After the interview.* However much one thinks one is able to
remember at the time, it may not be possible to commit important
facts to dictating machine or paper as speedily as necessary after
the interview. The life of the practising lawyer is full of hustle and
bustle. When a lawyer has spent sometime in an interview with a
new client, it is almost certain to mean that there are a number of
telephone calls which need to be returned. Something else may
intervene before the lawyer has a chance fully to note down the
interview. It is therefore clear that it is necessary to note down in
some form or other a fair degree of the information which comes
out during the interview itself, or to set aside a sufficient amount of
time immediately after the interview during which to do this.

(2) *Disadvantages*
In the literature of helping professionals a number of difficulties
are recognised in relation to the problems of taking notes.

(a) *Losing eye contact.* Perhaps the most important problem is
that one has to look down at the desk or a sheet of paper in order
to write clearly. This must result in the loss of eye contact between
the lawyer and the client, and since the lawyer will not be looking
at the client this may well affect the flow of the client's
conversation.

The act of writing down rather than listening is also an interruption itself to the interview and may stop the client from speaking. The lawyer's notes are personal to the lawyer and can only be seen by the lawyer at that time. The notes therefore become an intrusion into the relationship between the two.

(b) *False importance.* Some writers suggest that a client may give false importance to material which is noted by the lawyer, as opposed to material which is not so noted. This might encourage the client to give more information about those areas, which may not necessarily reflect their true importance to the case.

(c) *Threat.* For some clients, writing down things about them may present something of a threat. This is after all what happens in consultations with social workers or probation officers, and in supplementary benefit offices and other state agencies which they visit but may not considered to be on their side.

(d) *Command.* Writing notes can also be used as a powerful tool of command. Since the client may stop talking when the notes are being written it can become an effective way of arranging the pace of the interview. When the lawyer does not intend to use this tool in this manner, care should therefore be taken that it is not perceived by the client in that way.

(e) *Pace.* Just as in court when a witness is told to pay attention to the judge's writing hand in giving evidence, the pace at which a client will deliver a story will change if full notes are being taken of everything that is said. This pace may be very different from the normal speed with which they would speak in social discourse and this may make it difficult for clients to tell the story as they would wish. (A good example of this appears later, in Chapter Seven.)

(3) *Suggestions* _____
By way of balancing the positive and negative effects of note-taking during the interview, some suggestions are made for dealing with the problem.

(a) *Reading aloud.* Many new doctors have been trained to read out to their patients what they are writing in their notes. Although the clear import of this training is to try and be helpful it can have the effect of creating a too-submissive client or "patient". In most cases a lawyer will have to make copious notes after the interview and not all of these can easily be read back to the client at the time they are written. Reading the notes aloud remains, however, one method of dealing with the difficultly if it suits a particular lawyer's temperament and mode of operation, and the client seems particularly concerned about what is being written. Some lawyers dictate their notes on the interview, or a "statement" of the client in the client's presence during the first interview (see Chapter Seven). This may suit the lawyer's work system and it enables the client to comment immediately on any misunderstandings. However, it does seem to lend an impersonal tone to the interview and bothers the client unnecessarily with the lawyer's work method. This should probably therefore be avoided unless absolutely necessary because of imminent court or tribunal hearings.

(b) *Audio tape.* Some suggest that each interview be audiotaped and then listened to later by the lawyer transcribed by a secretary. This seems to be a counsel of perfection for those who have considerable amounts of time available to deal with each case. Though there may be certain types of cases where this would be useful most lawyers, and their clients, would probably be unhappy with this as a regular mode of operation. Certainty the client's permission must be obtained before any such use can be entertained. It has also been shown that some notes must, in any case, be taken for use in the interview itself.

(c) *Practice.* Many new lawyers have the utmost difficulty in remembering the details of each of the individual cases on which they work, when they begin their careers in the law. However, after some months of experience remembering the differences between cases becomes a great deal easier. Similarly, remembering what clients say in an interview does become easier with a little experience and it becomes less necessary to write down all of the facts. It is clear that certain facts will always need to be written down, including such formalities as names, addresses, telephone numbers, dates, places, parties and witnesses. What else needs to be written down during the interview is very much a matter for the judgment and experience of each individual lawyer. Experience helps with this and it becomes possible to make a few one- or two-word notes and to construct the sort of lists which are a helpful memory aid both during the questioning stage and after the interview when a completely full note can be made up.

(d) *Discuss the question.* Perhaps the most helpful of suggestions regarding the problem of note-taking is to mention the difficulty to the client and gain the client's understanding and agreement about how much note-taking will be necessary during the interview. Some interviews may need more notes than others and some clients may more clearly be upset by note-taking. Although mentioning this question may become mechanical if the lawyer does so at every interview, it may still be helpful to the client.

Note-taking, therefore, although perhaps not entirely desirable, is an unfortunate necessity. The lawyer's objective is to be conscious of the impact of note-taking during the interview and to act accordingly.

Conclusion

During Stage Two the lawyer has continued the approach of open questioning and developed the factual investigation into some more detailed questions on certain areas. The lawyer has spent time on determining the client's needs as well as the facts, and has checked back with the client to ascertain whether the lawyer's understanding of facts and needs accords with that of the client. The jigsaw puzzle is almost complete.

If the framework has been used as outlined the lawyer should by now be well set to suggest some possible plans of action to the client, and with the client's agreement initiate the legal work on the case. The lawyer is therefore now ready to move onto the Third Stage.

Chapter Four

ADVISING

This chapter examines the third and final stage of the interview. The Third Stage comprises the tasks relating to advising and counselling the client and setting an agenda for the lawyer's conduct of the case. This chapter also covers the conclusion of the first interview and preparation for work by both the lawyer and the client following the interviews termination. Before discussing how to give advice, however, it is necessary to consider what is involved in this crucial function .

The Lawyer's Function–Some Preliminary Thoughts

The literature relating to the function in society presents a number of differing role descriptions of lawyers. As with all stereotypes these offer a limited insight but do not provide a comprehensive working model. Indeed, some of the role descriptions appear to conflict with each other. The conflicts and the role descriptions themselves are illuminating in an attempt to understand what specific functions a lawyer may perform in an interview.

One of the classic lawyer roles suggested is that of a "gladiator" or a "hired gun" who fights on behalf of the wishes of a client regardless of right or wrong in the dispute. The "hired gun" is a "professional " who almost enjoys the antagonism of the duel and the victorious thrill of a "kill." In advising the client the "hired gun" is more likely to suggest antagonism than a conciliatory approach.

Another description of the lawyer is that of a "high priest" who hands down seemingly unalterable advice (see, *e.g.* Gawalt, *The New High Priests*, 1984). The "high priest" gives advice as if it has just been received from an unseen deity. The client must accept his advice, surrounded as it is in the mystique of the law, without question. There is no sense of collaboration in this relationship.

Some writers see the lawyer as simply "a business person" who happens to trade in the market of providing legal services, and whose major objective is to make a good living. Such a lawyer will not be deeply interested in the detail, both factual and emotional, of each case. This lawyer will be more interested in carrying on an efficient practice and getting out pieces of paper.

Yet others, more idealistically, see the lawyer as a professional to whom people bring their problems for solving, very much like a doctor, social worker or psychologist. Such a lawyer will be more involved in what lies behind each factual situation and interested in helping the "whole client". In the same way that a doctor might cure an ailment but still kill the patient, a lawyer could efficiently handle litigation which was not in the best interests of the client. "Problem solving" lawyers would only advise legal action if they think it is in the real interest of the "whole client", however lucrative.

It seems clear that no one lawyer exactly fits any one of these role characterisations but that all lawyers function sometimes more in one role and sometimes more in others. However, it is probably that for each lawyer there is a predominant self image which, in its extreme form, might be close to one of these characterisations. The characterisations can therefore serve as useful devices for describing how a lawyer may tend to act in carrying out specific functions such as advising and interviewing. They provide an opportunity for lawyers to match their behaviour against some of these given role models in order to help generate more understanding of what happens in an interview.

It may be that certain types of cases necessitate certain type of role. It may also be that certain types of lawyers or certain types of client prefer one role to another. Whichever role or mixtures of roles a lawyer decides to adopt in a particular case, the decision should be made consciously with full consideration for the alternatives. The role should also be performed with such clarity that will enable the client to understand and appreciate which role is being adopted.

Table 4.1–Stage Three Tasks

	7. State advice and/or plan of action and deal with question of funds.
	8. Repeat advice/plan of action *and* check for client's agreement or amend
	9. Recount follow-up work to be done by client.
Stage Three:	10. Recount follow-up work to be done by lawyer.
	11. State next contact between lawyer and client.
	12. Ask if Any Other Business and deal with it.
	13. Terminate, help out and goodbye.

With these thoughts in mind we can now approach the major task of advising the client.

Task 7:   State Advice and/or Plan of Action and Deal with Question of Funds

We have left the lawyer at the stage of having checked with the client that the lawyer now has a full understanding of the client's problem and needs. The task under current discussion seems to suggest by its title that the lawyer's mind leaps straight to the giving of advice or a plan of action. The gap which appears in this exposition seems to be the business of fashioning the advice or plan of action through application of legal rules to the given set of facts. This work is clearly occurring in the mind of the lawyer from the moment the client begins to tell the story. As has been seen, the questioning in Stage Two will initially have been questioning to develop the facts. But, as the questions and answers developed, there would also have been questioning pertinent to a theoretical framework which will enable the lawyer to apply law to facts. The plan of action or advice will not therefore suddenly jump into the mind of the lawyer at Task 7 but will have been developing throughout the first six tasks, and will probably continue to develop after the interview during the lawyer's handling of the case. At this period in the interview, however, the lawyer's thoughts must be crystallised sufficiently to come to a preliminary view of the facts and encompass them in some form of general legal relevance in order to provide the client with feedback on the lawyer's view of the legal problem and its consequences. The "advice" or "plan of action," stated here in terms of what happens in a first interview, is likely to be a preliminary view, in a generalised form, and not a statement which either the lawyer or the client would consider as a complete and binding view of the case.

Advising

We will look here first at the form and then at the content of the advice to be given.

The form of advice
Giving advice in the legal context involves broadly the giving of a general statement of the law relating to the "legally relevant" facts, applying that general picture to the background and circumstances of the client's case and discussing with the client which of the possible alternatives resulting from this application would be most desirable.

(1) *General statement of relevant law*
Sifting through the facts in order to find an overall subject categorisation which fits into the lawyer's legal knowledge is the familiar work of the lawyer. It is the same form of exercise as takes place at university and at the practical stage of qualification and which is normally referred to as "thinking like a lawyer". In simple terms this involves matching the given factual situation against paradigm fact situations remembered, or researched, from existing reported cases. It incorporates fine judgment of levels of gener-

alisation of fact in order to match new scenarios with old paradigms. It also includes some weighing of how the less obviously law based "merits" of a case interact with the more clearly relevant "law facts". "Thinking like a lawyer" is a subject in itself and a more detailed exposition would be out of place in a book of this nature. At any rate, legal education brings the law student to the stage of thinking like a lawyer almost unconsciously.

A general statement of the law relevant to the client's case should therefore be within the ability of even at the least experienced lawyer. It need only comprise of a fundamental area of law such as contract or negligence. The lawyer need not therefore, for example, be an expert on building contracts in order to give such a general statement of the law to a client complaining of a faulty roof repair. All that will be necessary for this particular part of the advice will be a statement such as that found in the first paragraph below:

> Lawyer: It appears from what you have told me that your probably had an effective agreement or contract, as it is known in law, with this builder. In general, a contract that is legally binding on both parties can be effective, even though it is not made in writing. What is agreed between the two parties in conversation can therefore stand as the terms of the contract.
>
> In your own case with Mr Green, if for example he promised that your roof would not leak after the repairs this would, it seems to me, probably stand as a part of the contract between you. (And so on . . .).

Knowing when one is not sufficiently competent either to give immediate advice, or even in some cases to take on the matter itself, its not so clearly taught in legal education and may come only with experience. It is probably better therefore to err on the side of caution. Where the subject is clearly outside of the lawyer's competence a referral should be made either to another lawyer within the same firm or to another firm. It is sensible to try and keep track with the new lawyer as to what happens after referral in order to know whether such referral was successful, and to be able to plan what to do within similar cases in the future.

(2) *Applying the law directly to the client's circumstances*

The exercise involved here is somewhat different from the work of answering a typical law examination-type problem. The general statement of relevant law mentioned above is very unlikely to be based on precedent which exactly matches the client's case. Neither is the lawyer, unless an expert in the field, likely to know the detail of all recent cases in order to be able to give a definite opinion. However, the more general statement of the law in (1) above can usually be explained and reviewed in the light of the client's fact-situation in a manner which is suggestive of how a court might decide the questions arising, but not (at this point) conclusive of such decisions.

For many new lawyers the task of giving advice is a frightening prospect. There is a strong urge to give the client some form of immediate advice that is both meaningful and helpful. The client has come, after all, in order to receive such advice and the lawyer may feel a sense of failure if formal and firm advice is not given. However, it must be realised that in most cases firm advice cannot be given at a first interview. Some would even suggest that it is quite wrong to attempt to give advice without checking completely the up-to-date picture of the law on that subject area. The law changes daily and no one person can hope to keep up with all of it. Neither is anyone likely to be able to retain the amount of knowledge that was present and available in their memory during the time of taking university level or professional examinations.

A client must feel secure and happy at having been given something to take away from the interview and the lawyer must feel also that some knowledge and information has been passed over to the client. However this knowledge does not have to be a definitive view of the case and a very general approach will suffice, provided the lawyer explains why it is necessary to do further research or find out further facts before giving a definite statement.

A short example of advice given in this manner, in a consume rcase, including both a general statement and an application of the law to the case, might go as follows:

Lawyer: Well, the general position in cases of this nature is that any article which one buys has to be of so-called "merchantable quality" which really means it has to be of a good reasonable quality, and it also needs to be "fit for the purpose" for which it is sold. This basically means, as you would imagine, that a tennis racquet should be good for playing tennis but does not necessarily have to be very good for straining spaghetti.

In your case you have only had this particular pair of rather expensive shoes for a week. I can understand your worry that you spent sometime walking in the rain in relatively new shoes. But if shoes must be of proper quality and fit for the purpose of walking, it would certainly seem that they should be up to the strain of getting some water on them

without falling to pieces. However, this is an interesting case and the law can be quite complex. I
would not feels safe in advising you with any degree
of certainty until I have checked up on any recent
decisions and also looked at things such as the
Code of Practice for the shoe industry.

The lawyer in this case could probably have been rather more
certain in the application of the law to the client's particular facts.
However, it is wiser to have the security of knowing the current
legal position. Even if the law has not changed in the opposite
direction, it would be helpful, in advising the client, to be able to
refer to recent decisions which go in the same direction as the
general advice. It is not difficult to formulate advice in this manner,
although some may feel that this is the very minimum of advice
that a client should be given.

(3) *Alternatives for action*
In some cases it will not even be possible to give a preliminary view
of the application of the law to the facts except in the most general
terms. Such cases might include where the facts appear only
vaguely to resemble existing legal categories, where the facts and
law are extremely complex, or where there is simply more information needed which the client cannot give at that time. In all cases
the lawyer may still give a "plan of action" to the client which will
lay out possible alternatives to the client and find out from the
client which of these are considered most desirable. These alternative plans of action need not necessarily be of final work strategies,
but could also be preliminary stages such as factual or legal
research. It is therefore not necessary to give clients a polished
legal answer to their inquiries. It *is* necessary, however, to discuss
what possible action to take, which may well include arriving at a
full legal opinion.

Discussing alternative modes of action, and even deciding what
the practical possibilities are, are not areas of expertise which are
taught in legal education. The task of discussing alterative possibilities with the clients sometimes referred to in the legal
interviewing literature as "counselling" the client.

It has been suggested in Chapter Three that in constructing
different alternatives for the lawyer's or the client's action, a
practical approach may be as helpful as an approach based only on
legal procedures. It is helpful to know that the law is on the side of
the client but it is often difficult, and may be costly, to ensure that
the client's rights are recognised, by taking the case to litigation. A
"practical" approach using the talents of the lawyer is not likely to
be eschewed by the client if it has a good chance of success. In
many cases the current legal position may not be helpful to a

client's case. It may still be possible to effect the client's wishes by simply making demands, or appealing to moral scruples, threatening bad publicity or suggesting some other form of (not illegal) retribution. Such practical or common-sense alternatives should also be presented to the client, and not treated as unimportant or as if they were bound to be within the client's own knowledge.

Strategies which include the use of law may be more complex to relate to a client unused to legal terminology and legal procedure. Counselling a client in such alternatives does mean that one should be as explicit as possible. This means the client should be told, as will be seen below, the exact nature of each step in the procedure, how long it will take and how much it will cost; how it will be likely to affect the client and what the likely chances of success are. It may be that all the details of each step in a lengthy procedure need not be explained immediately. However, the general import should be summarised and examples given so that the client is fully aware of what is likely to happen.

Above all a client should be given the absolute choice in making a decision. This is necessary not only because the client should feel totally involved in the case but because it is the client's decision to make. This should be a decision fully informed by legal advice and, if it is asked for, by the opinion of the lawyer. The question of which choices should be made by the lawyer and which by the client will be discussed further in Chapter Six.

Problems in giving advice
In the same way as the client's communications can be misunderstood by the lawyer, both the lawyer and the lawyer's communications can be misunderstood by the client. Indeed much of the concern expressed by clients about solicitors' conduct of their work relates to the manner, and amount, of communication from the lawyer to the client.

(1) *Jargon*
Perhaps the most obvious fault with which is noticeable in hearing least communicate with clients is the use of technical legal words or expressions which may not be immediately understood. Use of jargon in a legal office is not confined to lawyers. A client might use the vernacular of the factory shop floor in an unfair dismissal case, using terms for equipment which are adequate and precise for the context in which discussion of those terms normally occur but not sufficient for a legal case. In the same way, lawyers use legal terminology in order to maintain the precision of the trials and concepts which they expound. However, if the main object of giving advice is to present the client with information that can be readily understood, rather than giving the best technical account, legal terms and expressions might be translated into a vernacular form

or explained before they are used. This is an aspect of communication of which most lawyers appear to be aware. However, it is sometimes difficult to realise how much of one's speech is so tied into legal expressions which are used so frequently that it becomes quite difficult to speak in any other way.

An interesting point of imprecision which arises out of this two-way difficulty is that a client may use words such as "divorce", "arrest", or "mortgage" with only a vague understanding of the exact meaning of such terms. The client may also accept a lawyer's usage of those terms as having a similarly vague connotation. It is therefore helpful to include in advice definitions of all terms which are crucial to the advice being given so that they are fully understood with the precision of meaning intended. Client's understanding of legal terms they use should be clarified with them during the questioning stage.

(2) *Problems for clients in receiving and understanding advice*
Research in other fields, especially in doctor-patient communication, has shown that lay people have difficulty in understanding the advice or opinions of professionals even though they attend for the specific purpose of obtaining such advice or opinion. These problems seem to occur not simply in relation to the use of professional terminology but as a result of a number of other factors as well.

There may well be educational and class differences between the professional and the lay client, as a result of which the professional may use more complex sentences or speak in a form which is not usual for the client to hear in ordinary conversation. Intuitively, this is an explanation often relied upon by lawyers for lack of success in communication. Interestingly, where differences in social class and education have been studied in relation to recipients of medical care, there has been found to be no correlation between social class and education and satisfaction with the medical consultation (Korsch *et al.*, 1968). It remins to be seen whether the same is true for legal consultations.

Clients may also "freeze" when hearing the lawyer's or other professional's advice. They may be so anxious that when the advice is given their anxiety prevents them from fully hearing and understanding what is said. This is perhaps like the familiar experience of being a patient in a doctor's surgery. Patients may not fully understand the doctor's diagnosis, not because medical terminology is used or because the sentence structure is too complex, but simply because it is so important to hear and understand what is being said that the patients "freeze" and the words drift over them. As can be seen from the medical research, this phenomenon may occur in any class or educational level of client who, as a consequence, may not be able to take in what any doctor or lawyer is saying the first time around.

These difficulties can be alleviated somewhat by practice in speaking in plain and simple terms without "talking down" to clients or patronising them. It is difficult to know how to prepare for dealing with the problem of the client "freezing". One can usually see a glazed look appear over a client's face and deal with this and the problem of complexity by the *repetition of advice* which will come late under the heading of Task 8.

There are some tests measuring complexity of written information which use measures such as the relation between the number of syllables per 100 words and the average sentence length in words of the material analysed. "Readability scores" can be generated and related to the proportion of the population which is likely to understand a measured item. There may well be a difference between the way the mind perceives and assimilates written information as opposed to spoken informtion (Bergman, 1986). One helpful method for trying out by oneself a more simple form of explanation would be to try to dictate into a dictating machine the advice one has just given to the client. By analysing the explanation using those measures and then repeating the exercise it may be possible to make the advice simpler and easier to understand (details of how to work the Flesch Formula Readability Score are to be found in Chapter Seven).

(3) *Rehearsal and the lawyer's part*
Another difficulty which seems to affect the giving of advice an interview is that at the point of the interview when advice is given, the ideas expressed are still in the process of being formulated in the lawyer's mind. The vicissitudes of legal practice do not allow for a lawyer to spend too much time on an interview, or time within an interview in quiet contemplation. As noted above, the advice is beginning to form from the beginning of the interview at the Listening Stage and comes to a more defined metamorphosis by the Advising Stage. However, the first time advice is spoken it may still not be so well thought out that a clear and ordered expression of it is easily possible. Some may find it easier to "think on their hind legs" than others. Most people seem to need a repeated formulation of advice as should be undertaken in Task 8 below.

(4) *Remembering*
It is not only necessary to give advice so that it is understood at the time at which it is heard. The advice must also be given in such a manner that it will be remembered. This is especially so when alternatives are given which need to be thought about and discussed with other people. In all cases, advice which is given by a lawyer in an interview should be followed up by a full letter confirming such advice and stating plans of action (see Chapter

Six). But often decisions must be made or actions taken before the time it takes for a letter to be written and received.

There is a fair amount of literature on the subject of memory and recall generally, and specifically in relation to information and instructions given in the professional-lay person relationship. Among the concepts which appear in the literature which are helpful for the lawyer-client relationship are the findings noted earlier about primacy and recency. These findings suggest that things which are said at the beginning and end of a long speech or of a meeting are more likely to be recalled later than things said in between. This presents a clear problem, as *all* information and advice given in an interview, particularly different alternatives, will be important and will need to be remembered by the client.

Two methods are suggested for dealing with this problem and memory difficulties generally. They are, first to build the advice into a logical structure so that each part needs the other parts to be sensible, and secondly the use of "advance organisers". The first method takes advantage of the phenomenon of "learning by understanding". By explaining something in such a way that the whole is necessary for understanding each part, the listener is more likely to remember all of the explanation.

The latter suggestion of "advance organisers" also stems from some of the literature on education. Where material is categorised in advance by the lawyer and those categories are announced and repeated as each category is worked through, there appears to be more chance of clients remembering more of what they have been told. This is because the brain cannot apparently handle more than a certain number of units of information (Miller's number 7, see Chapter Two) at one time, but can hold a number of categories with a larger number of total units if presented in this manner. This is referred to as "chunking".

An example of this form of categorisation into advance organisers in a family law case would go as follows:

Lawyer: I am going to tell you:
What the basic grounds for divorce are;
What the system of custody, care and control in relation to children is;
What I think your chances of success are in keeping the older girl; and
What you will need to think about before we meet next time.
First, what the grounds for divorce are . . . (the lawyer would then go through the "grounds" for divorce explaining what these mean).
Secondly, what the system of custody, care and control of children is. (And so on . . .)

In the same way as information presented in this manner on a blackboard is more easily understood and remembered by students, such information presented even in the oral style with headings and categorisations has proved to be an important aid to memory. It may similarly be helpful to encourage clients to take notes during an interview. Alternatively, a lawyer may write out some headings for a client to take away and consider.

(5) *Achieving compliance*
A probable major aim of that advice-giving lawyer is going to be compliance on the part of the client with the advice or plan of action, or at least one of the alternative possibilities offered by the lawyer. Intuitively, one knows of many clients who do not seem to comply. Some do not do what their lawyers ask of them, some do not agree with advice and do not return to their lawyers after a first interview and many do not actually pay the bill of costs when it is delivered. The available research also has something to say about this.

What has already been stated about sharing control of the case between lawyer and client will have an important effect on the client's agreement with the advice or plan of action. Similarly, in order to agree, the client must both understand and remember what has been said (as explained immediately above). Compliance also correlates generally, at least in the doctor-patient sphere with the professional being seen as "friendly" rather than "business-like," "understanding a (client's) concern" and being a "good communicator". Two other matters were also found to be important in relation to compliance (Korsch and Negrete):

(a) Lack of thwarted expectations–where a client expected something to happen which did not materialise, such as a full explanation of the problem not being given by the professional.

(b) The length of the interview–where more time was given by the professional there was more compliance by the client.

The above serves to both underline and illuminate the importance of these other factors already mentioned in relation to the interview generally.

The content of advice and plan of action
We have looked at the form in which advice is given in order to understand better the functions of comprehension and memory of advice received by the client. We now turn to issues relating to the content of the advice. Issues arising here include how much advice to give, how clearly one should specify an evaluation of chance in

relation to an alternative and whether information about legal proceedings should include information of their likely effect on the client. This section then goes on to look at the Plan of Action, the problems of advising "bad news" and dealing with the questions of money.

(1) *The full story*
A legal decision or opinion can be argued at great length, and indeed arguing a case before a court is one of the foremost acknowledged legal skills. A lawyer is clearly not sufficiently prepared at the stage of a first interview to begin any such exercise for a client and it will not usually be necessary to do so (an exception might be a lawyer client). However, the *Which?* Consumers' Association Reports on lawyers and the Benson Royal Commission on the Provision of Legal Services tells us there are a number of other aspects of information which the client would like to know that lawyers do not often tell.

Sometimes the seriousness of a predicament is not fully informed to a client, or the seriousness of possible consequences are not fully informed. This is partly because the lawyer may not wish to worry a client unduly, or because it is considered not to be helpful to the client. Other instances are where details of procedure are not explained to the client. The result is that the client does not fully understand such matters as the tasks the lawyer has to perform, how long those tasks will take and what other people have to do in the process or how many court appearances have to be made before finality can be reached. Such aspects are clearly in the knowledge of the lawyer but are not mentioned, perhaps because the lawyer does not think they are important to the client or because thy seem too detailed. The argument is sometimes given that a client comes to a lawyer for the lawyer to carry the burden of worry and that passing this burden back to the client is therefore not fully or properly performing the lawyer's function.

We may be able to learn form Cartwright's research carried out in the medical context. In serious cases where patients were suffering from fatal illnesses, some 70 per cent of doctors felt that patients should *not* be told of the exact nature of their illness; whereas 78 per cent of lay people felt that they *would* like to be told if they where in such a position. Where the people questioned were already terminally ill, this number rose to 84 per cent who *wished* to be fully informed. In other cases, which where not life threatening, there was a general feeling that they would like to know far more information than they were already given. Dissatisfaction with poor communication in medicine is directly opposite to the very high level of satisfaction with the medical care itself. The findings of the Royal Commission on the Provision of Legal Services similarly show a high level of dissatisfaction with the communication of lawyers. Among items generally complained about appears to be insufficient communication of the details of the work involved in a legal case. Although this work may be second nature and "old hat" to a practising lawyer it is new and importantly relevant to a lay client. Detailing the procedure for clients is therefore necessary to ensure their satisfaction with the lawyer's work on the case and their agreement with the advice. These, as has been seen, lead to compliance with providing documents, evidence and finally funds. Indeed, research has shown that when expectations are met and information and explanations are supplied, satisfaction and compliance increases and often anxieties decrease (see Rachman, 1978).

A completely different aspect, which also suggest that the provision of the full story is best, is that of balance in an interview. Such studies suggest that if a professional spends the bulk of an interview in questioning the lay person but gives very little information back on the results of the questioning the client becomes very unhappy with the interview. Intuitively also one feels the need for some balance in the interview when a client has been closely examined for a long period of time. This is part of the lawyer's feeling of the need to give advice mentioned above. When advice or plan of action is given it should therefore be made as full as possible. Clients should not have the feeling that they have opened up their hearts to the lawyer, but the lawyer has hardly opened his, or her, mouth in return.

One further concern which also suggest the need for a full disclosure of information to the client has recently been developed by an American writer (Mark Spiegel) and which he refers to as "The Doctrine of Informed Consent." If the client is to hand over a great deal of responsibility to the lawyer in venturing the client's money, often with uncertain prospects, the client really needs to have as much information as necessary to be able to give a fully informed consent for the lawyer to begin that venture. Holding back any informtion which would be material to the making of that choice might well be considered as negligence if the lawyer's advice is taken and the suggested mode of action is not successful.

(2) *The lottery*

Litigation is often referred to as a "lottery". The results of litigation are nearly always uncertain. So much depend on the nature of the evidence, the nature of the witnesses, the preposition of the judge or other finder of fact or the expertise of the other side's lawyer. Nevertheless, lawyers still make decisions about the likelihood of success of a particular legal argument or a particular case in court or with other lawyers in settlement negotiations. In part, the job of a lawyer is to make such predictions in order to advise the client fully on the likelihood of success of failure of different alternatives.

It is perhaps questionable, however, whether such predictions can reasonably be expressed in clear terms such as percentage chances of success. It may be that a business person dealing with a commercial case would find a "70 per cent chance" form of prediction more helpful than the vague "very good chance" type of verbal prediction. Percentages are useful for a business person to weigh clearly two or three different alternatives whose chances of success differ. Some of the American literature on legal client interviewing does suggest that clear predictions should be given in such percentage terms (see Binder and Price, Chapter 9).

The problem with such clarity and definition, however helpful it may appear to a client, is that it is unlikely to be reflective of the level of accuracy which it appears to connote. It may simply not be possible to make the sort of predictions that clients would pefer. The question is therefore whether such predictions should be attempted even though they may be dishonest or unreliable, simply because they appear to a client to be more helpful. The reality is that law is but an inexact science and although this is a difficult lesson for a client to learn and a difficult responsibility to bear in relation to making choices, it may be better for the client to face this reality at the outset than to proceed in an imagined state of precision.

Another problem about the use of numbers in this context is that it may present to the client only a partial choice rationalised in those terms. Very often the ingredients of alternative possibilities for action on a case are highly complex. The reasons for choosing one alternative or another may not be capable of being turned into a numerical calculus, or may not be capable of being expressed in numbers such that the different choices can be compared. (Game theorists, such as Raiffa, have developed such numbering systems in order to prove theories of negotiation. This work does not, however, show how useful such systems would be in explaining uncertainties in real life.) By expressing part of a choice in numbers one may be forcing the client into a decision rationalised only on the basis of those aspects of the case or of an alternative mode of action which can be expressed in that fashion. Some equally important aspect which may be emotional rather than monetary may not be so easily counted if choices are presented in this form. A good example of this might occur in a family case where a choice might be between frequent visitation rights for a parent (without care and control of a child) as compared with a larger amount of weekly maintenance to be paid. Often such factors need to be weighed up or settlement negotiations between previous marriage partners in divorce proceedings. It would be difficult to reduce such different issues to a simplistic calculus and it is question able whether it is desirable to do so.

A verbal description of degrees of chance can give a sufficiently accurate picture to a client relative to the context in which it is given. Where absolute precision in judgment can reasonably be made, a lawyer should not hold back this information. It seems unlikely, however, that this will be frequent.

(3) *Knowledge of client reaction*
One area of informtion not often transmitted to clients is information about how clients generally react to the course of events being advised or alternatives suggested. For example, one particular course of events such as litigation may well be the most advisable in terms of its chances of success and the amount of damages that are likely to be obtained. But the client in question may be a particularly nervous person who prefers to avoid risk and might therefore prefer an agreed settlement even though it were for a small faction of what might be obtained by judgment in court.

The overall picture of the delays and uncertainties of litigation is usually communicated to a client. The sort of information that does not cross the lawyer's table is more the detail of how long the delays may be on a particular case and how that is likely to affect a client in emotional terms. Lawyers will have far more experience than their clients of how the progress of particular type of matter are likely to affect clients. This is important information for the client to consider in the choice of alternatives.

Under this heading will fall all types of informtion about a client's likely emotional reaction to the more emotive circumstances of legal cases. Examples would include being questioned by the police while under suspicion for commission of an offence; the problems of giving evidence in court on the question of custody or children or even discussing with the client the familial consequences of favouring one potential beneficiary rather than another in a will. Not quite so obvious in terms of discussing, or "counselling choices" (as it is referred to in the literature) will be those which do not appear to have emotional price tags on them. One example would be where the lawyer and company secretary consider one particular course of action to be best for a company, when the managing director feels otherwise. It is the job of the company secretary to try to persuade the reluctant managing director. However, doing so would have an important emotional ingredient which should be realised by the lawyer and included by the lawyer and company secretary in any calculus of choice. Similarly, such mundane and ordinary feelings as a house buyer's or house seller's natural anxiety and frustration with the conveyancing systems and conveyancing "chains" is something that could also be mentioned to client at the outset of a conveyancing matter.

Mentioning these items not only gives a client a fuller picture from which to make properly advised choices, but also gives the client the possibility of a stronger rapport with the lawyer who has shown understanding and interest in the client's feelings. Lawyers should therefore try to discover whether particular aspects are anxieties for particular clients. The result of this is likely to be a more satisfied client and a better run case. As has been stated above in relation to advice about law and procedure, the level of our satisfaction with any event is very largely affected by the nature of our expectation for that event. A client who is fully advised in advance of what is likely to occur not only with outsiders but with the client's own reactions, is far more likely to be satisfied with the final outcome than somebody whose expectations were quite different. This type of knowledge of what will occur before it occurs will also reduce anxiety for the client and make the lawyer's handling of the case a far less anxious period.

(4) *Preparing the client—"the work of worry"*
Some interesting findings have been made with regard to the way in which communications from professionals can also help to ease stress and promote recovery. Many of thee findings come from research on cases where medical patients are either about to undergo surgery or be exposed to painful or frightening procedures. It was found that those patients who had more information before hand about the unpleasant experiences they were about to face showed much better adjustment afterward than those that did not have information about the surgery or procedures. According to Ley:

> "They showed less fear during the hour before operation, less anger on the day of operation, more confidence in the (professional) when questioned, and less emotional disturbance when recalling the operation ."

According to Janis (1971) it is necessary to motivate the "work of worry" before hand so that there are no feelings of helplessness when the unpleasant event materialises; no vulnerability and disappointment in the protecting professionals and less intense fear and anger afterwards. Apparently, providing informtion beforehand gives a warning signal which arises some anticipatory fear; it gives information to clients which allows them to rehearse in their own minds what will happen and it prevents fear becoming too high owing to unrealistic or imagined danger or to alarming expectations (Ley, 1977).

If one may generalise from such patients to clients who go through unpleasant procedures in terms of delay and the court process in civil or criminal litigation, it seems useful to give clients the utmost advice from the beginning so that they do not suffer too much when worrying events occur. The more information that can be given to describe exactly what will happen, the less anxiety that the clients will suffer in advance, the less anger they will have afterwards, and the more satisfaction they will have with the whole process. Thus, withholding information in order to "protect" a client is shown to be counter-productive and indeed a small amount of appropriate worry is seen as beneficial.

(5) *Jeremiahs and other bearers of bad tidings*
One of the strongest lessons of legal education, with which most practising lawyers would agree, it that it is better to err on the side of caution in giving advice. A result of this is that legal advice is nearly always given in a conservative and measured manner. Such caution would seem to be an important part of the lawyer's function .

It is necessary, however, whilst remembering the need for caution and conservatism on the part of the lawyer, also to remember what the general effect of such advice can be on a client. Lawyers are often in the position of bringing bad news to their clients. This is an aspect of advice giving that does not receive much attention. Bearers of bad tidings were, as we know, in ancient civilisations themselves put to death. Nowadays, clergy, police officers, doctors and other professionals whose jobs may include telling bad news are often trained for this particular purpose. Lawyers have not so far been themselves as being involved in the same sort of process.

Advising a client who is an illegal immigrant that the period for a last possible appeal has passed and that the client can therefore now expect at any moment to be arrested and thereafter deported from the country is clearly bad news. The fact that in the lawyer's view of the evidence there seems little chance in a criminal case of escaping prison, or that a father is very unlikely to obtain care and control of this children in a divorce case will both come under the same heading. Whilst the legal profession sees itself as a group of exponents of the law, clients tend to think of lawyers more as actors within the situation who are themselves blameworthy if the advice is not "right" for the client. This is abundantly clear from many of the complaints against solicitors that go each year to the Lay Observer and to the Law Society's complaints panel. Clients will identify advice which is not helpful to them as being partly the fault of the lawyer giving that advice, unless the lawyer is more understanding of the function which is being performed and clients' perceptions of that function .

The coincidence of the need for caution and the aspect of imparting bad news can render clients' impressions of legal consultations somewhat depressing. We can perhaps, therefore, learn something from the approach of other professionals to those aspects of legal work. It appears that it becomes deceptively "easier" for professionals such as police officers to tell bad news.

Although the first few occasions are a harrowing experience for the giver as well as the receiver of bad news, people giving bad news often become used to the difficulties and more immune to the psychological burden. The result is that they tend to pass that burden over onto those they are informing, rather than sharing in that burden themselves. They do this by adopting a more distant, "objective" role and acting as a mere functionary rather than somebody who could provide "first-aid" sympathy and understanding. This description seems to conform with experience of how some lawyers also react. It is necessary to take into consideration the emotional effect of each piece of advice, whether good or bad news, on each particular client and to try to prepare for their reactions, both intellectual and emotional, to the advice given.

(6) *The plan of action*
In concluding this section dealing with the content and character of advice to be given, it should be emphasised that all that is absolutely necessary is for the client to leave with a clear plan of action agreed upon. Such a plan of action need not be complex, need not necessarily involve any "hard" law, and need not be definite. It can include the necessity to carry out legal research or for the client to carry out factual research or anything of even a preliminary nature such as the need for reconsidering the client's position. Giving such a plan of action is not so much a "fall-back" position or "safety-net", as a first step to be taken in completing Task 7, the Advising task. Provided that such a clear plan of action is given to clients, they will feel that they have been given something in the interview. Uncertainty on law or facts in the first interview is permissible, provided it is not accompanied by uncertainty on what should be done next by both parties. Even the most inexperienced lawyer can formulate, and advise the client on, such a plan of action. It is therefore surprising that in many cases clients leave their lawyers' offices without knowing what the lawyer is going to do next on their case.

(7) *Money*
"Information on Costs for the Individual Client

1.1. On taking instructions the solicitor should give his client the best information he can about the likely cost of the matter. The solicitor should discuss with the client how his legal charges and disbursements are to be met and must consider whether the client may be eligible and should apply for legal aid (including legal advice and assistance). The solicitor should also consider whether the client's liability for his costs may be covered by insurance.
1.2. When confirming in writing the client's instructions the solicitor should record whether a fee has been agreed and, if

so, what it is and what it covers and whether it includes VAT and disbursements. If no fee has been agreed or estimate given, the solicitor should tell the client how the fee will be calculated, *e.g.* whether on the basis of an hourly rate plus mark-up, a percentage of the value of the transaction or a combination of both, or any other proposed basis. The solicitor should tell the client what other reasonably foreseeable payments he may have to make either to his solicitor or to a third party and the stages at which they are likely to be required. Oral estimates should be confirmed in writing and the final amount should not substantially vary from the estimate unless the client has been informed of the changed circumstances and in writing.

1.3. If the matter is not to be undertaken under legal aid or covered by insurance so that the client is personally liable for his solicitors' costs he should be told in appropriate cases that he may set a limit on the costs which may be incurred without further reference to him. It should also be explained that it is often not possible to estimate the costs in advance. Whether or not the client has set a limit he should be told at least every six months the approximate amount of costs to date and inappropriate cases an interim bill should be delivered.

2.1. If the client is legally aided in civil proceedings he should be informed at the outset of the case and at appropriate stages thereafter:

(a) of the effect of the statutory charge in his case;

(b) that if he loses the case he may still be ordered by the court to contribute to his opponent's costs even though his own costs are covered by legal aid;

(c) that even if he wins his opponent may not be ordered to pay the full amount of his costs and may not be capable of paying what he has been ordered to pay; and

(d) of his obligation to pay any contribution assessed and of the consequences of any failure to do so.

2.2. If a case is covered by criminal legal aid the client should be told he may be liable to pay a contribution and the effect of not paying it.

3. If the client is not legally aided but the matter is contentious he should be informed at the outset of the case and at appropriate stages thereafter;

(a) that in any event he will be personally responsible for payment of his own solicitor's bill of costs in full regardless of any order for costs made against his opponent;

(b) of the probability that if he loses he will have to pay his opponent's costs as well as his own;

(c) that even if he wins his opponent may not be ordered to pay the full amount of the client's own costs and may not be capable of paying what he has been ordered to pay; and

(d) if his opponent is legally aided he may not recover his costs even if successful.

4. In all matters a solicitor should consider with the client whether the likely outcome will justify the expense or risk involved."

The Law Society's professional Standards,
Published June, 1985.

Perhaps the most unusual "bad news" which lawyers have to tell their clients is how much the lawyer's conduct of the case is going to cost. This is also, especially for inexperienced lawyers, a very difficult part of a first interview to handle. Talking about the money which the client will have to pay puts a rather different perspective on the "professional" obligations of the lawyer. From acting in the role of "helping professional", "counsellor" or as "high priest" of the mystical legal message, the lawyer has to descend to the position of an ordinary shopkeeper intent on selling goods or services at a price which will provide a good living for the lawyer.

Apart from the natural unease and embarrassment on both sides brought about by the discussion of money, the situation is compounded by the lawyer's difficulty in assessing how much a case will cost. Most lawyers give only a vague idea of the cost of a case, sometimes set between upper and lower margins or sometimes confining their assessment to the first or preliminary stages. Because legal costs can be high and may accelerate without warning as a result of opposition from the other side and legal or factual complexities, assessing the exact costs of a legal case can be extremely difficult, if not impossible. Where litigation is contemplated the differences between winning and losing case and the nature of costs awarded to each side will make any guess at costs more complex. Since the client only really becomes a client after agreeing to the suggested costs stated by the lawyer, discussion of these money questions are also crucial to the continuation of the case.

There are special instances where prediction becomes much easier. Where clients and their cases are entitled to legal aid then the limits of the clients' expenditure can be given to them on the basis of their income and capital. Even here, the existence and nature of the statutory charge will have to be explained to clients and this can cause some consternation. The question of how to administer the forms for the "Green Form Scheme" and for "Legal Aid" proper will be discussed in another section.

Some may question whether this is the best time in the interview to discuss costs. Some lawyers appear to favour discussing costs at a rather earlier stage and certainly before any preliminary advice or plan of action is given to the client. The argument in favour of doing so is that if a client is given preliminary advice there is then no need for the client to pay for that consultation itself. However, it would seem that it is not possible to make any realistic assessment of how much a case is going to cost without having full information on the case from the client. Clearly, the later in the interview the discussion of funds takes place, the more information the lawyer is likely to have gleaned. Also, different alternative modes of action must be discussed in order to explain to the client how much each mode of action would cost. Since this is an essential piece of information in making a choice, it does not seem possible to avoid outlining some overall advice in detailing different plans of action. It seems doubtful, in any event, how much use preliminary advice could be to a client, in view of all that has been said above. Other lawyers appear to put clients at rest immediately they come to them by explaining that they make no charge for the first interview anyway, or only make a nominal charge for the first half hour.

The English Law Society's view of methods of costing is well set out in their pamphlet entitled "The Expense of Time." My own view (see (1982) 45 M.L.R. 598–602) is that it should be possible right from the outset to give a client a clear expectation within narrow margins, and providing for different possible alternatives, or what they can expect to have to pay. Unless a case is unusual, or a firm is very small and unused to handling such cases, it will be possible to gauge from looking at the past five to ten cases of that nature handled by the firm how much the new case is likely to cost. In these days of computer accounting it should not be too difficult to put up on a screen the cost of some of the most analogous cases in the recent past. Taking an average of these cases should give both the client and the lawyer a fair price. If the sums are calculated correctly, on average over all the cases that come into the firm, the lawyer should receive about the same amount of money compared with work done as would have been received if the client had been left in almost complete ignorance of the final figure and had the lawyer worked out a bill of costs in the usual manner. All of this would reduce in great part the uncertainty regarding what appears to be one of the most worrying aspects for clients of attending a lawyer's office. No other service profession or industry manages to get away with such vague predictions of cost. It seems more reasonable that lawyers should estimate what their costs are going to be and stick to that estimate than the clients with far less experience should have to make the same sort of judgment.

Assessments of costs which are based on an hourly rate stated to the client, do have the impression of giving a more exact approach. However, unless this hourly rate is the only charge (and the bill of costs does not include items such as letters in and out, telephone calls in and out, photocopying and travel costs) and the lawyer also states a precise number of hours to be spent on the job, this does not provide a very exact assessment for a client.

Making such assessment can be an especially difficult task for inexperienced practitioners, not only because they may not know what the cost of such matters has been in the past, but also because they may not be in the position of fixing the cost when the time comes for the bill to be sent out. New lawyers in this position should try and obtain from their seniors or senior partners a definite statement on the question of costs so that they are in a proper position to answer the client's questions on the subject.

Task 8: *Repeat Advice/Plan of Action and Check for Client's Agreement or Amend*

It follows from what has been said above that the process of advice, both for the adviser and the advisee, is complex. A well presented legal opinion is unlikely to be given easily off the cuff by the lawyer. A first statement of advice is unlikely to be completely understood or appreciated first time round by the client. It therefore seems advisable to make certain that the client has heard, appreciated and understood the main object of attending the lawyer's office, by having that advice repeated.

If it is to be given, such repetition should be contemplated by the lawyer in advance of the previous task, Task 7. Some lawyers may even introduce Task 7, the "Advising" task with a statement such as,

Lawyer: I would just like to explain the legal position quickly in outline and discuss the question of cost with you and then I will be able to talk to you in more detail about my advice to see what you think.

The main intention of the repetition is not so much to amplify previous advice, although this is a possibility, but more to sort the advice into a presentable form for the client from which choices can be made, and with which the client may criticise or agree. If more than one alternative option is being suggested to the client by the lawyer, and this should in almost all cases be so, it will be essential for the client to hear the different possibilities more than one time. Where the choice is complex and involved, the client may well have to wait for the letter confirming advice before giving agreement or making a final choice. But very often some preliminary decisions need to be made regarding the plan of action a the first interview.

The literature on decision-making shows us an interesting distinction between two types of information processing strategies (Janis and Mann, 1977): "vigilant" and "non-vigilant" strategies. According to Morely and Hosking (1984) in the "vigilant" strategy the decision-maker:

(a) Seriously considers more than one policy or course of action.

(b) Carefully considers the full range of objectives to be met, and the values implicated by each choice.

(c) Carefully works out the costs and benefits of each of the alternatives.

(d) Intensively searches for new information which may change his or her opinion of what is important, and what is not.

(e) Is sensitive to new information or expert judgement, even when the new information is unpalatable and does not support the option initially preferred.

(f) Re-examines the consequences of all known alternatives (including those initially discounted) before making a final choice.

(g) Makes detailed provisions for executing the policy chosen, paying special attention to contingency planning.

From this it is clear that the "vigilant" decision-maker is attempting to make the best choice within the constraints of the task and not simply allowing precedent or natural bias to make the choice for them. On the other hand the "non-vigilant" decision-maker avoids the uncertainty which comes from insufficient information, and the cognitive strain of handling a full range of options. The non-vigilant:

(a) Considers a restricted number of alternatives, sometimes only one.

(b) Considers a restricted number of consequences, sometimes only one.

(c) Evaluates each alternative once only. Options are evaluated sequentially as they arise.

(d) Regards each consequence as either acceptable or unacceptable. The actor is looking for a decision which is acceptable (good enough) rather than optimal (the best overall).

Each of these strategies is appropriate to different kinds of decision, and where decisions need to be made quickly and can be reversed easily a "non-vigilant" strategy approach will be more acceptable.

In the legal setting, were some of the job of decision-making is shared between lawyer and client, the lawyer must choose which form of strategy is necessary for each decision to be made by the client. Where the more "vigilant" approach is needed the careful repetition of advice and plan of action in fuller detail will be called for.

Task 8, "advice repetition", is mot simply the restating of the advice so that the lawyer can be pleased with the way in which it is formed. The other objective is to give a chance for the client to exercise judgment on the advice and alternatives for action, to criticise and suggest amendments where necessary and finally to give agreement on the final choice. From watching lawyers (in our research) giving advice, and reading transcripts of such consultations it appears that many do repeat their advice, but much fewer give time to a client to agree or disagree with advice or alternatives proposed. Where clients are not completely cowed by the force and impact of the lawyer's words they may well ask questions of the lawyer in relation to the advice or alternatives given. These questions may be real questions asking for further information, and they may also be a disguised form of suggested amendment to the advice. Often at this stage a client will mention a "new" fact which had not yet emerged in the interview but which is importantly relevant to the case. This sometimes occasions a reaction of impatience in the lawyer since the whole suggested advice had been given in ignorance of this fact and may now need to be changed. For example, a client may have mentioned everything about the home situation except that the mother-in-law also lived there. A lawyer's suggested advice might well have to be revised taking into account the new extra fact of mother-in-law's residence.

Full time must be given to this stage of the interview and it would seem of little worth to repeat the advice too quickly to a bemused client. This task involves much interactive discussion between the two, and the client may need to interrupt the lawyer with questions of detail during the course of the repetition. The lawyer should not move from this stage unless the client has expressed with some certainty, agreement with a possible course of action and with the costs involved in that course.

Task 9: *Recount Follow-up Work to be Done by Client*

The next three tasks are, in a sense, a summary of elements which will already have been mentioned at Tasks 7 and 8 but need to be repeated and organised in a different format so that they can be remembered and acted upon by both parties. In one sense these are set out in the form of "advance organisers", as mentioned above. There will also be occasions when both client and lawyer may wish to take short formal notes of these details to be sure that both understand what they have agreed and what each should do. There are many types of follow-up work which a lawyer may ask a client to perform as a result of an interview. The most usual would be finding and bringing in a letter or other document to the lawyer's office, or locating a witness or perhaps making a preliminary move in relation to the other side before the lawyer is fully involved in the case. Experience shows that unless such items are pointedly mentioned to the client towards the end of an interview in the context of actions which the client must take, they tend to be forgotten in the client's catharsis of having unloaded the problem to the lawyer.

The letter confirming advice may well remind the client to carry out this work (see Chapter Six) but once again it may be some time before that letter reaches a client and the delay involved is not necessary. Indeed, full commitment from the client on working together with the lawyer in the style suggested by Rosenthal can be commenced successfully only in this way. The consultation between lawyer and client is therefore treated as a business meeting of equals, at the end of which each agrees what the other needs to do next, or before their next meeting. Clients often seem to delay before coming to a lawyer with a problem and it is useful to use the impetus of the interview itself to push them into further considering what has happened and involve them in doing something about it.

It is not suggested that work is manufactured for the client to perform. However, the feeling of being involved in one's own destiny and therefore having some control over what happens to one-self is an important aspect in dealing with any difficulty. Handing over the problem entirely onto the shoulders of a professional is too much of a burden for the professional to bear. It is also unlikely in the long term to help solve the real problem, which is the effect of what has happened in each individual client themselves.

Task 10: Recount Follow-up Work to be Done by the Lawyer

Whereas many lawyers seem to understand the necessity of repeating the client's follow-up to the client in those terms before the end of the interview, far less seem to explain to the client what work they themselves will be doing on the case.

One of the most unsatisfying aspects of solicitors' work for their clients, appears to be that solicitors do not explain to their clients what is happening on their cases (Benson). This approach seems to conform to the "high priest" lawyer model rather than any collaborative model of the lawyer-client relationship. A client probably has a right to know exactly what the lawyer is to do because the client will usually be paying for that work. Where a case is funded by public funds a client may still be paying a proportion of the costs, or will have paid towards the Legal Aid Fund in taxes previously, or may well pay towards the Legal Aid Fund out of the proceeds of any court judgment or award under the statutory charge.

There are other, more cogent reasons with more practical effects than this claim of right. Where a client's collaboration is requested in carrying out follow-up work it is right that the client understands similarly what the lawyer is to be doing. When a client appreciates the work the lawyer will be carrying out and how long that work is likely to take, then the client's expectations of delay are more likely to be met and the client is more likely to be satisfied. A few minutes well spent on this may save much time later. Otherwise, a client uncertain of what is happening on a case may pester a lawyer with telephone calls and letters unnecessarily.

It would appear, therefore, that legal work need not remain under a cloud of mystification (see F. Rodell, *Woe Unto You Lawyers*, Chapters 1 and 8) but can be explained at least in outline to the client with full details of how long each item is likely to take. This will also form the other side of the coin in the collaborative approach. It would be a poor collaborator who stated what was required from the other person but was not prepared to state what they themselves were going to do. "The law's delays", so well charted by Shakespeare and Dickens, remain one of the greatest difficulties and one of the greatest fears to be faced by a client. Clients therefore need to be reassured that delays occurring on cases is the fault of the law itself and its procedure, rather than the fault of their lawyer.

Task 11:   State Next Contact Between Lawyer and Client

As noted in Chapter 1, the tasks are fully delineated in numbers 9 and 10 are individually mentioned because, from experience in teaching new lawyers, they tend to be items which otherwise go unmentioned in an interview. It is for this reasons that they merit such explicit mention in this text.

There has been some research (Sherr, 1986; Bergman, unpublished) directly on the question of whether clients know when they leave their lawyers' office when to expect the next contact from their lawyer. It has shown that only about 30 per cent of clients leave a lawyers' office knowing when that next contact is likely to be. In order to remove some of the anxiety engendered by the other uncertainties of a legal case the client should be very clear when the next contact between the lawyer and client will be and how that contact will take place. If the lawyer is to write to the client this should be stated and an estimate made of when the letter will be received. This estimate should of course subsequently be kept to or the client informed why not. If the communication is to be in some other form such as a telephone call or meeting then this also should be stated and it should be made absolutely clear whether it is intended that the lawyer or the client should initiate the communication.

Lawyers' workloads often change dramatically from day to day and cases which appear to be quite formant have a habit of suddenly waking up with a vengeance. It is therefore convenient for a lawyer to be vague about when things will happen. However, there is no excuse for not making some communication even through a secretary, when promised. The effect of certainty on a client will make such a different to the client that any inconvenience or extra communications arising out of such a promise are worthwhile.

Research with clients in other fields shows that the immediate "blush" or satisfaction at the end of a consultation begins to change during the few days afterwards. Clients tend to review in their minds what occurred during the consultation and may become more anxious than they were on leaving the professional's office. It therefore seems good policy to give the client something to look forward to in terms of the next contact.

Task 12: Ask if "Any Other Business" and Deal with it

By Task 12, the "Any Other Business" task, the interview appears to be completed. The client has told the whole story to the lawyer who has replied by giving advice and setting up a plan of action. This after all, is what the client came for and what the lawyer was there for. It might well seem to be high time to move to the final task of termination of the interview.

Before terminating, however, a final check may be necessary in order to be sure that everything the client wished to tell the lawyer has been mentioned and whether in fact the problem situation outlined is the real problem on which the client most needed advice. Research, once again in the medical field, shows that clients very often do not reveal their expectations or worries to the professional from whom they seek advice. In one study (Korsch *et al.*, 1971) 65 per cent of patients' expectations were not communicated to the doctor and only 24 per cent of their worries were mentioned. It remains to be seen whether this is also true of the legal profession.

Similarly, in a number of cases, patients came to doctors and presented a completely different set of symptoms at first, and only after having dealt with these symptoms did the patient mention far more serious anxieties about a more serious problem. Doctors sometimes refer to this as the "hand on the doorknob syndrome" where a patient actually tells the real reason for attending the doctor's surgery with one hand on the doorknob as they are about to leave the room. There are no figures of how often this occurs in legal practice though experience suggests that it does occur. An example of such an incident in which I was involved as the lawyer was a visit by a young married client and her mother to inquire generally about the possibility of divorce. Only towards the end of the interview did the client mention that when she left her mother's home to attend the interview her husband had been "hanging around" the house. She had left her young baby there with a younger sister and her husband had previously threatened to take the baby away with him. Their confidence in the power of the law regarding the general situation in the future had completely blinded them to the important practical needs of the present, and the precipitating event which caused them to consult a lawyer.

For these reasons it appears to be advisable to give clients one further occasion too say anything that they wished to say. Clients should therefore be asked if there is anything else that they wanted to say, and to give a little time to think about this before the interview is terminated. Some of the literature suggests that a minute or two spent in conversation about non-legal topics may also help to calm the client and give a chance at this stage for the client to think about anything else which they might have wished to say (Korsch *et al.*, 1971).

If a completely new problem is presented at this stage it can cause great difficulty for the lawyer. All the lawyer's energy systems have been switched off after listening so attentively and advising so carefully. It can therefore be most frustrating and annoying to realise that the whole process may have to be gone through again from the beginning. Nevertheless, there is usually some good reason why it was difficult for the client to mention the real problem at the outset. Also the fault, if anybody's, may in part be the lawyer's for not having sufficiently noted the client's needs earlier, or any non-verbal communication that some other concern was not being addressed.

The "Any Other Business" task concludes the business of the interview. It gives an opportunity for clients to think again either about any facts, worries and expectations which they have not yet conveyed to the lawyer or to reconsider whether to mention a more pressing and more important problem that they have not been able yet to bring themselves to state in this interview. It is a task that should not be rushed or treated mechanically. There will nearly always be something extra that a client wishes to mention, given a little time and patience from the lawyer. It is also a helpful period during which the lawyer's role reverts from the "high priest" adviser image back to the "helping professional" image and this is therefore a more pleasant way to end the interview.

Task 13:   Terminate, Help-Out and Goodbye

We have seen in Chapter Two how poorly the normal social skills involved in greeting clients was practised in research on inexperienced lawyers. The same was found to be true at the end of the interview (Sherr, 1986). Seventy per cent of new lawyers carried out these tasks badly, many of them remaining seated at their desks as the client withdrew from the room and they crouched over their notepads hurriedly making up their notes of the interview. The lasting impression for the client was of a harrowed and busy lawyer not sufficient concerned with the client personally to say goodbye and see them out effectively. The lawyers' intentions had been to do a good job of noting the interview. They did not sufficiently consider the effect of this on the client.

In a society in which it is common to shake hands at the end of a meeting it is necessary for a lawyer to get up from behind the desk and shake the client's hand. The normal social decencies including helping clients on with their coats and seeing them out through, what may be for them, a maze of offices is an important aspect of making the visit to a lawyer a more pleasant experience. These are minor issues, but they may well make a major difference to the client's feelings.

The interview covering, as it often does, extremely important and sometimes emotional issues for the client may well have been an exhausting experience. A pleasant ending will make all the difference to a client's memory of what occurred and therefore a client's continuing activity on the case. One writer (Shaffer) even refers to the need for a "sunshine termination" of the interview.

Conclusion

The "Advice" Stage has therefore concluded the interview in a collaborative manner. The lawyer has performed the function of giving advice and made sure that the advice given or alternatives proposed are understood and fully agreed by the client. Both have work to do with regard to the problem and both know what each, and the other, need to do next. They have a deadline set for the next contact had have had a moment to reflect on whether there as anything further to say. At the termination of the interview the client should feel some relief at the prospect of help with a difficult problem, and the lawyer should feel confident that enough information has been gathered for the immediate tasks ahead.

With the main framework for a first interview now completely set out we can turn in succeeding chapters to using the framework with the intention of learning from each interviewing experience, and taking a look at the continuing relationship between lawyer and client.

＋ Chapter Five

SOME SPECIFIC INTERVIEWING PROBLEMS

This chapter contains a "pot-pourri" of more specific problems which can occur in legal interviewing. In the first part of this chapter we will look at interview interruptions, documentary information including forms, and interviewing witnesses. In the second half of the chapter we will consider briefly three difficult interviewing situations: clients with mental health problems, clients who threaten suicide and the problems involved in interviewing children.

Confidentiality, privacy and interruption

The lawyer-client relationship is, as stated in the Solicitors' Code of Professional Conduct, and by its own natural ethics, a relationship of confidentiality. Most clients immediately appreciate this, although there are particular cases where it may be important to mention the issue directly. Sometimes clients appear to be reticent about giving certain information, and explain that they do not wish anybody else, apart from the lawyer, to know what they are about to tell. In such cases it is well to assure the client that the lawyer will not, and may not by the Solicitors' Code of Conduct, pass the information to anybody else without the client's permission. This appears to be especially important in criminal proceedings, but may be equally important even in the negotiation of a civil matter. Much of the client's information to which a lawyer is privy could well have the effect of lessening the value of the client's case if it were told to the other side. There will be circumstances where a solicitor will feel that being privy to certain information would make it difficult for that solicitor to work on a particular case. The client's confidentiality should still be maintained but it may be necessary for the matter to be taken over by another lawyer or another firm. Such conditions might include where a client is determined to fight a vigorous defence of a criminal prosecution, impugning the validity of police evidence, at the same time as admitting fully to the lawyer that the client is nevertheless guilty of the actual charge.

For most cases it will be an easy matter for the lawyer to treat the client's confidences as such. What is important for our purposes here is to note how the atmosphere of confidentiality, and the image of a lawyer interested in the client's matter, should be engendered in the interview itself. It seems trivial to state that all interviews should be carried out without any interruption. It would seem that all lawyers would immediately agree with such a proposition. However the vicissitudes of legal work often cause lawyers to act counter to such principles.

In research on lawyers with differing levels of experience interviewing clients in their own offices, out of 18 cases considered there are 14 interviews with interruptions of some sort, usually a telephone call (see Chapter Seven). In some cases lawyers will spend between five to ten minutes on a telephone conversation with another client or other third party whilst a client they are interviewing for the first time is sitting in front of them, waiting to begin, or in the middle of an interview. Often a commercial case is given precedence over a matrimonial matter. Although it may not be true, the client being interviewed could well have the feeling that the interruption is considered to be more important by the lawyer than the case in hand. It would be impolite in normal social circumstances to take a telephone call in the middle of a conversation with somebody one has only just met. It seems equally, or more, impolite to do so in the legal office setting, however busy the lawyer or office is. Each client should be shown the courtesy of full attention from the lawyer whilst the lawyer is dealing with that client's case. Switchboard telephonists, receptionists and secretaries should be alerted when a lawyer is in consultation with a client. Modern technology allows for the telephone systems which enable the lawyer to divert all calls to a secretary. Advantage should be taken of such aids where at all possible.

Documents and forms-the written word in the interview
Problems arise for both lawyer and client in a first interview where documents are handed over or where forms need to be filled out. When a client comes to an interview with a letter, summons or other document, unless it is a long document it will usually be necessary for the lawyer to consider this during the interview. As soon as the document is mentioned by the client, or placed on the table it acquires the status almost of another persona in the interviewing room until the lawyer has read it, glanced through it or promised to look at it afterwards.

Often a client will continue to refer to the document in the presentation of the facts in the Listening Stage and the lawyer may well feel the necessity to consult the document rather than listen to the client. Where possible, this inclination should be avoided and the document should only be looked at during the Questioning Stage of the interview (the stage at which in a doctor's surgery a physical examination might take place). Until then the document should, if possible, be treated as a major item in the list of "issues for attention" for the Questioning Stage. This is a counsel of perfection and it would not be desperately wrong in certain circumstances to glance at the document before listening to the client.

The problem that may arise as a result of doing so is that, as mentioned above, the immediate attention of the lawyer is lost, and the lawyer's inclination will be to pigeonhole each case under a legal subject heading. The written word has probably clearer and more obvious effect than other types of evidence and so immediately becomes of great importance in the lawyer's mind. It is therefore preferable to hear the client's story before concentrating too much on a document that the client has brought along. Clients also have a tendency to talk whilst the lawyer is reading the document, which means that the lawyer does not pay sufficient attention to either the document or the client. It is difficult under these circumstances to ask a client to be quiet until the document has been read. On the other hand, if the lawyer spends some time reading the document in silence, it can also have the effect of making the client somewhat subdued for the next part of the interview. On the whole, therefore, it is best to hear the client out first and to read any documents subsequently.

It is often necessary for forms to be filled out in the course of any interview. The "Green Form" needs to be filled out where legal advice and assistance are being claimed, and legal aid forms may need to be filled out for financial assistance for work in court. In social security benefit cases, some tax cases and any case where an affidavit of means has to be prepared, a large amount of detailed factual information has to be processed with a number of short, closed questions. Where some of this information can be considered beforehand it is well to get the client to prepare answers to the necessary questions. This can sometimes be done with an explanatory leaflet in a waiting room, or information can be sent to a client ahead of time where a lawyer knows that such questions may need to be asked. At any rate, filling out forms, or answering questions from forms, especially those regarding financial circumstances, are not very pleasant tasks for clients to perform. Because of this, where possible, forms should not be filled out until after the major part of the first interview, probably when the Advising Stage has been reached. Clients will feel much more satisfied when they have been given something in terms of advice or a plan of action before they have to start filling in forms requesting money for that very advice.

Interviewing witnesses
Potok, in describing the social organisation of an ancient Sumerian city, notes how the judges sat at the city with the citizens assembled nearby. He notes a Sumerian stone inscription of the period advising that citizens keep a fair distance from the judges warning, "They'll pull you in as a witness, and you'll get involved" (*Wanderings*, 1984).

This book concentrates mainly on the subject of lawyers interviewing clients. The investigation into the facts of a case, and the interviewing of witnesses (other than clients) in particular, stand as subjects by themselves and cannot be dealt with in any detail here. However, a little may be said about some of the distinctions between client- and witness-interviewing which, it is hoped, may shed some light on both of these processes.

We will first consider the major motivational differences between clients and witnesses as interviewing subjects. Clients have made a personal decision to come to see a lawyer and to be interviewed by that lawyer on the facts of a problem case. They therefore know why they are being asked questions. Witnesses (other than clients) will usually have made no such conscious decision to have come to a lawyer or to be involved in this process. Very often a witness has just happened to be at a particular place at the time when the event occurred. Witnesses may not otherwise be affected by the event, and therefore do not have the same understanding of why they should be involved.

Clients therefore clearly *want* to be involved or have made a decision that they have to be involved. In most cases witnesses do *not* wish to be involved either in being asked questions by a lawyer or with the prospect of some day perhaps having to go to court. Both clients and witnesses tend to be wary of lawyers but clients will have more of a feeling that they can control what is happening. They are, after all "paying the piper" and will therefore be more likely to "call the tune". Witnesses have no such say in the matter. Lawyers will usually be pleasant to their own witnesses because they want to persuade their witnesses to give evidence useful to "their side". The other side's lawyer may not be quite so kind in cross-examination in court. For some witnesses the amount of time spent on such matters is a deterrent to becoming involved, but also important in the minds of many prospective witnesses is the idea of being made to look a fool in court.

Lastly, clients see very clearly the possible rewards of helping the lawyer establish the facts. No such rewards exist, and should certainly not be offered, to a witness.

Witnesses can however be properly motivated by their interviewers. In an appropriate case of an appeal to the altruism of a witness can be most effective. Many people will be swayed by being told it is their public duty as honest citizens to assist in the course of justice. Some may be encouraged by being invited to stand in the shoes of the client: "How would *you* feel, if *you* were in this predicament and nobody came forward to help *you*?" Others still will be excited at the prospect of publicity. There is also always the threat of a possible *subpoena ad testificandum* to compel a witness to attend at court. However, a reluctant witness is unlikely to make a very good witness and it would seem to be far better to motivate with encouragement rather than with threats. It may sometimes be possible to suggest to witnesses (as pointed out in Binder & Price) that if they are prepared to give a full statement of facts at an early stage, the lawyer might be able to negotiate an adequate settlement of the case without the necessity of going to trial.

There are also differences in what the lawyer is trying to achieve in interviewing a witness as opposed to a client. By the stage of interviewing witnesses the basic outline of the case is known and the lawyer is searching for particular evidence which will be useful for the client's case. Client-interviewing is, as we have seen, open-ended, at least in the early stages. Witness-interviewing is far more directed to specific instances and desired conclusions. In an earlier chapter the analogy of carving a sculpture out of a block of marble rock was used. It was there stated that, in direct contrast to sculpture, in client-interviewing there should be no perceived form inside the mass, to which the lawyer as sculptor is aiming. With a witness, however the analogy is far more apposite. The lawyer knows exactly what types of evidence will be necessary and helpful for the client and what shapes to form from the witness's facts. The exercise of fact gathering and presentation beyond the first client interview can be seen as much more of an exercise in stage management of existing factual material. Witnesses will therefore be far more closely "managed" than clients.

There will also be an immediate need to test how a witness will face up to giving evidence in court, when the witness is being interviewed for the first time. Since this may be the only chance before trial of meeting witnesses it will be necessary to test out how they are likely to perform in the witness box and react to examination and cross examination. Despite all of this, witnesses should be treated with kindness and courtesy and not as mere "artillery" or "gun fodder" in the lawyer's "armoury". Witnesses, even the other side's witnesses, are far more likely to react best to lawyers who treat them with respect and courtesy.

Special Interviewing Cases

In the latter part of the chapter we will look at some especially difficult interviewing situations: those involving interviewing the mentally disturbed, people who threaten suicide and also interviews with children. This is a rather strange group to be encountered in the same package. They are all interviewing situations which are not uncommon for lawyers to face, and which may cause particular difficulty where a lawyer has not contemplated the problems involved in such interviews before encountering them for the first time.

The mentally disturbed

Lawyers, unless otherwise trained, do not have any special skills in handling the mentally disturbed and this book in no way suggests that lawyers should become involved as amateur, or unskilled, psychologists or psychiatrists. However, clients who are mentally disturbed may well come to lawyers for help and it is important to be aware beforehand of this possibility so that the lawyer can be prepared to make adequate referrals and succeed in handling clients in an appropriate manner.

In dealing with the mentally disturbed it is important to distinguish between those who are "mentally handicapped", who were probably born with some congenital defect which leaves them in this condition, and those who are "mentally ill" and may with treatment be helped to recover. There is a particular body of law relating to the capacity and responsibility of people who are mentally disturbed, as well as a body of law dealing with questions of mental health review concerning the release of people under institutional care. It is not intended to deal with such questions here. This section will instead be looking at the case of a client who approaches a lawyer to deal with subject matter which does not clearly by its nature expose the mental health condition of the client.

In order to consider that case, if it first instructive to learn a little more about mental illness so that the limits of a lawyer's involvement can be more clearly delineated. Mental illness can be further divided into those suffering from "neuroses" and those suffering from "psychoses" (Myre and Sim, *Psychiatry*). There is no exact definition to be found for either of these terms. "Neuroses" appears to cover the condition where people are so nervous of worried that they are not able to deal with life or a particular problem. "Psychoses" seems to cover a more common view of someone who is "mentally unbalanced" and will therefore be suffering from delusions of grandeur, or be paranoid.

Much has been written recently about the more controversial aspects of mental illness especially by Dr Thomas Szasz in *The Myth of Mental Illness*. He there suggests that society tends to label people as "mentally ill" when they present society with difficult social problems, or do not think in quite the same way as the rest of us. However, such literature is not helpful to a lawyer who faces for the first time a client who does not appear to be mentally well. No strict definitions will be attempted here, and it may often be difficult to draw the line between normal and abnormal behaviour. Some clients may need help from another professional such as a psychologist of psychiatrist to assist in recovering from a particular problem such as injury, bereavement, divorce or even the psychological effects of a criminal conviction. It may be necessary for lawyers at times to suggest to a client, carefully, that such help is available. It is therefore useful for lawyers to ascertain and have available the names, addresses and telephone numbers of possible providers of such help in the locality.

A rather more upsetting instance for an inexperienced lawyer is to be presented with a client with a normal problem to which the lawyer reacts accordingly, only to find about half way through the interview that the client is probably mentally disturbed. Clinical advice given to doctors under such circumstances is as follows. When there are two of you in a room and you begin to feel that one of you is mad, it is a good working hypothesis to begin with the presumption that it is the other person rather than you yourself (Watson).

Some cases of this nature which appear to come to lawyers would probably be diagnosed as showing paranoid schizophrenic symptoms by a doctor. The first example sounds very much like a good case of nuisance and breach of planning regulations. A kindly, elderly lady complains about the neighbours next door who have begun some sort of manufacturing process in their cellar. This process apparently causes an unpleasant smell and lets loose a white deposit which the lady claims has fallen on the leaves of the trees in her garden and on parts of the railings in front of her house. On inspection the white deposit turns out to be bird lime. The lady is widowed and has few visitors.

A second example looks like defamation. A young man presents himself to the lawyer complaining of damaging statements made about him by other people. The statements have affected his employment, which has been terminated as a result, and turned some of his friends against him. As the interview continues the client explains that the damaging, but untrue, facts about him have even been relayed by astronauts from outer space through to the mission control centre at Houston. When asked directly by his lawyer, he admits to being under treatment for these delusions and gives the name of his doctor.

A third example is that of another elderly lady who complains that the people upstairs are somehow interfering with her television signal and arranging for unpleasant things to appear on her television set. In this particular case it becomes obvious from the initial facts that it is unlikely that the clients story is the product of a completely sensible mind.

In all of these real cases, where these clients have come to the writer, or lawyers known to him, it has been quite difficult to ascertain where the reality ends and the delusions begin. It may of course be that there was some truth in some way in each of the allegations. Often the greatest problem for the lawyer facing this sort of client is the unpleasant realisation that the case is probably not a regular nuisance action against a neighbour or an action of defamation. This can be something of a shock the first time it occurs and it therefore seems sensible to have such cases in mind as a possibility.

It is not known how common it is for such people to present such problems to lawyers, but on the basis on intuitive findings it does seem to happen occasionally. Such people may still have legal problems tucked away within their delusions, or they may have other difficulties which are susceptible to legal help. They should therefore not be simply turned away or referred to a more appropriate helping professional without some attempt to ascertain whether this is so.

In the examples mentioned above it was found possible to give help in a number of different ways. The first lady was helped by regular visits from workers in the legal advice centre she had first approached. These visits were aimed at checking whether she was physically well, and providing occasional company. Such services could in other circumstances be provided by some local voluntary "welfare" group or even the social services department of the local authority. Subsequently she returned to the centre with an interesting probate problem. She appeared, as previously, to be lucid in her account. The facts were checked with a relative whose name she provided and were found to be entirely correct. That case was dealt with in the normal way. She sent a Christmas card to the centre each year.

In the second case, the young man's story, when it had reached its conclusion, seemed so disturbed that the lawyer (with the permission of the client) made a telephone call to the client's doctor. The lawyer explained the circumstances and the doctor, who was a specialist in the treatment of the mentally ill, confirmed that the story was largely delusion. He also confirmed that the client was undergoing a long course of treatment but was not confined to an institution. The doctor's advice was that it was safe for the client/patient to make his own way home. The lawyer therefore suggested to the client that he may have been mistaken about some of the facts, they discussed the matter and the client agreed. The client left looking a little happier and no follow-up was given.

In the third case the lawyer decided to involve the social services department to check generally on the client's circumstances, with the client's permission. They provided her with a "meals on wheels" service which gave her food and a little daily friendly contact.

Each case will be different and reactions will have to be tailored to the presenting facts and person. What is necessary to note here that these instances occur and a lawyer should be prepared for them.

Suicide

A less frequent occurrence (once again no statistics are available and this judgment is made on an intuitive basis) is that a lawyer is witness to a threat of suicide by a client of another party. Suicide is a highly emotive subject on which most people have strong beliefs.

In this section the intention is to discover whether learning in other fields is of assistance to lawyers in reacting to such a threat. Once again, it is not suggested that the lawyer is in any different position from any other lay person in this regard and should certainly not play the amateur psychologist/psychiatrist. However, there may be certain professional responsibilities such as confidentiality involved and the circumstances in which lawyers' clients often find themselves may be high-risk situations for suicide.

Durkheim's classical work on suicide divides suicides into those which are "egocentric", where the suicide lacks a support grouping, and those which are "anomic", occasioned by sudden crises in people who may already be predisposed to suicide (Shaffer).

There is also some ethnographic information. Shaffer notes that men, the elderly and single people are most likely to commit suicide in the USA. For this country, one can add that the higher professional classes are also more likely to commit suicide.

The research conducted by the mental help professions on suicide is, by its nature, retrospective. Two major groups appear: those who are only attempting suicide in order to gain attention (Group B in Figure 5.1), and those who fully intend to take their own Lives (Group A). Within each of these two major groups there are sub-groups of those who die, and those who do not die.

Figure 5.1

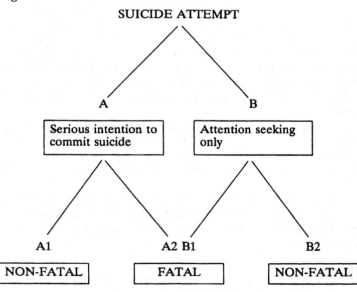

SUICIDE ATTEMPT

A — Serious intention to commit suicide

B — Attention seeking only

A1 — NON-FATAL

A2 B1 — FATAL

B2 — NON-FATAL

All the retrospective studies are carried out on those in the two sub-groups who do not die (A1 and B2). It is not therefore clear how reliable all the information is. It does, however, seem clear that about 80 per cent of those who finally succeed in taking their lives, have given warnings which can be understood as such after their deaths. A similar proportion of those who take their lives have attempted to do so on earlier occasions. It seems that the decision is usually made in a sudden, short-term crisis (Shaffer). The crisis will pass, and although it may recur, equally it may not.

We can learn from all of this that no threat of, or attempt to commit, suicide should be ignored. The lawyer has the responsibility to refer the client and if the client refuses to make contact with someone else the lawyer should perhaps get secondary help to advise the lawyer how to handle the client and the predicament. A lawyer should certainly not take responsibility for such a client's actions when the lawyer is not competent so to do.

Some interesting recent research has shown that the spouses of suicides have more difficulty than other widows or widowers in coping with the bereavement. Lawyers may well come into contact with such people in relation to probate matters. These spouses are apparently not given the same consideration afforded to others who have lost a partner because of society's difficulty in discussing the question of suicide. The spouses themselves suffer a measure of personal guilt for what has occurred and are uncertain about whether they were at fault. They therefore need a great deal of understanding.

Some other recent research shows a larger proportion of the younger people committing suicide than was previously the case. Included in these statistics are some who seem reckless about their behaviour, such as those who become involved in drugs or drink in such a way that it is a matter of pure fate as to whether they live or die. Lawyers may well come into contact with clients on criminal charges related to such behaviour. Reference to a mental health professional, wherever possible under these circumstances, seems to be a sensible step to take. If the client refuses such help, the lawyer should attempt to obtain secondary help from such a professional to advise what the lawyer should do. Except in the most dire circumstances where a client appears unable to exercise reasonable choice, confidentiality should be maintained.

Children

It will be unusual for many lawyers to be interviewing young children as clients, although this does sometimes occur. It will perhaps be more usual for young children to be interviewed as witnesses. Once again it is not intended to deal with legal questions of capacity or responsibility in relation to children, but more to concentrate on the problems of interviewing them.

Two, almost opposite, approaches appear in the research on children. One approach is to treat children as simply small adults.

A second approach is to treat children as a different sort of animal altogether. Much of the latter approach results from the work of child psychologists such as Piaget who have shown different stages in the physical, mental, emotional and moral development of children. In Piagetian cognitive theory, below a certain age children do not have the cognitive ability to understand certain abstract ideas, such as being able to see something from another person's point of view. In terms of moral development children may have a very different sense of where blame or guilt lies from an adult.

One cannot lump together children in a large age-range. The cognitive ability of, say, a 15-year old child may be almost the same as an adult, but peer group pressure might be far stronger on such a child than on a five-year old. A lawyer cannot be expected to be an expert at determining which stage of ability any particular child has reached. However, a lawyer should remember that there is different social, emotional, cognitive, physical, perceptual and linguistic development at all stages.

Some recent work on children as witnesses (Dent) shows that children are much more open to suggestion than adults. Children want to please and may say what they think is required in order to do so. Younger children are encouraged to have their own private dream worlds of fantasy and it is sometimes difficult for them to differentiate between their dreams and reality. It is therefore sensible to double check as much as possible any information gained from a child and to return to a child with more questions if what has been learned elsewhere seems not to agree with what they have already said. Linguistic sophistication of adults may mean that a question has quite different significance in its intention to the way it is perceived by a child.

Such issues have become even more important recently with the growth of cases dealing with child abuse and especially sexual abuse of children. In a recent case in California a number of children in a day care institution gave completely different stories in their statements to those which they finally gave on the witness stand. It is questionable how reliable a child's evidence is going to be. However, there are some cases where such evidence is the only evidence available and may have to be introduced.

All that has been stated above in relation to making adult clients feel at ease is especially applicable to children. A special attempt to make them feel happy and at home in their surroundings should be made before interview is begun. They should be given as much time as possible to tell their story in their own way and special care should be taken not to "lead" them or suggest to them which answers are preferred. If possible they should be interviewed in their own homes, or in familiar surroundings with a parent, or some other adult they would consider friendly, present. If appropriate they should be assured of their own innocence and no threats of heavy cross-examination should be made. It may be necessary to meet children on a number of occasions in order to gain their confidence, before hearing a full account of particularly traumatic circumstances.

Conclusion

In this chapter we have looked at a number of disparate but specific interviewing problems.

Interruptions, especially telephone calls, should be avoided whenever possible so that clients feel that they are being given complete attention and that their case and problems are important. The difficulties of handling documentary information and evidence in an interview were also considered, and in general it was suggested that documents be viewed only during the Questioning Stage of the interview. Forms should be filled in only when the interview has progressed so far that the business of filling them in will not unduly affect the client's flow of information.

The differences between interviewing clients and witnesses were next considered. In general, witnesses are reluctant to be involved, and need a good deal of encouragement. They cannot see any obvious benefits to them in assisting the lawyer, and fear being made a fool of in court. Witnesses may also have to be tested on the first occasion the lawyer meets the witness to see how they are likely to react to being questioned in court. Gathering facts from a witness usually involves aiming at providing specific evidence for a case and is therefore different from the more open-ended interviewing of a client.

The chapter ended by considering the problems of interviewing the mentally disturbed, suicide threats, and interviewing children. Lawyers should be prepared for some of the difficulties in dealing with clients who are mentally ill and who may need referral to another agency for specific help. Lawyers should be aware of the possibility that they will meet such cases in the course of their general practice.

Any threat of suicide by a client or a third party should be treated seriously and not ignored. Help should either be obtained for the client, with the client's consent, or the lawyer should seek advice on how to deal with the client. Children can be difficult clients and witnesses because their cognitive, social, moral an linguistic levels of development are not the same as adults. As much as possible, corroborative evidence should be found for any information obtained from a child.

Having considered these more specific problems relating to lawyer's interview, we can now turn to the lawyer's ongoing relationship with the client.

Chapter Six

THE CONTINUING RELATIONSHIP

This chapter looks at the ongoing relationship between lawyer and client during the period after the first interview. It begins by examining the construction of a file note of the interview, and the writing of a letter to the client concerning the interview. The chapter then goes on to consider the counselling of different alternatives with clients, and deciding which choices should be made by lawyers and which by clients in the continuing relationship.

Note of Interview for the File

As soon as possible after the interview a full note should be made of everything that occurred during the interview for the lawyer's file. Since the note must be legible to any person who may need to pick up the file, a typed note is best. The easiest method will probably therefore be to dictate a full note of the interview to be typed out and to remain on the file.

Some firms, law centres and advice centres have their own forms or format for making such notes. These can be extremely helpful as a reminder for common factual details such as names, addresses and telephone numbers. It immediately becomes clear when an essential basic piece of information such as this has not been obtained in the interview. However, any more complicated checklists, which will be discussed subsequently, are not so useful in the interview itself. As has been demonstrated above, going mechanically through any list of questions is a poor way to elicit information from a client in a personal interview. Such checklists become useful at this stage, after the interview, when the lawyer has more time to think of what extra information may be necessary and what information should be requested from the client in the letter confirming the interview.

Whatever general format is used for constructing a file note, certain major headings will be helpful in directing the mind of the lawyer towards the solving of the client's problem. The file note will be discussed here under three headings: factual information, the lawyer's impressions and the suggested work to be done.

(1) *The factual information*

Foremost among the three topics is the factual information which has emerged from the interview as a result of what the client has stated, or as it appears from documents which the client has brought along. Headings for such factual information applicable to any form of contentious matter can be found in the information checklist which follows. This is a fuller version of the information headings which were mentioned in Chapter Three above. By working through this list *after* the interview the lawyer can check which items may have been missed and how they need to be followed up.

Table 6.1

1. Client personal information

(a)	Full name(s) (maiden)	(i)	Children
(b)	Full address	(j)	Parents
(c)	Telephone number(s)	(k)	Age
(d)	Circumstances of residence	(l)	Income
(e)	Work (or not) and address	(m)	Health
(f)	Work history	(n)	Education
(g)	Supplementary benefit or other welfare	(o)	Previous unrelated legal problems
(h)	Marital status		

2. Other Parties

(a)	Full name(s)	(e)	Job
(b)	Full address and telephone number(s)	(f)	Age
(c)	Solicitor(s) instructed	(g)	Background
(d)	Connection/relationship with client		

3. Witnesses

(a)	Full name(s)	(e)	Job
(b)	Full address(es) & telephone numbers	(f)	Age
(c)	Witness for client, other side or both.	(g)	Background
(d)	Connection/relationship with client.		

4. Problem Subject Categorisation

e.g. commercial, conveyancing, crime, matrimonial, probate, tax, unfair dismissal, etc.

5. Events

(a)	Dates of major events	(g)	Persons involved
(b)	Times of major events	(h)	Course of incident(s)
(c)	Venues of major events	(i)	Parties affected
(d)	Parties present	(j)	Property affected
(e)	Witnesses present	(k)	Subsequent course of
(f)	Precipitating incident of events		events

6. What the Client Wants

(a)	The main problem	(e)	Other organisations/ persons to be notified
(b)	Desired outcome		
(c)	Difficulties in achieving desired outcome	(f)	Precipitating incident to visit lawyer
(d)	Persons to be affected		

7. Previous Advice and Assistance

(a)	Who consulted	(d)	Action taken by consultant
(b)	Address and telephone number(s) of consultant	(e)	Action taken by client
(c)	Advice given	(f)	Effects/further events

8. Legal Proceedings

(a)	Character	(e)	Last hearing
(b)	Parties	(f)	Next hearing
(c)	Court	(g)	Pleadings/papers seen
(d)	Date begun	(h)	Pleadings/papers requested at interview

9. Next Contact Between Client and Lawyer

(a)	Date or event	(b)	Nature of contact

10. Work to be Done by Lawyer

(a)	People to be contacted	(d)	Factual research
(b)	Letters to be written	(e)	Warnings to be given
(c)	Legal research	(f)	Date of report/return

11. Work to be Done by Client

(a) People to be contacted
(b) Letters to be written
(c) Telephone calls to be made

(d) Papers to be brought in
(e) Date of report/review

12. Advice Given

(a) Unconfirmed advice given (general statement of law applicable).

(b) Confirmed advice details

Some adaptation of the above table is necessary for non-contentious matters. This will involve removing headings such as "witnesses" and "hearings". However, the remainder of the checklist will still be useful, especially to the new lawyer.

More specific checklists exist in published form for particular types of cases. These can also be useful for checking with after the interview, provided of course that they are not used as the only means of researching and applying the relevant law.

(2) The lawyer's impressions

Whatever format is used for setting out the strictly factual information obtained in the interview and any legal advice or plan of action stated by the lawyer, the file note should also detail the lawyer's impression of the client, the client's problem and any special client needs. Some of this information will already have appeared in the factual outline, provided that the lawyer has asked direct questions of the client on these subject areas during the interview. However, there may be much more which the lawyer has learned about the client and the client's needs than can strictly be included as factual information. These will be the lawyer's impressions of the client as a person and what may be necessary in handling the client and dealing with the particular matter. This form of information less often appears in lawyers' files. One possible reason is that, by its very nature, it is based on opinion and is tentative and changing throughout the course of the case. Another possible reason is that it may be considered irrelevant to the dispassionate role which lawyers feel necessary in handling legal work. Some may also worry that any adverse information about a client may fall into the hands of clients themselves or somebody else who may misuse that information. It is therefore considered by some lawyers that it is better for such information to be left in the head of the lawyer and not to be put on paper.

A lawyer's file is the property of the lawyer and it is unusual for a client ever to see the file, or its contents. In the exceptional circumstances that a client decides to remove work from one lawyer to another it is only necessary for correspondence and original documents to be handed over. The lawyer-client relationship is covered by absolute privilege and it is therefore not permissible for even a court to demand to see the contents of a lawyer's file unless the lawyer's work itself is called into question by the client in a contract of negligence suit. In such circumstances, provided the comments and opinions stated by the lawyer are not based on sheer speculation and the evidence for them is stated, it seems more likely that mentioning such issues would only redound to the benefit rather than to the disadvantage of the lawyer. However, the arguments that there are some dangers involved in including such information is an important one, although the benefits should be weighed against the unlikely disadvantages.

The other arguments are more easily met. The fact that opinions are tentative and changing does not mean that they may be less important. Any lawyer taking over the matter and able only to read the file will be immensely helped by the previous lawyer's opinions. They will be useful not only as a means of assessing the client but also as a means of assessing the original lawyer's legal and practical solutions against that lawyers feelings about the client. They will be useful for the original lawyer also in writing them, to help explain why certain alternatives were suggested in particular for this client for this particular case. Any such opinion should clearly be viewed as part of the continuing process and should be added to, amended and completely changed if necessary as the relationship and the case progress. However, as suggested by Andrew Watson (*The Lawyer in the Interviewing and Counselling Process*, pages 16–27), the first impressions of the client gained by the lawyer, even if they do change later after getting to know the client more, are important indicators of how the client has reacted and will react in other situations. This sort of information will therefore be important in reviewing the case subsequently. It will help in deciding such questions as how the client will stand up in court to examination and cross-examination, how a client will react to family strife resulting from an unexpected testamentary bequest or even any necessary last minute bargaining on the price of a house the client wishes to purchase or sell. It is not easy for lawyers to remember all such details about all their clients without some form of reminder, and an effective file note including this information can serve well in this regard.

The view that such information should be actively ignored by a lawyer whose job it is to be "objective" is quiet strongly held by many. There is no doubt that it is the lawyer's obligation to act for all clients whether they are likeable, pleasant, innocent, or not. There is also no doubt that it is part of the lawyer's function to assess from a dispassionate point of view what a court would think of a case and what the law strictly says. This may be totally unrelated to the bona fides of a client. However, the lawyer's reactions are an important part of such decisions. It is not possible for the lawyer to be entirely objective. More objectivity can be obtained by openly declaring impressions and feelings, than by suppressing them in a pretence of being a dispassionate observer, unaffected by one's own feelings. The importance here, therefore, is not to rely totally on such impressions or opinions, but to state them openly so they can be dealt with and taken into account in any overall calculus of the client's case.

The following is an example of such a note by a lawyer advising a company in a commercial matter. Only the section of the file note giving the lawyer's impressions of the client is here hypothesised.

> *The client.* Mr. Sharpe seems to be a confident "new broom" at Harvey Vehicles. Although we have dealt with this Company for some time, this is the first occasion we have met their new financial controller. He does not seem quite to match the more staid and traditional image of the Company, although perhaps he was hired for that very reason. I found him quite forceful in wanting to push ahead in suing Newford Haulage and then arranging to have them declared bankrupt. He expressed doubts very clearly that it was unlikely his view on this would immediately be accepted by the rest of the Board and especially the Managing Director. But, he seemed confident he could sway them—which might be more difficult than he thinks.
>
> I feel that we should probably check back with the other members of the Board somehow, without upsetting Mr. Sharpe or make sure that any decision to go ahead and sue Newfords was one that was made by the Board of the Company itself, before we proceeded in this matter. It is possible that if we follow Mr Sharpe's speed we might not be acting in the best, long-term interests of the Company, which is after all our real client in this matter.

(This hypothetical note is based on the facts of the second play-let "Extremely Competent But . . . " in the Law Society's video film "Solicitor/Client Relations").

From this example it will be seen that this form of note can be highly useful in documenting the reasons for taking actions in the conduct of a case which might otherwise not be explained in the file.

(3) *Proposals for work to be done*

The third aspect which should appear in a file note concerns the lawyer's preliminary legal opinion and view of the alternatives available to the client in the particular matter. Some lawyers prefer to carry out initial legal and factual research before committing any such thoughts to paper. However, a few preliminary views will almost certainly be held by the lawyer, if only which avenues to research. By including a heading of proposed work in the file note the lawyer may adopt a work pattern which prevents a file being put aside without a preliminary decision being made about what immediate work is necessary on the file and how that work will be carried out. Each time a file is put aside and picked up later, some rereading time is necessary to refresh the memory. Whilst the lawyer is writing the file note, whatever musings come to mind on possible alternatives should be noted. These will be useful to look at and adopt, or reject, later when they can be fully considered. Encouraging such work habits is useful for the lawyer when the file is picked up again. It will remind the lawyer what was to be done, and will be especially helpful to another lawyer taking over the file if this becomes necessary after the first interview. Such a file note in the case used as an example above might appear as follows:

Suggested work. Write to Mr Sharpe a letter confirming the interview and the information he gave me especially pointing out his insistence on moving ahead with suing Newford Haulage. Set out in the letter all the other possible alternatives to suing them and making them bankrupt, including perhaps:

(a) A form of arrangement enabling them to get back on their feet again by giving them time to make staggered payments.

(b) That the Board should consider whether to take over or merge with Newfords—if Harvey Vehicles is owed so much money by them, they are clearly an important customer and it would be a shame to lose them unless absolutely necessary. Since they are both local firms there may be other advantages for this sort of option.

(c) Working out something with Newfords' bank and other creditors, which would "put the squeeze on" generally but would not close them down.

Harveys is a highly responsible and socially conscious firm and it may well be that they would not like to see the local consequences of Newfords going bust. This should be canvassed with B.G. (our own senior partner) and he should consider, take the responsibility for and take, whatever action we, as a firm, suggest. Perhaps an informal approach to Mr Harvey, the founder and Managing Director of Harveys would be the best idea.

In the meantime we should ask for more information on the debt and full particulars of it in writing from Mr Sharpe in the same letter.

(d) Carry out some legal research sending one of the articled clerks just to check on the dates by which we could sue, have judgement if undefended, and then proceed after an unsatisfied judgment to bankruptcy. I should also just check how much this would all cost and if it is still necessary to brief counsel to appear at the hearing of a petition for the winding-up of a company.

In summary, it will be seen that a file note has three major parts. The factual information section records everything that was said or understood from the client or any documents brought to the interview, as well as any legal advice or plan of action stated by the lawyer. The section on impressions of the client and the problem allows the lawyer to put in writing some of those things that are felt but not directly stated in an interview. Lastly, the suggested programme for work forces the lawyer to think about what should be done next at the time of writing up the initial interview, enabling further steps in the handling of the case to be carried out with more efficiency and less delay.

The Letter to the Client Confirming the Interview

The lawyer should always confirm in writing what occurred during an interview to the client, together with an idea of what work has been done since and what is going to be done, within a few days after the interview itself. The letter serves a number of purposes, some practical and some symbolic.

The most important practical purpose is to confirm what happened at the interview and what the lawyer understood of the facts and the client's desires. At this stage the lawyer has either begun or is about to start work on the case, contacting third parties drafting wills, contracts or pleadings and in other ways relying on what the client has said. It is therefore very useful to have an agreed form in writing of what the client has told the lawyer about the facts and also instructed the lawyer to do. Even if the lawyer has been exceptionally careful in the interview to check back with the client at each stage, the client may not have felt able then to contradict the lawyer or may have had second thoughts about something since. The letter gives the client a reminder and a chance to think again.

The letter will also be confirming that the lawyer is instructed or retained by the client as the client's legal representative. It is useful for the lawyer to have this in writing both in relation to the client and in relation to third parties. More symbolically, the letter is the first formal step in the lawyer's handling of the matter. Its speedy delivery confirms to the client the lawyer's efficiency, and ability to keep to the early promises made in the interview of times for next contact and work to be done. The character, as well as the content, of the letter, will therefore be important to the client. The client will be looking for signs of the lawyer's ability to communicate well in writing, as well as some feeling of warmth and understanding to engender confidence in the client's relationship with the lawyer.

"Lawyers have two common failings. One is that they do not write well and the other is that they think they do".

C. Felsenfeld, *The Plain English Movement in the United States,*
extracted in *Plain English for Lawyers,*
National Consumer Council.

Drafting of legal letters is a subject in itself and cannot be dealt with in depth in the context of this work. A few basic guidelines are, however, worth noting.

(1) *Style*
The style of the letter should show a fairly traditional "professional" stance, at the same time as appearing friendly and understanding. There should be no attempt to mystify the client with legal verbiage, but the client should be impressed (although not subdued) by a confident writing style.

(2) *Tone*
Legal letters, even letters to clients, often operate on more than one level. The actual meaning of the words is supplemented by the manner and form in which they are stated. Sometimes the words can have a totally opposite effect to the tone of the letter. One should therefore be very careful how one uses such skills in writing to a client, to ensure that both tone and content are appropriate.

(3) *Why?*
Committing oneself to written communication is an important step and it can be a dangerous one. It is essential to think out very clearly why the letter is being written, what it is absolutely necessary to say, what should be said also once one is writing and what should not be said. Very often new lawyers find themselves writing almost everything that is in their heads into a letter. It is important to understand exactly the objectives in writing and to keep to them. Constructing a file note at the same time as the letter will perhaps help to differentiate what material should appear in each of them.

(4) *The other side of the table*
One way of visualising the effect of a letter is to try and see what it might look like from the point of view of the recipient. Reading

the letter from "the other side of the table" as the addressee can cause a writer to think again about how to say the same things. This is a useful method of assessing whether the letter conveys both the message and feeling intended.

(5) *The third constituency*
Legal letter writing differs from other letter writing in one material aspect. A lawyer's letter should always be written with the background thought that it may not simply be for the readership of the lawyer or of the client. There always lurks in the background a third constituency, that of the court, which may under certain circumstances read a letter to a client in an action against the solicitor. Even if, as in this case, it is unlikely that a letter would ever go to court, every piece of writing emanating from a lawyer's office should be written (even letters to clients), as if they might at some stage be seen by somebody else. This particular view of letter writing is helpful in encouraging a useful caution.

It is often necessary to outline a set of procedures of likely procedures in a letter to a client. For this purpose it is helpful to develop a set of office precedents which can either go out with a letter as photocopied sheets, or can be included in a personalised form in letters with the aid of a word processor. Such procedural outlines might include the normal progress of the purchase or sale of a house, the procedure involved in instituting proceedings and prosecuting them to a hearing or trial, or something more detailed such as the duties of the client in relation to discovery of documents. It will help to have an agreed form available and this will cut down on time spent in informing clients, whilst still giving them the utmost information possible.

Here is an example of a letter written to the fictional John Sharpe in the Newford Haulage case used as an example above.

FIRKIN, GLASS AND BARREL
Solicitors

Robert Glass	68, Market Street,
John Sawkins	Casilton,
Alex Grey	Surrey SPG 5QT
James Barrel	
Caroline Elliot	February 30, 1986

Our ref:
Your ref:

John Sharpe, Esq.,
Harveys Vehicles Ltd
57 George Street,
Casilton,
Surrey SPG 6

Dear Mr Sharpe,

Re: *Newford Haulage*

I am writing to confirm our meeting today to discuss Harvey Vehicles' problems with your largest creditor Newford Haulage.

From our discussions I understand that your Company has been selling vehicles to Newford Haulage, a local haulage contractor, for some years. You are currently owed by them some £150,000, about half of which has been outstanding for more than six months. You are apparently their major suppliers of vehicles.

Your own strong recommendation to the Board of Harveys is that you sue Newfords as soon as possible. I understand from you that there is no apparent legal defence to such a suit. You then wish to go straight ahead with proceedings to wind-up the company and try to obtain as much as possible in the winding up. You feel that waiting any longer might allow Newfords to get into further debt and thus leave even less money available if they had to be closed down later. The recent redundancies which were reported in the press leave you even more worried about the situation.

By your calculation you might realise between 15 and 30 per cent, of the debt owed to you on the winding up. This comes to something between £22,500 and £45,000. I pointed out to you that our costs, including taking Harveys all the way through to running the creditors' meetings and appointing and advising the liquidator could all come to an amount in the region of £5,000, even if the case were to be undefended.

You pointed out that there was some dissent on the Board on the question of how to deal with Newfords. Other members of the Board were more inclined to give Newfords time to get back onto its feet. I understand from my partners that Harveys is certainly a firm which has been keen on showing social responsibility in the neighbourhood and one can quite understand the force of both points of view.

I feel that you should canvass with your Board of Directors some of the major possible alternatives open to them. We will on course be pleased to act on your behalf whichever course you choose. The major alternatives appear to be:

(i) *Winding up by compulsory liquidation*
   This is the alternative we have discussed quite thoroughly at our meeting and in this letter. I am confident that you will report our discussions on this to the Board.

(ii) *Making an interim or long-term settlement with Newfords*

Another alternative is to face up to the fact that you will not be able to get back more than 30 per cent of the debt even after costly proceedings.

In light of this the Board might consider the desirability of agreeing a figure such as £45,000 with Newfords, or something even higher, in interim settlement of the debt. Once Newfords are released from the larger obligation the might in the longer term be able to get re-financing from the bank, and get back on their feet again. They might even be able to repay more of the debt in later years. At any rate, provided you receive something of the order of £30,000 to £40,000 within a year you will still probably be better off than if you had to pay for legal costs and wait for the legal machinery to grind away slowly.

(iii) *Merge with Newfords or take them over*
The most intrusive possibility seems to be to merge with Newfords or to take them over. If they are your largest creditor and you are their major supplier it would seem that you do have some stake in the continuation of the Company. This alternative would obviously need a great deal of research but it might well provide all that the Board wants in the longer term.

We did not discuss the latter two alternatives in any detail at our meeting and I would be pleased to give you or the Board more information on these possibilities should you so require. Once again, we will be pleased to act on whatever choice is made by your Board.

In the meantime I would be grateful if you could find the original invoices and correspondence with Newfords so that we will be ready to take urgent action if this proves to be necessary.

I do hope this letter will be helpful in setting out the situation regarding Newfords. Please do not hesitate to contact me if you would like any further information.

I look forward to hearing from you with your Board's decision.

Yours sincerely,
Caroline Elliot.

The letter illustrates a number of the points already mentioned. It was necessary to confirm what Mr Sharpe had told Mrs Elliot at the interview. It was also important that Mrs Elliot carry the work for the client a stage further into advising a number of possible alternatives, and not just the one which Mr Sharpe had suggested. The letter attempts to do this without annoying Mr Sharpe, or showing any disagreement or dissatisfaction with his preferred course of action. The tone adopted, as well as some of the repeated wording, points Mr Sharpe back to obtaining definite instructions from his Board before Mrs Elliot is prepared to go ahead with the case. The letter sounds business-like but is not cold, and is quite encouraging. This is a case in which it might be a good idea to send out some form of procedural outline showing what steps would occur in the compulsory liquidation of a debtor company. Mrs Elliot might decide, however, not to send one out in this particular letter since it might draw further attention to one alternative above the others.

Having set the lawyer-client relationship on an ongoing footing by opening and starting work on the file and sending out the letter confirming the interview, we can now turn to considering some of the longer term issues in conducting the relationship.

Client Counselling and the Question of Choice

This section considers how the lawyer may manage the relationship with the client in such a way that the client is kept fully informed with the development of the case and able to make all the necessary choices when they arise.

Counselling—an introduction

The term "counselling" should first be explained. A distinction can be drawn from the American writings on legal interviewing between two concepts: "advising" and "counselling" clients. "Advising" is taken to mean the situation where a lawyer suggests to a client one particular course of action which the lawyer considers best for the client. On the other hand, "counselling" is used to mean the presentation by the lawyer of a number of options for the client and helping the client go thoroughly through those options whilst allowing the client to make the final choice. The term "counselling" does not therefore borrow strongly from ideas based in the psychotherapeutic relationship. It is probably its association with that relationship which seems to have made it less acceptable to English ears. The word "counselling" does not appear in any of the English short practitioner guides, although almost all American texts refer to both "interviewing" and "coun-selling" [sic] in their titles. Presenting options and allowing the client to choose among them seems essential to a more collabora-tive relationship along the lines of the model suggested by Rosenthal.

The American works on legal interviewing and counselling (such as Binder and Price, Watson, Freeman and Weihoffen, Shaffer) do not generally seem to differentiate between which tasks in client communication need to be carried out in the first interview, and which tasks in subsequent interviews. The major work of counselling a client is more likely to occur in a subsequent interview when all legal options and practical options have been researched by a lawyer and all necessary facts obtained. Our discussion in this chapter therefore looks more towards the work of counselling clients in subsequent interviews.

The major complaints which have been noted so far in this book are largely those which have emanated from clients and have been discovered through consumer research. One of the major complaints made by lawyers about their clients, however, becomes important in the current context. A frequent complaint is that clients, or some clients, do not do what the lawyer would like them to do, or what the lawyer suggests to them. Intuitively, one often hears this complaint posed as a question at seminars on interviewing for lawyers: "How can I get clients to do what I suggest?" It is a complaint not confined to a particular social class of client or even to clients who do not return to the lawyer. It seems to be an occasion of some annoyance and frustration to the lawyers concerned, and it tends somewhat to shake their confidence in their own judgment.

The solution to this problem would appear to be found directly within the distinction between "advising" and "counselling" mentioned above. Where advice is given in the form of only one alternative, a client is given a simple, but limited, choice: to accept or reject the advice. But in legal work, there is always more than one option available. The psychology of choice shows that clients are far more likely to accept a decision which they feel they have made themselves than one which they feel has been made for them. Rosenthal in his book, *Lawyer and Client: Who's in Charge*, excerpts an interesting paragraph from Sir Isaiah Berlin's essay "Two Concepts of Liberty":

> "I wish my life and decisions to depend on myself, not on external forces of whatever kind. I wish to be the instrument of my own not of other men's, acts of will. I wish to be a subject, not an object; to be moved by reasons, by conscious purposes, which are my own, not by causes which affect me, as it were, from outside. I wish to be somebody, not nobody; a doer—deciding, not being decided for, self-directed and not acted upon by external nature or by other men as if I were a thing, or an animal, or a slave incapable of playing a human role, that is, of conceiving goals and policies of my own and realising them . . . I wish, above all, to be conscious of myself as a thinking, willing, active being, bearing responsibility for my choices and able to explain them by reference to my own ideas and purposes."

Rosenthal goes on to suggest that this view of life and of oneself is quite opposite to what he calls "the traditional lawyer model" of direct advising which "encourages passivity, dependence, and absence of responsibility for choices," as opposed to the counselling approach.

The process of counselling

In order to discover what methods to adopt in carrying out the work of counselling in the legal setting a review of the American texts on legal counselling helps to provide some clear programmes. There is also some interesting material generally on the making of judgments under conditions of uncertainty (such as Kahneman, Slovic and Tversky), materials on the psychology of risk avoidance, and a great deal has also been written on the subject of decision-making generally.

A number of similarities appear from reading in these areas. For all of them a spectrum is drawn of types of decision to be made, ranging from decisions which would be more susceptible to "vigilant" than "non-vigilant" decision making processes (see Chapter Four). One of the more popular books, written by Edward De Bono (De Bono's Thinking Course for the BBC) also suggests a "preframe" for the decision concentrating on the "context, need, time scale and type of decision".

De Bono's approach echoes the more academic writings in directing any decision maker's attention towards "the situation in which the decision is to be made: calm, panic, conflict, competitive pressure, or what?" He also points out the important question of whether there "needs" to be a decision at all, and takes into account the time scale in which the decision and its effects must take place. He then directs attention to whether the decision is to involve a small adjustment or a major change; to stop or start something; whether it depends heavily on others to be implemented and whether it is irrevocable. These questions will be important to note before even beginning the work of making the decision itself.

The works on legal counselling as well as those on problem solving all seem to advocate a separation between the two stages of suggesting or identifying alternatives, and choosing amongst those suggested. If the suggestion and rejection of alternatives is carried out at the same time there is a tendency to reject too quickly, or even to miss entirely, the less obvious alternatives. Even if such alternatives prove to be inadvisable subsequently, a reasoned approach to their applicability is very helpful in identifying elements or conditions of the choice which might not otherwise be noticed. A list should therefore be made which includes all possible alternatives, even those which seem unlikely. By later going through this list in a careful way, and noticing why each proposal sounds useful or otherwise, one learns more about the nature of the decision which has to be made.

Where the decision is to be made by a group of people, much of the research suggests that alternatives be proposed through a "brain storming" session. This is a method of generating alternatives in which all group members are encouraged to call out headings of ideas, as they occur to them, without anyone being allowed to comment on those ideas at that stage. This is a model which is especially proposed for decisions to be made in the business context. For the professional-client relationship (except perhaps between people who know each other very well) this does not seem to be ideal. The formality of the occasion and the fact that there will often be only two "players" make this an unlikely "game," at least for English lawyers and their clients, to play. The best approach would appear to be that the lawyer suggests all the alternatives that the lawyer can think of, and then asks the client for any additions to this list. It appears actually to be helpful to write out such a list (or present a typed list) for the client so that both parties can then work together with the same headings and ideas.

With the list of all possible alternatives in front of them, the lawyer and the client can go through each one in turn. Binder and Price suggest that the client should be asked which of the alternatives the client would like to discuss first. In this way, what is most on the client's mind will be dealt with immediately.

A "vigilant" approach (as described in Chapter Four, above) necessitates the careful discussion of each choice. This involves the lawyer describing what each alternative involves, and predicting the probable consequences of each alternative. All of this entails a good deal of thought and preparation beforehand by the lawyer to ensure that each alternative and all of its possible consequences have been covered.

It may be helpful to work through an example of counselling a client in a contentious matter arising out of an accident. These are the facts of an hypothetical case:

(1) *Counselling example*

You are a young lawyer representing an infant victim of an automobile accident. You have tried only one case before, and not in the area of personal injury. You were approached by the mother of the infant to work on this case because she is a personal work colleague/friend of your own mother (who has boasted about you all through law school to her). The infant's mother is highly active within her own local community and success in this case might mean more work for you, which you need.

Unfortunately, the legal subject matter of the case is complicated and the law is uncertain. It involves, amongst other things questions of contributory negligence, a "thin skull" problem of an existing medical weakness and an extremely difficult "measure of damages" issue regarding capitalisation of future amounts to present day value.

The lawyer on the other side is an "old hand" working for the insurance company of the other car driver. He seemed bored when you put your emotional plea to him at your first meeting. He was very shrewd and spent a long while scaring you out of you wits with talk about the complexity of the case, and comments about procedural tactics you had never heard of. However, he did make an offer of settlement on a final, "take it or leave it" basis.

You issued proceedings a year ago and now it is a week before trial. His offer is that you accept £50,000 in "full and final settlement" within three days or proceed to trial. His comments about the case make it clear to you that there are defects in your pleadings—and you are worried about your evidence.

You think that the mother will probably be quite pleased with £50,000, because it is more money than she has ever seen. But you sense she would like her day in court and to speak from the witness box. You are not sure you can control her there, and you suspect your medical evidence is not as good as the insurance company's.

If you win in court you could get £100,000 or more, good publicity and lots more money. If you lose there on the contested issues you may only get £10,000.

The example (which is taken from Warwick University Legal Practice course materials) is intended to show some of the problems which can face the lawyer as well as the client in making choices. Most choices will have implications for the lawyer, if only in terms of the amount of work they involve, as well as for the client. The lawyer must therefore be careful not to allow those implications unnecessarily to affect the counselling of the client's choices.

In this example it appears that there are some four possible alternatives for this stage in the case, all of which need to be counselled with the client. These are:

(a) To proceed to trial

(b) To accept the offered settlement

(c) To push for a higher offer before trial

(d) To abandon the case.

Of these four alternatives (more could be generated but are not necessary for the sake of this exercise) only the first two are likely to be important or realistic, judging from the facts. There might be situations where alternatives (c) or (d) would be preferable to certain clients and they should therefore be proposed to the client. The process of rejecting them will still be useful to this client in understanding her position. The lawyer should therefore begin the meeting with the client by introducing all the alternatives.

Lawyer: "Well, Mrs Watson, I thought it was best that we met again to discuss all this rather than talking on the telephone. I hope you don't mind having to come in at such short notice but we really have some difficult decisions to make today, and I thought it would be best to do it in this way.

Client: No, that's fine. Thank you for calling me in so promptly.

Lawyer: Good. Well, as I see it there are some four or so possible alternatives open to us at present. I thought I would go through these with you and then see if you had any other suggestions. [Offers her the typed list].

Client: O.K.

Lawyer: First, we could to ahead with the case next week, ignore the insurance company's offer, and go on with the trial looking for a larger sum of damages. That's one option. [pause] Secondly, we could accept the offer of £50,000 from the insurance company, with is after all a "bird in the hand." [pause]

Thirdly, even though they said it was a "final offer" we could try to push it higher. [pause]

Lastly, I just wanted you to know that you could still pull out at this stage, if you feel the trial will be too painful for you and Johnny, and rely on the state benefits such as they are.

Those then are the four options *I* could see. I've had them typed here so that we can review them together. Are there any others that you feel we should consider?

Client: Well, as you know, I've been in favour all along of setting up some kind of pressure group for infant accident victims like Johnny because I think the state really ought to make such payments, not individuals. But I don't really see an alternative which could assist that at this stage. I feel, in any case, too bound up with Johnny's own problems now that the trial, that we have been waiting for so long, has finally come.

Lawyer: Yes, perhaps that is something we could return to in a few weeks time. I agree that we should probably concentrate more on Johnny's own problems at the moment. Well—which of the four alternatives would you like to discuss first?

Client: Well, I don't want to abandon anything. So you can probably leave that one 'till last. From what you said on the telephone it didn't sound as if there would be any success at all in trying to get a higher offer from them before trial. Their lawyer sounds like a rather hard nut to crack. No, I think I'd like to look more closely at taking the current offer, and going to trial, and, I think, lets look at trial first.

For each of these alternatives the possible consequences will then need to be discussed. Binder and Price suggest a vigorous and detailed approach to describing consequences which involves going through five separate headings of possible results for each of the major alternatives. These headings are: "(i) The best possible, (ii) The best likely, (iii) The most probable, (iv) The worst likely, (v) The worst possible" results. This approach bears careful scrutiny. Although it may seem over-detailed initially, such a full analysis of consequences is necessary in giving the client the full picture. These results headings are not part of a continuum or range which could adequately be described by indicating only the outer ends of the spectrum. Taking this approach with the example above, it may be applied to the alternative of proceeding with trial.

Lawyer: Well, lets look at trial then. We have discussed this often before so I know I don't need to tell you that litigation is a lottery and one can never be sure what will happen. But let's look at the parameters.

If we got judgment in our favour all the way down the line it is possible that we could get something in the region of £100,000 or, at least, that is what our counsel has suggested. He thinks there is only a small percentage chance of that though, but that is the *best* we could get. [He writes the figures down on paper they can both look at.]

He feels we are more likely to get something in the region of £65,000 to £70,000 even if our medical evidence is accepted. [He writes again.]

But, just as possible is the likelihood that we only get something in the region of £35,000 to £40,000, if our medical evidence is not quite so persuasive. [As above.]

At *worst* we might only be awarded £10,000. [Pause.]

Overall the most likely result seems to be that we will recover about £60,000, in court. Mr Johnston, our counsel, thinks that we will probably lose on the question of Johnny's prior medical condition but win on the contributory negligence point. That means we will not then have to go against you brother-in-law as the driver of the car Johnny was travelling in. [pause]

I know that all sounds rather complicated. But the most likely result at trial would be an award of about £60,000.

Remember that even though legal aid is footing your lawyers' bills for the present, the statutory charge will take back some of that if you win. I reckon that the trial itself could easily cost a further £5,000 to £8,000 depending upon how long it goes on for. So you would have to discount any likely gain from going to trial against what it will cost you in legal fees up to the limits we have discussed.

I think that deals in outline with the strict financial consequences of trial. There are of course other consequences too. I sense you would really quite like to have your say on the witness stand. You should remember though that your evidence will only relate to Johnny's health before and after the accident. You won't have much chance to rail against the state benefits. Cross-examination can also be quite wearing, since the insurance company's counsel will be trying to make you look like a liar or at least a stretcher of the truth. . . .

Carrying out the work of counselling properly and fully means a full investigation of each option. This must cover not only the direct effects which can often be measured in financial terms, but also the emotional and personal consequences for the client. A counselling meeting with Johnny's mother should continue on to go through all the advantages and disadvantages of each option, invite her ideas, comments and questions at each stage and give her some time to think about it afterwards. The Binder and Price programme of five possible results for each option proves a helpful guideline as used above. Possibly any such system which is rigorous and exhaustive, will be useful.

Care should be taken that a client does not reject, without full consideration, an important available option. However, it will not be necessary to apply such a rigorous approach to all options. Options such as option (d) "abandonment of the case" in the Johnny example, are not in the client's interest and the client has already indicated how strongly she feels about that particular choice.

Many of the American works on legal counselling dwell at some length on the problem of clients who will not make a choice, or (what the lawyer considers to be) the "right choice." None of the writings seem particularly satisfying on these questions. However they are more constrained by a legal position which leaves lawyers open to more negligence actions as a result of errors in advice even where trial is contemplated. This is perhaps why the American literature, and the professional rules of conduct (see ABA Code of Professional Responsibility EC 7–7, 7–8) are so clearly in favour of the client making the choice and bearing responsibility therefore. The position is not quite the same in the United Kingdom (see *Rondel v. Worsley, Sauf Ali, etc.*). However, a lawyer may still be sued for negligent advice not relating to the conduct of a case at trial, and for this reason as well, it is a good idea to counsel clients through all their options and to invite *them* to make the final choice.

Some reflections on the counselling role

Having been introduced to what is involved in the process of counselling we should reflect a little on its implicit nature. Any such reflection takes us back to the stereotypes outlined at the beginning of Chapter Four which forced us to clarify our own conception of the necessary roles for a lawyer to play in handling the affairs of clients.

The best account of such issues appears in the work of T.L. Shaffer and R.S. Redmount. Their prescriptive work on *Legal Interviewing and Counselling* (Matthew Bender, 1980) seems to take into account much more of the commentating and descriptive writings on lawyers, than any of the other works. They note, as Johnson, Bankowski and Mungham and Cain have also noted, that:

> "Legal counselling does not occur in a vacuum. It operates in a context and it is not just legal. It is a form of political control, or, as a directed activity, it participates in a process of political control. The lawyer, in one sense, is an instrument for the translation and utilization of law, and of appropriate response to it, by citizens otherwise engaged in the pursuit of their private affairs. Law, the standard and the directive, impinges or may impinge, and lawyers are utilized to maximize or minimize the effects of law on a personal well-being and on different kinds of transactions."

Shaffer and Redmount go on to describe legal counselling as "an exercise in value choices", including such choices as those "between legality and authority, between historical tradition and immediate needs and circumstances, between transcendant social values and immediate private preferences, between possibility and compulsion, between humanistic concern and values of rigour and discipline", etc. They see counselling as a form of intrusion or intervention in client affairs and discuss the importance of deciding and planning when, where and how best to enter into counselling with each particular client on each particular matter. They also point out the imbalance in the relationship which comes from the need of the client for the lawyer's help. This imbalance may leave a client vulnerable and uncertain, and easily led by the lawyer's preferences. This is an area where it is too easy to adopt the "high priest" role and deliver mystical pronouncements of legal knowledge. The problem is the client's problem, and the solution must also be that of the client.

De Bono points out how easy it is for people to accept decisions once they have been made by themselves, even though they may have been made only as the result of the person throwing a dice. Any feeling of the client that the decision was forced either by the lawyer or by circumstances, and was not actively taken by the client, can rebound on the lawyer at a later time. The effect of reliance can also set up an enormous emotional responsibility between the lawyer and client which can also cause difficulties in the continuing relationship.

Shaffer and Redmount mention how easy it is for a lawyer to approach the job of advising and counselling cynically. It appears to be easy to discuss options, other than the lawyer's preference, in a poor light. The lawyer can never know completely the mind of a client. Only the client can hope to make a choice appropriate to that client and with which that client can live.

A somewhat different emphasis, however, can be found in the words or Nizer in his book *The Implosion Conspiracy*, about the trial of Julius and Ethel Rosenberg for treason against the USA:

> "[A] . . . philosophical question . . . was whether a client should be permitted to make a decision of strategy contrary to the judgment of his counsel . . . .
>
> I have in the past struggled with this problem. At first I distinguished between matters which were legal, where I insisted on my view, or the client was invited to get another lawyer whose judgment he would accept, and non-legal questions such as the amount of settlement, in which instance, I offered my judgment, but permitted the client to decide. I found later regrets by the client, combined sometimes with lack of memory, as to who was responsible for the decision. So I tried recording the difference of views in writing, and stating that the client was making the decision despite my advice. Even this did not avail. When he regretted the result and was confronted with the letter, he would reply, 'I know, but after all, you knew more about it than I did. Why did you let me do it?'
>
> Perhaps he was right. I have since taken the full responsibility of decision even in non-legal matters."

As excerpted in Bellow and Moulton, *The Lawyering Process*.

Choice

Although the major choices and the basic direction in the handling of the case should be made by the client, it is not suggested here that all possible choices should be so made. Wherever a choice is available on which a client might have particular feelings, this choice should be offered to a client to make. Decisions about how best to implement the client's major choices by using legal skills and techniques should be made by the lawyer. In cases where, however, a client has expressed a desire regarding the particular details, or a particular detail, of the handling of the case, the wishes of the client should be followed where it is possible to do so without affecting the proper running of the matter. A familiar problem occurs when a client asks the lawyer not to approach a particular witness who might be very useful to the client's case. The lawyer should explain to the client why that particular witness's evidence might be useful, but in the final analysis the choice should be that of the client. In the event that the lawyer feels badly affected by the adverse wishes of a client these problems should be counselled carefully with the client. In the most extreme case a lawyer may feel it necessary to withdraw from continuing to handle the client's matter.

For the most part clients leave the general handling of cases to their lawyers. There are a few notable exceptions which should be mentioned. Certain business clients, or companies with "in-house" lawyers, may request sight of all correspondence or material in draft form before it is sent out of the office. This should not be considered as a threat to the judgment or discretion of the lawyer concerned but should be viewed as a somewhat different relationship in which both lawyer and client have an equal role to play even in choosing among legal measures.

Where a client insists on hearing the lawyer's view of which among the given alternatives is preferable before making a choice, the lawyer's preference should not be unreasonably withheld. However, such a statement of preference should be couched within an overall review of the other major alternatives, and the lawyer should conclude with a reminder for the client that only the client can know what is best for that client.

Conclusion

In this chapter we have noted:

(1) *The file note of the interview* which should be written up and typed as soon as possible after the interview, is in three basic parts:

   (a) An account of the factual information of the case given by the client to the lawyer followed by an account of the information in the form of advice or plan of action given by the lawyer to the client in the interview.

(b) An account of the lawyer's impressions of the client and any necessary information which was not stated directly in the interview or appeared from papers, but which may be helpful in deciding how to handle the client's case.

(c) An account of the lawyer's suggested proposals for the immediate work to be done on the case.

(2) *The letter to confirm the interview* which should also be written as soon as possible after the interview. Its main objectives are:

(a) To confirm in writing facts of the case understood by the lawyer from the client, and on which the lawyer is about to act or give advice.

(b) To confirm the existence of the lawyer-client relationship.

(c) To act as a symbolic beginning of the work on the case, demonstrating the lawyer's keeping to the promise of immediate attention and efficient work.

(d) To sweep up any questions which on reflection after the interview, or after legal research, need to be asked immediately of the client.

(e) To confirm asking for any further papers or documentation repeating them specifically in the letter.

(f) To explain what work the lawyer is about to do on the case and when the client will next be contacted.

(3) *Counselling the client's choice* which looked at the process of offering alternatives to the client and helping the client to analyse both legal and practical consequences in order to facilitate the client choosing which course to follow. The major points mentioned were:

(a) The distinction between "advising" and "counselling"— giving more than one alternative and discussing all of them.

(b) Consequences should be analysed in detail.

(c) The background to each decision including its context, need, time scale, and type should be considered.

(d) Giving clients the choice overcomes the problem of the client who will not do what the lawyer wishes.

However, there are problems with the counselling relationship including:

(a) It forms part of the "politics of control" in which law and lawyers are involved, in relation to their clients.

(b) It is a relationship of strong emotional responsibility on both sides and therefore difficult to handle, but

(c) A beneficial and efficient handling of the counselling relationship is crucial to the proper handling of client affairs.

Chapter Seven

GETTING GOING: THE BEGINNING, NOT THE END

This final chapter concentrates on how best to put the learning of the earlier chapters into practice. It notes the difficulties involved in making the behavioural changes necessary for good interviewing and looks at some practical methods for assessing interviewing skills. The chapter discusses how to learn from experience and ends with some proof for the pudding, in the form of the results of some research on training lawyers.

The Learning Process–Cognitive and Behavioural Change

Experience in teaching the ideas contained in this book and training new lawyers in their performance has demonstrated an interesting factor in the learning process. Most new lawyers seem to learn to understand these ideas in a cognitive sense, and agree with the general approach quite quickly. However, changing their behaviour to conform with their new ideas, has been a more gradual development over time. It appears to be quite difficult to adapt behaviour for major changes at a first attempt. The ingredients of a different approach have to be added more gradually and confirmed with some success, before they can become fully integrated into a person's natural repertoire.

"Modification of behaviour involves isolation and repetition, internal and external reinforcements consistently applied, and establishment of consistency in skilful behaviours. Behaviours to be learned must be experienced as isolated from other aspects of the context, including other behaviours, in which they occur of they are to be focused upon and experienced as rewarded. A behaviour must be repeated many times if it is be firmly established/if the habit is to be adopted."

Greenebaum, *Understanding Clinical Experience*,
(as yet unpublished, 1986)

A common reaction by the new lawyer to what occurs in those early attempts to change interviewing approach is that for some reason it was difficult, or not possible, to carry out the schedule of tasks that had been intended. Every interview, just like every lawyer and client, is idiosyncratic to itself, and some excuse can always be found for not having carried through an attempted change in that particular case. This reaction seems to occur quite regularly and appears to be natural precursor to a further progression in change on subsequent occasions. However, it is necessary, in order to progress subsequently and not to forget this learning, to review each interview after it has occurred to assess how closely it conforms to the interviewing model. Any initial lack of success, or feeling of unease with the performance of such new ideas is therefore not unusual. It is necessary to work at them in order to provide the expected benefits. The material covered by this book is not a prescription for instant success. Interviewing and counselling skills, as can be seen from the earlier chapters, are subtle and detailed. Changes in behaviour to bring about a new approach cannot be donned as easily as a new overcoat.

It seems that the cognitive aspect of understanding the tasks and skills involved leaves a new lawyer with a confirmed feeling of "common sense" of the approach,. Not being able to put the new approach into practice, despite agreeing with it, tends to be irksome. The knowledge that this is a common reaction seems to have the effect of helping new lawyers through this unease to subsequent success.

Monitoring Performance

How then can one tell if one's performance of interviewing is progressing well? In this section we look at a number of possible checklists which will help the new lawyer to assess performance at interviewing and counselling, or may be used by a third person such as a supervisor to assess performance. Three different schemes will be considered. The first two are complementary in that either could be used. The last the Flesch Formula, has a very specific use in relation to complexity of language.

The ideal method for operating a system of assessment is to have the interviews which are to be assessed either videotaped or audiotaped and then to arrange for a colleague to help assess them by looking at or listening back to what occurred. However, it is unlikely that either of these will be possible for many new lawyers. Not quite as ideal, but certainly much better than no form of monitoring, is for the new lawyers themselves to remember and assess what they have done, after the interview is over.

(1) *Tasks and Skills monitoring*
The framework of Chapters Two to Four of this book follows the 13 major tasks which were set out in full in the first chapter. One form of monitoring involves a simple checking back at the end of an interview to see whether these tasks have been successfully completed.

Table 7.1–Tasks Checklist Monitoring Table

Interview with . . .	Mark Scale 1–10
1. Greeting, seating and introducing.	
2. Eliciting a story with opening question or helpful silence.	
3. Obtaining basic outline of personalities and case from client's own unhindered words.	
4. Questioning on facts for gaps, depth, background ambiguities and relevance.	
5. Summing up and recounting lawyer's view of facts, and checking for client's agreement or amending.	
6. Note-taking.	
7. Stating advice and/or plan of action.	
8. Repeating advice/plan of action and checking for client's agreement or amend.	
9. Recounting follow-up work to be done by client.	
10. Recounting follow-up work to be done by lawyer.	
11. Stating next contact between lawyer and client.	
12. Asking if "Any Other Business" and dealing with it.	
13. Terminating, helping out and goodbye.	
Total	

These Tasks and Stages were developed to mesh in with a list of Skills and techniques which would not necessarily be confined to a particular stage of the interview but would carry on throughout (Sherr, 1986). Looking at the Tasks by themselves may omit these aspects of interviewing. It will therefore be useful also to consider the headings of Skills to be used in an interview and perhaps to give an assessment against each skill of how well one performed for that heading. The Skills headings are themselves explained in more detail elsewhere (Sherr, 1986), but should be understandable from a reading of the earlier chapters of this book.

By using both the tasks and skills checklists to assess performance of the interview a good overall assessment should be obtained. A mark (say) on a scale of 1 to 10 could be given for each item. Comparing performance over successive interviews should show where any major deficiencies lie, and where progress is being made.

Table 7.2–Skills Checklist Monitoring Table

Interview with . . .	Mark Scale 1–10
1. Handling personal and confidential topics.	
2. Not accepting client's jargon.	
3. Not over using legal terminology.	
4. Precision in obtaining information.	
5. Efficiency in obtaining information.	
6. Picking up client's verbal cues.	
7. Picking up non-verbal cues.	
8. Clarifying gaps or confusions.	
9. Controlling the client in a helpful manner.	
10. Facilitating the client to talk.	
11. Not using leading or closed questions.	
12. Not using complex questions.	
13. Ease with client.	
14. Empathy with client.	
15. Reassurance of client.	
16. Time control throughout.	
17. Opening/closing ease and control.	
18. Advising and counselling.	
Total	

(2) *Byrne and Long's monitoring system*
In 1976 the Department of Health and Social Security published a study of the verbal behaviour of general practitioner doctors consulting in their surgeries entitled *Doctors Talking to Patients*, P.S. Byrne and B.E.L. Long. This was the result of some years of observation of doctors, and work in training of young general practitioners. The "behaviour checklist! which was developed out of their work has been adapted here for use with lawyers. The checklist was intended for "practical use by any who have as a professional requirement, personal interactions with people".

The behaviours in the checklist have been divided into three major categories. "Lawyer Centered", "Client Centred" and "Negative". As set ou below the checklist can be used to give a new lawyer, as objectively as possible, a quick score out of three for each behaviour item, depending on the amount that behaviour was used.

0	No use during this interview
1	Used a little
2	Moderately used
3	Used a lot

Table 7.3—Behaviour Checklist

Lawyer Centred Behaviour		Client Centred Behaviour	
Introducing oneself		Giving recognition to client	
Relating to some previous consultation		Offering observation	
		Broad question or opening	
Direct question		Concealed question	
Closed question		Encouraging	
Self answering question (rhetorical)		Reflecting	
		Exploring	
Placing events in time or sequence or place		Answering client question	
Correlational question		Accepting client ideas	
Clarifying		Using client ideas	
Doubting		Offering of feeling	
Chastising		Accepting of feeling	
Justifying other agencies		Using silence	
Criticising other agencies		Summarising to open up	
Challenging		Seeking client ideas	
Summarising to close off		Reassuring	
Repeating what client said for affirmation		Terminating (indirect)	
		Indicating understanding	
Giving information or opinion		Pre-directional probing	
Advising			
Terminating (direct)			
Suggesting			
Apologising			
Suggesting or accepting collaboration			

Negative behaviour

Rejecting client offers	
Reinforcing one's own position (Justifying oneself)	
Denying client	
Refusing client ideas	
Evading client questions	
Refusing to respond to feeling	
Not listening	

Table 7.4—Fact Finding Behaviours

Client Centred → ← Lawyer Centred

STYLE

USE OF CLIENT'S KNOWLEDGE AND EXPERIENCE		USE OF LAWYER'S SPECIAL SKILL AND KNOWLEDGE	
SILENCE LISTENING REFLECTING	CLARIFYING & INTERPRETING	ANALYSING & PROBING	GATHERING INFORMATION
Offering observation	Broad question	Direct question	Direct question
Encouraging	Clarifying	Correlational question	Closed question
Clarifying	Challenging	Placing events	Correlational question
Reflecting	Repeating for affirmation	Repeating for affirmation	Placing events
Using client ideas	Seeking client ideas	Suggesting	Summarising to close off
Seeking client ideas	Offering observation	Offering feeling	Suggesting
Indicating understanding	Concealed question	Exploring	Self answering questions
Using silence	Placing events	Broad question	Reassuring
	Summarising to open up		Repeating for affirmation
			Justifying self
			Chastising

Table 7.5—Advice Giving Behaviours

	Client Centred				Lawyer Centred	
STYLE 7	6	5	4	3	2	1
Reflecting	Giving information	Giving information or opinion	Giving information	Giving information	Giving information	Directing
Encouraging	Answering client questions	Advising	Directing	Directing	Directing	Terminating (direct)
Seeking client ideas	Seeking client ideas	Clarifying	Advising	Reassuring	Terminating	
Using client ideas	Using client ideas	Reflecting	Answering client questions	Seeking client ideas (but not using them)		
	Summarising to open up	Exploring	Seeking client ideas	Terminating (direct)		
	Pre-directional probing	Seeking client ideas	Indicating understanding			
		Using client ideas	Using client ideas			
		Offering collaboration				
		Terminating (Indirect)				

USE OF CLIENT'S KNOWLEDGE AND EXPERIENCE

USE OF LAWYER'S SPECIAL SKILL AND KNOWLEDGE

The exercise should be repeated with subsequent interviews to see if there has been any change. The intention is first to try to eliminate all negative behaviours and therefore to have a reducing score level on that heading. It is also intended to try and move from lawyer centred to client centred behaviours where this is possible. The score for client centred behaviours should therefore grow as interviewing experience is gathered and the score for lawyer entered behaviours should diminish.

A clearer understanding of the exact meaning of the headings for different behaviours can be obtained from the original publication by Byrne and Long. Most of the words describing behaviours can however be understood with a little circumspection. Many are intended as opposites, *e.g.* "Introducing oneself" in the Lawyer Centred section is almost to an opposite behaviour to "Giving recognition" in the Client Centred section.

The commitment involved in making this sort of assessment is not long. The checklist will take only about 10 minutes to fill out and administer.

Byrne and Long analysed the work of the professional consultation into two separate parts. Adapted to the legal context these may be called "Fact Finding" behaviours and "Advice Giving" behaviours. Within each of these they characterised certain "styles" which were made up of clusters of the behaviours in the above checklist. Tables 7.4 and 7.5 show the constituents of these clusters for both fact finding behaviours and advice finding behaviours.

Style descriptions for Advice Giving Behaviours (Table 7.5)
Below is a list of style descriptions for Advice Giving behaviours:

Style 1	Lawyer makes a decision about the client and his/her case and then instructs the client what is to be done.
Style 2	Lawyer makes decision and announces it.
Style 3	Lawyer sells his/her decision to the client.
Style 4	Lawyer presents a tentative decision subject to change.
Style 5	Lawyer presents the problem, seeks suggestions and makes decisions.
Style 6	Lawyer defines the limits and asks the client to make a decision.
Style 7	Lawyer permits the client to make his/her own decision.

The Byrne and Long monitoring system may initially seem somewhat complicated. With a little practice it becomes quite easy to administer and presents a set of useful, interrelated measures building towards a comprehensive assessment of style and approach. It provides detailed information and inbuilt guidelines which should aid constructive criticism.

(3)   The Flesch Formula Readability Score
Unlike the preceding two sets of measurements this particular form of assessment was designed for something more specific: to assess

how easy it would be for the general population to understand and read a particular item. The Flesch Formula deals specifically with written material and would therefore be most useful in assessing the "readability" of letters, outlines of procedures, and other written materials sent to clients. The formula has also been used in relation to spoken information. In order to assess as section of speech a transcript would have to be made to apply the formula.

Flesch's work (1948) has been extensively tested and correlates with standardised reading tests, the speed with which a passage can be read, knowledge of contents after reading the passage and the probability that an article in a newspaper will be read (Ley, 1977).

In order to apply the formula two counts have to be taken. A measurement has to be made of the number of syllables per one hundred words, which is referred to in the formula as "W". A second measurement referred to as "S" must be taken of the average sentence length in numbers of words. Once these counts have been taken the formula may be applied as follows:

$$\text{Reading Ease} = 206.04 - 0.85\,W - 1.02\,S,$$
where W = number of syllables per 100 words,
S = average sentence length in words

Example. Looking at the first paragraph printed above under the heading (3). There are 177 syllables for the first 100 words. The average sentence length in words of the four sentencess 25.25. Therefore, for that paragraph:

$$\begin{aligned}\text{Reading Ease} &= 206.04 - (0.85 \times 177) - (1.02 \times 25.25) \\ &= 206.06 - 150.45 - 25.76 \\ &= 29.83\end{aligned}$$

Ley (1973) also provides a table for interpretation of Reading Ease scores, which is reproduced below.

According to Ley, this table can be used "Cautiously to provide estimates of the percentage of the population who would understand a given piece of writing and the IQ level required for understanding."

For our own example the first paragraph of this section with a Reading Ease score of 29.83, falls just within the highest score levels of the chart at "0–30." This means that probably only 4.5 per cent of the population would understand it with ease, and they would probably be confined to those with IQs of 126 and above.

Table 7.6–Interpretation of Reading Ease Scores

Score	% who would understand	under-IQ required for comprehension
0–30	4.5	126 +
31–50	24	111 +
51–60	40	104 +
61–70	75	90 +
71–80	80	87 +
81–90	86	84 +
91–100	90	81 +

The Flesch Formula therefore provides a possibility for a lawyer to check on how easy it would be for a client to read, understand and perhaps remember a given piece of writing. A judicious use of such a measuring scheme on occasion may be a helpful means of overcoming some of the problems faced by clients in handling legal language.

Understanding and Learning from Experience

It is assumed that we learn from experience. That is, in our present context of learning skills, it is assumed that simply by doing something we actually "get better" at doing it. It is not clear that this is in fact correct.

Repetition certainly gives one a sense of familiarity with a procedure and familiarity in turn enables one to produce strategies for dealing with the next occasion. What is not certain is that such strategies are necessarily progressive in objective terms. Although many lawyers may become more proficient in certain respects in relation to their usage of interviewing skills as their experience grows, the results may not necessarily be entirely beneficial to either lawyer or client. It appears from our research that some experienced lawyers' feelings of proficiency in conducting an interview are based largely on an approach which involves a great deal of narrow questioning and constant control. This is an approach which we have seen may not be the best approach for a first interview with a new client.

If there is any truth in the saying, "practice makes perfect" then it is only because the practice itself is monitored and assessed at each stage from an objective point of view, that "perfection" can be achieved. In order to learn properly from one's own experience it is necessary to be an *active* participator in the learning process. Experience, by itself, can be a bad teacher of it is not planned, monitored, reviewed and understood.

Planning experience
It is not really sufficient simply to place a new lawyer into an interview, or any new legal work, without planning for this

beforehand. Whilst there may still be some advocates of the old method of teaching children to swim by throwing them in the deep end, a new lawyer gaspingly splashing around in the deep water of a first interview is unlikely to be of much help to the client, the firm, or the lawyer's own sense of learning.

(1) *Preparatory readings*

Hopefully, a book of this nature will be a sufficient introduction for a new lawyer before undertaking the work of interviewing clients. Even with the help of this or similar work, it is necessary for a supervising principal or colleague to spend more time in discussing the adaptation of these ideas to the circumstances an setting of the individual firm, lawyer and client. Time should be given for the new lawyer to discuss any particular fears about the interview, and perhaps the main objectives of a first interview should be reviewed.

(2) *Skills training exercises*

There are numerous other ways to prepare. Goodpaster in an excellent article in the *Journal of Legal Eduction* (1975) sets out a particularly in testing programme of skills-training exercises related to client interviewing. These exercises break down the parts of the interview and concentrate on listening skills, repetition and paraphrasing skills, and general skills of awareness. The exercises are arranged to conform with five principles for such skills training:

> "1. The exercise must provide a means for making the student aware of his current level of skill and of the need for and the uses of the new skills.
> 2. It must identify the behaviours involved in the new skill.
> 3. It must provide opportunities to practise the new behaviours.
> 4. There must be some mechanism for providing the students with feedback concerning how well they are performing the behaviours.
> 5. The final condition–that new behaviours must be integrated into the student's behavioural repertoire."

Goodpaster's exercises are primarily intended for a course of study at an institution of learning, but can easily be adapted for more informal processes. In his course the students begin by interviewing each other to find out why they have decided to study law, what they want to do after leaving university and about their "most significant recent experiences". Subsequently, in a small group of six or so students, each interview introduces them in interviewee to the other members of the group. This form of exercise is intended to demonstrate the responsibility involved in asking people questions about their confidential lives and aspirations. The exercise works quite well, even in an English setting, and interviewees are very quick to correct those "introducing" them, if their views have been misrepresented or they have, in some other way, been misunderstood. From this type of exercise which is intended to increase the sensitivity of interviewers, Goodpaster moves on to skills-training itself. Students talk for one minute without interruption on a controversial subject and their partners then repeat to them what they have said. Practice is given form summarising and repeating and an opportunity is provided for the speaker to correct any misconceptions. One exercise involves a group in which each participant is told to try and wrench the subject matter round to their own way of thinking, whatever has been said immediately prior to their own interjection. This is intended to show everyone in the group the experience of being ignored whilst the speaker carries on with the same train of thought. This is something which seems to occur frequently on the part of lawyers in interviews, and sensitising the law students to this may aid them to realise when they are doing it themselves.

Some people find it quite difficult to be involved in such exercises and are unable to shake off the unreality in order to learn from them. However, even reading the exercises does convey their intention, and will provide some substitute for those who are so minded.

(3)   The "pre-construction" role play
Apart from the planning of a first interview for a new lawyer, consideration should be given to the planning of further consultations between that lawyer and the client. As a part of the review procedure (see below) in interviews, where difficulties have been experienced in handling or understanding a client, the work of a subsequent consultation should be planned carefully before hand. One method of planning involves a discussion of the difficulties experienced by the lawyer. A far more helpful method, which has been used most successfully in the training of new lawyers in the Warwick University Legal Practice course, has been the "pre-construction" or "role-play" of the projected interview. In this method, the supervisor takes the role of the lawyer whist the new lawyer takes the role of the client. They agree two or three types of approach for the lawyer to try out. The "client" enters the room and the " interview" begins. After about ten minutes they stop and start again with a different approach. They then evaluate which approach worked better and carry out a final role-play with the new lawyer assuming the part of the interviewer and the supervisor as the client.

Many people have a feeling of unease in beginning to act out such situations, and some clearly take to it far better than others.

However, this form of trial role-play seems to be by far the best method of preparing and practising for a specific interview situation which a new lawyer has already experienced. It is difficult for the new lawyer in a discussion to be able to be objective about the performance of the lawyer's part in the past interview. But, acting out what is intended to occur in the next interview, and criticising the supervisor's performance of that same role enables the new lawyer to view what is needed from a much more objective position.

(4) *Planning the range*
Apart from the detailed planning of the ingredients of an interview and client handling, it is also necessary for a supervisor to plan out a new lawyer's experience over a range of topics and a range of clients. The vagaries of legal work may make it difficult to plan experience exactly along ideal clients. However, more attention can be paid to this subject by those who allocate work in a firm, than normally occurs. The spread of experience should cover different types of client as well as diffident types of matter.

Monitoring experience
Systems, in the form of checklists, have been detailed above for helping to assess and monitor experience. This is an highly important aspect of the training and professional growth of a new lawyer. The psychology of learning shows very clearly that the greatest progress can be made only when full feedback is given on how well, or how badly, a person is learning and performing.

Providing such feedback is in itself a skilled task. Intuitively, many new clerks in articles are given feedback in an unpleasant, harshly critical form. Supervisors may not need to suffer fools gladly, but there is nearly always something praiseworthy about a performance as well as something which merits criticism. It is much easier to be critical than to be full of praise. Lawyers especially are better at criticism, and seeing what may be wrong, than finding what is right. New lawyers are frightened, untrained and keen to learn. Any approach which does not take these factors into account in the presentation of assessment or monitoring will render much of the time spent as wasted. Just like clients, new lawyers will understand what they are being told only if it is explained to them kindly and clearly and if they are allowed to comment on the assessment and discuss it with the assessors. All of this needs a person who is interested in training or teaching. Time well spent in such assessment can reap enormous benefits in a new lawyer's performance within a short period of time.

Reviewing experience
We have said that experience must be planned beforehand and assessed afterwards. In this section we look at how the experience

of interviewing should also be "reviewed" from a wider aspect than just the assessment of how well the lawyer performed.

Monitoring, as shown above, is one form of "review". However, the ego of the new lawyer is highly threatened in the process of assessment and it may be difficult for the interview to be viewed objectively in this form of review. Other forums should therefore be provided for such review under less threatening circumstances, than with an assessing supervisor. It is very useful to discuss what has occurred in an interview with a wider group, such as other new lawyers, or other lawyers in the office. What is suggested here is something along the lines of a "Case Discussion Group" (Sherr, *New Law Journal*, April 22, 1982, p. 397 *et seq.*). Other professions that include as a major part of their training some supervised "fieldwork" utilise a form of regular seminar group for trainees with one "trainer" or "seminar leader" leading the discussion. In the seminar, some of the new lawyers should be encouraged to bring forward for the information of the group the details of interviews on particular cases which have caused them some difficulty. The difficulty should rather involve the practical skills of handling the case, or a problem of professional etiquette than a problem regarding the law. The other clerks would be invited to offer suggestions on how best to deal with the difficulty, which might be a client who is not liked, or a client who challenges their lack of experience, or a possible conflict of interest.

As the discussion develops the other new lawyers will begin to mention their own experiences in similar situations, and the issues involved in interviewing can tumble forward for easy handling by the trainer and the rest of the group. This gives a great opportunity for sharing new experiences and also allowing new lawyers to see that their own fears, worries and anxieties are also shared by others in a similar position. The group can also help each of its members to learn about discussing cases and issues among themselves, and learning when to trust their own knowledge or reactions and when not to do so. It enables the experience of a few to become the experience of the many. It develops a wider repertoire of approaches, than would be possible if interviews are discussed only with a supervisor (see, *e.g.* Abercrombie, "The Anatomy of Judgement" (1960) M.L.J., Pt. 2). Where any anxieties involve problems of professional etiquette and responsibility, the group discussion can aid the development of a keener sense of the correct priorities for future cases which might be met by all the members of the group, and not just by the individual concerned with the particular case.

In summary, this form of review should have no special personal threat for the new lawyer. It is an atmosphere in which everyone can be open (whilst still maintaining the confidentiality of clients) without fear of being reprimanded for having acted wrongly. In this atmosphere lawyers are able to look at themselves more critically and also to see how their colleagues might handle a similar situation. In this way, even a few interviews can throw up a great number of issues about interviewing, and confidence can be built in a fuller awareness of the work in which they are involved.

Understanding experience
Having carried through some planned experience, suffered its monitoring and enjoyed the easier discussion of a review session, the experience should be well on its way to being "understood". However, rather like the fifth and final condition in Goodpaster's skills training table (above) the full integration and understanding of experience also needs time in personal reflection and personal integration of any result in changes in attitude and behaviour. The learning of such important skills as interviewing and counselling cannot be rushed. The absorption of such new ideas needs time and effort. It also needs the correct atmosphere of encouragement and understanding of a positive approach to the first efforts of new lawyers.

"Understanding" according to Greenebaum "is the process of attributing meaning to our experiences" (Chapter Four). The pattern of daily toil gives little opportunity to view each client as a new learning experience rather than an added difficulty to an already hectic day. But it is possible to learn a little from each new client that we meet; a little about ourselves and our abilities as well as a great deal about *them*. All of this is very different from the more traditional mode of learning in which a clerk watched a superior interviewing a client to learn how it was done. "Watching Fred" was fine if Fred was good at his job, not so fine it he was not.

Dessert–Some Proof of the Pudding
We will end then with a little "hard" information from some empirical research. This is divided into two parts. The first part showing the effects of training lawyers how to interview, and the second part being an extract from a sub-sample of current research on more experienced lawyers interviewing which should help to show us now "Fred" or "Freda" are likely to perform.

Research into training methods
In this research (reported more fully elsewhere: Sherr, 1987) teaching as given by traditional lecture/seminar means as well as audio-visual replay in order to improve interviewing skills. Twenty seven new articled clerks were randomly assigned to three groups. All of the lawyers carried out an initial interview and then were given on of three forms of treatment. Group A received interview training in the form of traditional teaching and audio-visual replay. Group B received traditional teaching but no audio-visual replay.

Group C, the control group, received no training. All groups then carried out a further initial interview.

It was hypothesised that the trained groups would show significant improvements in their interviewing abilities. It was of further interest to compare the different forms of teaching in order to understand any different contributions which might be made by different teaching methods.

(1) *Procedure*
The lawyers were instructed to interview a client who was drawn from a pool of real clients attending local legal advisory centres, they were videotaped during their interviews and were instructed to see the client for 20 minutes and to make case notes for the file. Subsequently, in their three different groups they received the treatments enumerated above. Finally, a further videotaped interview with a different client form a similar pool of real clients was undertaken by each lawyer.

(2) *Assessment*
The interviews were assessed in a number of ways. The videotapes themselves and the case notes made up by the lawyers were analysed on the basis of information emerging in the interviews, and information noted by the lawyers. The interviews were further analysed in accordance with the checklists for those tasks and skills enumerated in this chapter (above). Judging was carried out, scoring on seven-point scales, by four practising lawyers.

The results were analysed by comparing performance in the first interview to performance in the second interview, and by comparing the performance in the second interview across the different groups.

(3) *Results*

Section 1. Comparison of fully trained group (Group A) with control group (Group C).

A detailed analysis of the total scores showed that the fully trained group performed significantly better than the untrained group. Although there is no significant difference in the amount of information emerging in the interviews, the untrained Group C did not *record* that information as well as Group A. The fully trained Group A also carried out the tasks and skills related to the interview in a significantly different (better) manner.

By comparing their first and second interviews one can similarly compare gains due to experience alone by the control group (Group C) compared to the gains by Groups A resulting from both experience and full training. Half of the individual members of the control group actually decreased in their treating scores. Those in group A, on the other hand, showed no decreases individually and most–though not all–increased their scores. The fact that some of the control group increased their scores also shows that there can be some gains as a result of experience alone for some individuals, although some may similarly get worse. Training, however, clearly enhances the beneficial effects of experience and no decreases were found in the fully trained group.

Section 2.–Comparison of Training Styles (Group A with Group B) to look at imputs from teaching with and without audio-visual feedback.

Group A, who were given traditional training and were also given the opportunity of seeing their own first interviews on videotape, performed significantly better on most measurements in their second interviews than Group B who were trained by readings, film and teaching alone (the "traditional" method). In this case there was no significantly difference on the information noted by the lawyers in each group. However, the way in which the information was obtained and the interview conduced in terms of effect on the clients seems to have been improved somewhat by the use of audio-visual techniques. This was reflected in the significant differences found on the tasks and skills measures.

(4) *Discussion*
It seems that legal interviewing skills can be taught as a separate entity from legal subject matter. By analysing the interview into its constituent parts and noting the common items in the first interviews (as has been shown in the earlier chapters of this book) an understanding of interviewing can be successfully taught, and this can improve the quality of subsequent interviews and enhance the information the lawyer obtains from such interviews. As far as this (limited) research showed, experience alone without training may mean that some individuals decease in quality in performance. Those receiving training showed increases in performance and no decreases in performance were noted. Although some form of audio-visual feedback, showing lawyers how they have performed, is useful; it is not essential in a system of training in interviewing. The more traditional methods of training by readings, seminars and practice also make a significant difference to performance in subsequent interviews.

Experienced practitioners–a sub-set search
In the second piece of research which forms part of this "proof of the pudding," a sub-set of 18 transcripts of interviews (chosen at random from 85 of such transcripts) was searched for obvious errors along the lines indicted in this book.

(1) *Interruptions*
In four interviews no calls or interruptions occurred. In two cases telephone calls were made during the interview by the interviewing

lawyer regarding the client's own case. In three interviews the lawyer dictated a file note or statement into a dictating machine in the presence of the client during the interview. In a further three cases there were short telephone calls in, which were immediately denied by the lawyer. In one of these the lawyer also ignored the client for some minutes whilst the client was in the room at the beginning of the interview, and the lawyer was reading something not to do with the client's case. Similarly in another interview, having shown the client in, the lawyer walked out for ten minutes to "see to his mail".

In the remaining six interviews significant interruptions occurred. In one, although the lawyer told his secretary to hold all calls "unless essential," five telephone calls into the office were received (in one of which the lawyer talked for one and a half pages of transcript regarding another client) and one telephone call out was made in consequence of the later telephone call for a half a page, also on the other client's case. In another interview the lawyer left the room for some minutes in the middle of the interview in order to find the client's file, took a half-page telephone call into the office on another matter and there were a further four telephone calls in, which were all denied. The other three cases are similar, involving incoming calls taking up a quarter of a page to one page of transcript, dealing with colleagues in the office standing at the lawyer's door and a secretary who comes in with a telex in the middle of the interview. The overall picture given by reading these transcripts is that many lawyers are fairly lax about allowing interruptions and following through with telephone calls relating to other matters in the presence of new clients on their first interviews. This may certainly not convey to the new clients the necessary feelings that their confidentiality would be observed of they were telephoning the lawyer, and may also be quite unnecessary interruptions to their own interviews.

(2) Listening
Some of the other interesting examples also emerged. One interview beings in this manner:

1. Lawyer: Right, have a seat. Now, what's it all about?
2. Client: Um.
3. Lawyer: What've you been up to?
4. Client: Well I haven't been up to anything actually.
5. Lawyer: Well I'm pleased to hear that.
6. Client: [Laughs nervously] Err, I'm supposed to have been accused of being involved in an accident in um in the er Jordan Square E.C.1.

Watching the beginning of this interview on video-tape, one can see the client quite taken aback by the lawyer's intendedly friendly approach at no. 3 above. The client's answer at no. 4 is made quite pointedly, and out of style with what one might have expected from an easy exchange of pleasantry. The client hands over to the lawyer a Summons at the point at which the above extract ends. The lawyer is so beguiled by this piece of legal documentation that he does not listen to the client's explanation. As a result he forget the pointedness of the immediate response at no. 4 above and therefore does not realise until five or six pages on that the client has had nothing to do with the accident. The client goes on to tell the lawyer five times in the course of as many minutes that he did not even have a car at the time, but the lawyer does not appear to hear this until the finally looks up from the Summons. The lawyer's fault is not so much that he misjudged when to be "friendly" at the beginning of an interview with a new client, but that he failed to take note of its effect when out of the ordinary, and became so enmeshed in the dates when the Summons had been served that he could not think clearly around the issue itself even though the client was trying desperately to tell him.

(3) *Questioning*

Another interview concerning a claim for an industrial disease exhibits in epic manner some of the difficulties resulting from the wrong style of question. In this interview, the one in which the lawyer walks out to sign his mail right at the beginning, the lawyer asks the client to spell out her full name and address as soon as he returns and starts the interview. The transcript of some 24 pages shows one answer given by the client lasting more than one and a half lines. Most answers are one word answers of "yes" or "no." Only in one case does the client talk for three and a half lines. At one point in the interview, where the client begins to try and explain the process in which she was involved at work and the client says more than five or six words at a time, the following exchange occurs:

Lawyer:	Slow down, slow down, slow down. You had to wet the leather?
Client:	Yes.
Lawyer:	What does that mean?
Client:	I had to put it in water.
Lawyer:	So did the leather come in strips already?
Client:	Yes.
Lawyer:	Cut? The leather was already cut for you?
Client:	They were in strips, but we had to slice them and make them.
Lawyer:	Slow down again. So you had the cut pieces of leather all at the side of you ready for use?

Client: Yes.

One can only imagine the frustration the client must have gone through in not being able to explain generally the process of the work and then subsequently to answer more detailed questions from the lawyer as notes were taken. It seems clear that this particular form of questioning might work in the court room but is inapplicable at the first stage of the interview.

(4) *Advising*
In a case involving an immigrant who had once entered the country under a false name, and therefore illegally, the following exchange occurred at the point at which the lawyer was giving advice:

1. Client: Now what do you think of the whole situation what's the possibility of it, percentage?
2. Lawyer: Quite high.
2. Client: Quite high for what, deportation or er?
4. Lawyer: They'll let you stay, because on the one hand it is the Home Office policy to allow foreign husbands married to English wives to stay here . . .

Here, a vague and poorly thought our remark at no. 2 above could have been taken either way by the client, who suddenly saw the prospect of deportation looming over him. More care in answering the question would have saved the client some immediate anxiety and removed a great deal of the awkwardness from which the remainder of the interview suffered.

(5) *Showing understanding*
In the last example of more obvious faults found in this sample, as in many of the other interviews, the interview begins in this way:

1. Lawyer: Right I'll just take down a few details.
2. Client: O.K.
3. Lawyer: Erm. What's your full name?
4. Client: Beatrice Anna Smith.
5. Lawyer: Smith with an "e"
6. Client: No.
7. Lawyer: And your address?
8. Client: 7, Yellow Close.
9. Lawyer: Yellow Close?
10. Client: Thats (naming the area)
11. Lawyer: NW10?
12. Client: mm mm.
13. Lawyer: Right. And er your problem is?
14. Client: I'm um an unmarried mother and I now want to make somebody, er my brother and his wife, legal guardians should anything happen to me.

15. Lawyer: I see.
16. Client: And secondly,
17. Lawyer: What's the name of your brother in law?
18. Client: He's my brother.
19. Lawyer: Your brother.

The lawyer appears to businesslike and not very caring here, that he could well be filling in a form and reading the questions to the client from the form. The lawyer's attention to the details of everyone's names cuts quite across the client's story at no. 16 with the lawyer's interjection at no. 17. No emotional significance is given to the fact that the client has had to violate her own privacy by giving facts about her private life to a stranger with whom she has only spent two or three minutes.

Each of these examples appears, by itself, small in significance, but may have an important effect on the interview and could equally be avoided by some thought or a little training. If these are the "Freds" that our new lawyers have to watch, then it might be better for them to learn their own interviewing in another manner.

Conclusion

This chapter had discussed the process of learning about interviewing by combining training with experience. It has set out a number of schemes for such training and learning which it is hoped the reader my easily follow. The chapter ended with some "hard" facts to show how poorly even some experienced lawyers interview and clear evidence that young lawyers can be trained to do so better.

Chapter 8

CLIENT AND CASE MANAGEMENT TECHNIQUES

This chapter considers client interviewing and the further lawyer-client relationship, as well as work on behalf of the client, through sets of new techniques for managing both clients and cases. The chapter considers methods adopted by two firms which have now closed, and whose approaches are therefore more open to public view. It also considers how commercial firms and others may operate client and case management techniques.

The techniques and management of lawyering have changed considerably in the last 10 years, as has the legal profession (Sherr (1993) *International Journal of the Legal Profession* 1, Editorial). Among the changes within professional work has been a move towards specialisation according to subject categories of law and also towards specialisation within subject categories, as to the level of work undertaken by each qualified lawyer, trainee lawyer and paralegal. In many firms especially the larger firms, an approach has been taken to rationalise the system of work within the law firm. The effect of this is often that the early part of the case, or matter, is carried out by one individual at a particular level, and later parts by different individuals, often at different levels, or different lawyers at the same level. The notion of "each case handled by one lawyer" within a firm is fast disappearing. This clearly has major consequences across all features of both case and client management, and must also affect the context and nature of client interviewing and the continuing client relationship.

It is instructive to consider three models of "industrialisation" of the legal process as practised in the United Kingdom in two of the largest legal aid firms existing in 1992 and in many larger, commercial firms. Each of the named legal aid firms, for very different reasons, has since ceased to exist, although the systems which they used have been, to some extent, adopted elsewhere.

The Deacon Goldrein Green Model

DGG was a firm in Merseyside with some 35 different offices and a central litigation unit (see, *e.g.* Sherr, A.H., Moorhead, R., and Paterson, A., *Lawyers—the Quality Agenda*, Chapter 10; Dirks, J. *Making Legal Aid Pay and Franchise Development* (Sweet & Maxwell, London, 1994). Clients would attend at their local office of DGG and if a case moved towards litigation it would be passed on to the Central Litigation Unit which was located in the centre of

Liverpool. Clients would continue to be dealt with through the local offices who would maintain communication between the Central Litigation Unit and the client. In this particular model, the people who carried out initial client interviewing and diagnosis, were all qualified lawyers. The work pattern was highly organised to a format of structured interviewing and case diagnosis, which was set out in the DGG "red files". This was a form of quality assurance system organised to promote the asking of all appropriate and relevant questions for each type of case. The system acted as something in between a structure and a checklist for client interviewing and case handling. The "red files" were updated as the law and procedure changed.

Grahame Durnford Ford and the Family Law Bureau

At almost the opposite end of England in Hastings another quite large firm, which also handled a considerable amount of legal aid work, had developed a somewhat different approach in relation to family law work. Noticing how difficult it was to work on legal aid rates and maintain a good client service for family law, they evolved a system of work based around an expert computer system and highly devolved work allocation.

There were no satellite offices under the GDF system but the "intake" was carried out by paralegal "counsellors" who had been trained in the art of "counselling" clients and had also received some basic training in the elements of family law. They were forbidden to give any advice. In this system the computer would generate all the questions and the answers given by the client to those questions would be entered onto the computer. The computer would then generate the next questions for the counsellors to ask, depending upon the answers to those above. It was an algorithmic system which operated through a set of diagnostic routines, narrowing down to more and more specific questions. Since all the answers of the clients to these questions were typed into the computer by the "counsellors" the computer was also able to make some sense of the information given. By the end of the first interview, the computer would automatically produce a draft letter to the client confirming the information obtained, draft letter to the other side, draft Affidavit, etc., and draft Pleadings, all of which would be checked by a higher level operative.

The Commercial Firm Model

Each of these systems can be contrasted with devolved work patterns existing in larger commercial firms. Often a fairly senior lawyer, perhaps the "client partner", will carry out a first interview, sometimes together with a "matter partner" and sometimes not. Once the basic details are received, further elucidation is the responsibility of the matter partner or a more junior assistant solicitor. Different elements of the ensuing work might then be delegated to a range of lawyers, including trainee solicitors, solicitors and legal executives, either in the matter partner's department (legal subject based) or not. The continuing relationship with the client would be handled by whoever was carrying out the work at any particular time, although overall supervision would be in the hands of the client or matter partner.

It is not intended here to make any assessment of the worth of each of these systems, each approach or certainly the work of each of the named firms. The intention of describing these systems in basic outline is to report their existence so that a reaction to the client management and client interviewing issues can also be recorded here.

In general, where each case is not to be handled by a single lawyer from start to finish, this author's preference is for a managed system in which a qualified lawyer carries out the initial and any continuing diagnosis of the relevant facts and legal issues in a matter. Legal diagnosis is the most complex and the most crucial of the skills which lawyers learn. It includes all that is involved in "thinking like a lawyer", analysing cases, dealing with legal problems and fashioning practical solutions which are dealt with in undergraduate and vocational legal education and during the Training Contract. To place these tasks in the hands of non-lawyers, even with the support of structured procedures, or computerised questioning systems, is to underestimate the difficulty involved in carrying out those tasks, and also to underestimate the value of the bulk of legal education and training. Legal diagnosis, probably both an art and science, needs a wide range of both general and special knowledge, strong practical skill in all the areas mentioned in this book and the ability to solve problems by suggesting a number of alternative solutions from which a client may choose. A case worker with the same level of knowledge, training and experience as a qualified lawyer could certainly handle this, but not somebody at a lower level. In DGG above, a lawyer was involved at the beginning and in GDF a more senior level of staff, probably a qualified lawyer, considered the information once obtained. This author's preference would be for the involvement of a fully qualified lawyer at the earliest stage. Whatever system is in place, the management of proper, effective and reliable diagnosis at the beginning is essential.

Similarly, the management of clients at later stages needs to be considered carefully in any such process. Although it may be a counsel of perfection for the heavily industrialised firm of the future, clients should not receive information at second hand from those making the decisions on which the information is based. This would not just be tiresome, but also inefficient and impractical. Either the continuing level of information and advice would be

minimal and insufficiently client-centred, or the number of itera-
tions between the different players would be considerable. In either
case the system will not be working at an optimal level.

Information from the London Insurers Bureau who operate the
Solicitors Indemnity Fund negligence insurance on behalf of the
profession seems to suggest that it is the three to five partner firm
which is proportionately more likely to have negligence claims
made against it. It is interesting that sole practitioners, with low
resources and no other partners from whom to obtain a second
opinion, are not the group with most claims. Neither, does it seem,
are the larger firms with often better systems of management.

Sole practitioners are probably much more aware of their own
areas of knowledge and lack of knowledge. If the firm really is one
single person, they are more likely to know and remember whether
they have done something or not. In the medium sized firm the
problems of sharing work may mean that responsibilities between
different people are not absolutely clear. Yet work is likely to be
shared or moved around between different lawyers and levels of
lawyers. The same could, of course, be true for even the largest
firms. This author has carried out a survey of negligence cases in
some larger firms (unpublished). The problems that arise do not
seem in general to involve mistakes of law. Only one case was
found where updating on the law would have been helpful. The
greatest problem was poor communication either with the client or
within the firm.

Poor communication within the firm included insufficient information or agreement about responsibility for clients and cases.
This was especially a problem on changeover of staff, at holiday
time, or when someone was ill. Although it might be imagined that
these would be obvious sources of difficulty and that everyone
would be aware of them, often this was simply not the case. Issues
of poor communication with the client were sometimes similar.
These included cases where the client thought the lawyer was going
to do something and vice versa.

More usual were the cases where the lawyer had reached a
particular point of view which affected the client's position, and
believed that this had been communicated fully and effectively to
the client. However, there was no evidence of this in writing either
by way of a communication with the client, or even by way of a file
note. Therefore, when a client's memory was different, or selective,
it became difficult to substantiate that they had been warned of a
possibility or an issue which might affect a transaction, or their
rights in litigation.

Communication then is not simply a means of obtaining client
information, or of giving advice to clients, it also involves the
management of cases among lawyers. Poor communication can
lead not only to poor factual information, dissatisfied clients and

bad case outcomes. It can also lead to firm mismanagement, breach of conduct rules and negligence actions.

Prevention

Two approaches seem to be applicable for the prevention of such problems: one involving management techniques, and the second involving training techniques. These may be expressed as incorporation of supervision and review techniques within the management of cases and the adoption of comprehensive and specific training systems.

The most common general system for management of cases is outlined in the Law Society's Practice Management Standards and is also reflected in the Legal Aid Board's Franchising Specification. A copy of the Practice Management Standards is included in an Appendix at the back of this book. Reporting to clients is dealt with separately under Rule 15 Issues (see Appendix 1). The Practice Management Standards include the contemplation of a system in which junior staff are supervised in their work on cases, which includes their communication with clients and there are clear agreements between the different case workers or fee earners regarding who has responsibility for which elements of the case. In addition, everyone's files should be subject to a review process, which need not take place in relation to every file, but should involve an independent review of a proportion of files for problems in case handling and client handling, or issues which might lead to negligence actions.

Training techniques in relation to managing client interviewing inside the larger firm with devolved work patterns should in future be a matter for consideration by those teaching interviewing skills at the Vocational Course level and beyond. Teaching and training in client interviewing skills has come of age and will now need to reflect the changing circumstances in which lawyers carry out their work. This, clearly, does not just affect the person who carries out the interview. It also affects the junior lawyers in a firm (or senior lawyers in one of the models above), who have not had the advantage of the direct client contact and client relationship which would allow them to understand all of the issues, and the hopes and desires of the client which may not be set down in the notes of the first interview. Those carrying out interviews under such circumstances must be trained to think of recording more of their understanding of the client, the client's needs and the facts of the case than they might otherwise have done if they were the only lawyer working on the matter. A model is shown in Chapter Six above of how a file-note might record issues other than the simple facts.

Those receiving the notes of interview and asked to carry on discrete tasks to take the case further, must be aware of the difficulties of working with "sanitised" sets of facts and be prepared to question the lawyer who carried out the interview wherever necessary in order to gain more depth and breadth. Those who supervise and review such cases must be on the alert to notice the sorts of problems that occur in a devolved process. Client contact should be frequent and open, so that any gaps or slips in understanding can be remedied; and copies of correspondence, etc., should almost invariably be sent to the client. This may sound like a heavy price to pay for a devolved system, but much of it is good practice anyway and its generation of continuing client involvement will be beneficial.

Such issues cannot just be "managed" through supervision, monitoring, assessment and review. They must also be trained within the firm itself. This system is very different from that of the idealised, archetypal single lawyer who is fully trained, fully qualified, with a wide base of general knowledge about the law, enormous common sense, close personal knowledge of the client, as much time as is necessary, brilliant precedents, perfect support staff and, no other cases or management responsibilities. Quite probably this sepia tinted "golden age" of lawyering never did exist. But the technologist of the new millennium will certainly be at the other extreme. Training must accommodate these new work practices and be directed specifically towards the ways in which each person will operate at different stages in their legal careers. In the larger firms, where such practices predominate, there are also likely to be proper training systems and even training partners or directors of training. Instead of training on induction the very newest trainee solicitors as if they were going to handle a client interview, this group should now be trained to deal with working on cases at second hand. Qualified solicitors should be the group to be trained more on how to handle client interviews, and more senior solicitors should be trained in delegation and supervision under the effects of a devolved process whose parameters must be clearly stated at all times.

In effect, this represents a separating out of the different skills involved in the task of interviewing and a devolution of separable elements of the process to different case workers. Sometimes the diagnosis will be carried out by somebody separate from the interviewer. This is a most difficult system to operate and training for this should include the necessity of checking back with the client on all assumptions of fact, as well as the diagnosis and possible options.

This account is not intended to be a commendation, or any form of comment, on such devolved systems. Such comments and analysis need to be made elsewhere. What is important is that where such systems operate, the old paradigm of legal work in the hands of the individual lawyer cannot be blindly adhered to if it no longer exists. Both management and training must take into account what is actually in place.

Supervision and Review of Files

Both supervision and review of files are essential mechanisms for ensuring the quality of work. They will be especially important under a devolved case system. Supervision is the process which occurs when a senior member of staff overlooks the work of a junior member. Supervision can include:

(a) Reading outgoing letters.

(b) Reading incoming letters.

(c) Periodic file checks.

(d) Periodic discussions about work and work overload with a supervisee.

(e) Open door policy—come for supervision when you need it.

Any combination, or any one of the above may be used as a means of supervision. Which are the most appropriate, depends upon the nature of the work, the experience of the supervisor and the supervisee, the numbers of people being supervised, etc.

Supervision systems are now quite familiar in almost all firms and appear to be a natural progression from the apprenticeship nature of the training contract and responsibilities of partners towards work carried out by other staff. They are sometimes haphazard in both smaller and larger firms, although larger firms have tended in the recent past, to set more clear rules for supervision. Because the concept of supervision within legal practice has the provenance of articles or the training contract, the degree of supervision as between a more senior and more junior member of staff is carried out on an highly individualistic basis. The degree of supervision necessary for one trainee may be quite different from the degree of supervision necessary for another. Similarly, a supervisor with greater experience both of the work and of supervision, may be able to take a more light-handed approach than one who is less experienced. He or she may have a clearer idea of what the warning signs should be for supervising more closely. They should also be aware that haphazard, or too individualistic, supervision of both work and people can render the whole system useless.

Review is often taken to mean a somewhat different process, which is necessary for all lawyers and legal workers whatever their experience and whatever the nature of the work. It involves a random check of files, often on a proportionate basis, in order to see that time limits are being well kept to, clients' communications answered and reasonable decisions are made. Review might involve looking at 5 or 10 per cent of each person's files at random. Any specific problems found might be followed up with a more comprehensive review.

File review is a much more recent phenomenon and it is one which has only taken root where quality systems such as legal aid franchising, practice management standards and ISO 9004 have demanded it. Because file review is ubiquitous, relating to all files of all partners and staff, and because firms are organised on a hierarchical basis, setting up a system of file review which will include more senior members of staff is unlikely unless there is a strong external impetus.

Each of these methods of supervision and review will help to ensure the quality of the work being done including the client handling elements of that work, where they are evident from the file or from discussions with the lawyer concerned. Issues arising often on supervision and review should become the subject of training or another form of corrective action. Noting such issues in a methodical way will allow the assessment of themes subsequently. They can then be used as an analytical tool to fashion a more appropriate or more competent system in the future.

Risk Management

Such issues as client management techniques in the larger, more industrial firm, and supervision and review are major elements of any risk management system within the firm. At present, the Solicitors Indemnity Fund through the London Insurers Bureau, runs what has been a "mutual fund"—the entire profession supports the rest of the profession through insurance. The differential rate of claim for different subject areas and as between different sizes of firms has begun a move away from the mutuality principle, and different limits on the disregard element of claims now exist for different firms, largely based on turnover. Such elements of claims have to be insured on the more general insurance market, as does any top-up beyond the limits of the compulsory scheme. In addition, the compulsory scheme does not appear to cover all the actions of a person who is not a partner in a firm.

Since so much insurance must be organised on the open market, issues such as claims history and risk management systems become much more important. Insurance companies take an interest in the systems for controlling such issues before they agree annual insurance premiums with each firm. Insurance companies querying management structure will often ask about client handling techniques, especially in relation to supervision and review of files.

Clients are rarely immediately aware of negligence which is covered by insurance. Clients' awareness is much more geared to understanding when communication is absent or is poor from lawyer to client. In other words, clients' awareness of problems relates to this issue, but, it may also be the case that lawyers who are negligent are also not careful when handling client issues.

Client Questionnaires and Client Reviews

All firms should consider some method of discovering what their clients think of their service. It is often very difficult for lawyers to put themselves in their client's shoes and see how the clients perceive their work and the service they provide.

In firms which have a high turnover of clients who may come "off the street" and may be dealt with in one visit on advice and assistance, client questionnaires can be a very good method of discovering the client's view of the service. Such questionnaires should ask about how long it took the client to gain an interview; how the reception staff performed; as well as what they thought of the lawyer, the advice given and the general service. Questionnaires on performance can also be useful for cases which take rather longer. But there are problems about securing the completion and return of the questionnaire at the completion of a matter and there are also difficulties about deciding exactly when it should be delivered. If a questionnaire is delivered fairly early on in a long case, at a point in time when the lawyer has made an assessment and perhaps some promises, the expectation/satisfaction level may appear prematurely high if the promises are not ultimately achieved. In order to decide in a meaningful way how performance changes over time, it is essential to send out the questionnaire at the same time for each case.

Another system which may be used for firms which have a number of repeat clients, or clients with a large number of files, is the periodic service review. This involves a meeting, perhaps annually or every two years between the client/partner and other lawyers within the firm who carry out a large proportion of their work for the client company or individual, and representatives of the client. The object is to find out whether there are any ways in which it would be possible to change the approach of either or both parties so that the joint performance can be organised optimally.

Such meetings can often be a major revelation to both sides. Generally, the clients will be sophisticated in their dealings with lawyers and have an awareness of the legal and practical problems involved in their transactions or cases. There will also be a relationship history through which many of the smaller difficulties of communication may well have been ironed out. Nevertheless, both sides learn an enormous amount from such contact. The revelation often includes issues of behaviour or work patterns which can easily be managed in a different way in order to achieve the desired objective. Perceptions of each other can often be quite different from the perceptions each holds of themselves. As this interactive reflective relationship grows it becomes possible to organise specific regimes of client service for different clientele. This largely would reflect what is mentioned in the first three chapters of this book. Learning in this way from one client can also be enormously helpful in learning how to deal with all clients.

Conclusion

This chapter has considered how clients and cases can be managed in firms where more than one lawyer or paralegal will be involved in dealing with a case or a client.

Where a number of lawyers handle different elements of the same case, then it is sensible to organise a case management system to ensure that client communication is properly organised and safeguarded. In addition, supervision of less experienced lawyers and a sample review of all lawyer's files are important ingredients of any good case management system. Some models have been set up in the chapter for approaches which have been used by different sorts of firms. These, together with Practice Management Standards of the Law Society, or the Legal Aid Franchising Standards, should provide assistance in understanding how best to ensure that clients are properly served and that work is properly and effectively carried out in the medium sized and larger firm.

Chapter 9

REGULATION AND GUIDANCE FOR LAWYER COMMUNICATIONS WITH CLIENTS

This chapter details how both regulation and guidance have entered into ethical behaviour for solicitors carrying out both initial client interviews and further communication with their clients. The chapter considers the relative merits of regulation, contracting, and guidance and then presents the major elements of each now present within the professional context.

There has been both specific conduct regulation and a number of elements of guidance for the manner in which lawyers communicate with their clients. Direct regulation is now enshrined in rule 15 of the Solicitor's Code of Conduct which was incorporated into the Code Of Professional Conduct in its current version in February 1991. Rule 15 itself incorporates written standards of guidance largely relating to the provision of information on costs. An update incorporating the information on costs into the Rule is due late 1999. (Rule 15 and the Written Standards of Guidance are printed in the Appendices to this book). A separate regime of guidance also persuades solicitors in general to operate within Practice Management Standards and recommends that solicitors who work on legal aid adhere to the standards promulgated by the new legal aid regime of franchising. Both direct regulation and guidance have proved to be important and useful.

Conduct Regulation

Direct regulation sets an atmosphere of certainty. It makes a clear statement of professional interest in dealing properly with clients, and in the worst cases, it would allow the Office for the Supervision of Solicitors to take action on a breach of conduct rule against the solicitor concerned. But the system has no policing mechanism, other than relying on clients or other solicitors to complain. Clients have difficulty in complaining about their solicitors. Whilst the case is still in progress they would be worried that this would affect the solicitor's work or charges, and possibly the outcome of the case. To move a case from one solicitor to another, especially on legal aid, can be quite difficult and is likely only to add to costs. Clients will often be uncertain about what is, and is not, acceptable behaviour in terms of legal service and they therefore cannot assess the validity of their own complaint. Finding the appropriate people within the firm or the external body to receive a complaint is often awkward. Articulating the complaint and pursuing it are time consuming and difficult for those who do not have expertise.

Contracted Systems

The alternative method of exhortation through standards which are not mandatory has worked more through contract than coercion. Firms sign up to Legal Aid Franchising and are thereafter monitored on their compliance with the conduct laid out in that scheme. Recent announcements for the future of legal aid suggest that it will become exclusive to those firms who will be contracted with the Legal Aid Board under the continuation of franchising. Although firms will be at liberty not to work on legal aid, this will certainly provide more of a coercive feel to the system. The Law Society has recently announced a system called Lexcel in which firms may sign up to compliance with the Practice Management Standards. They would be monitored on their compliance with these and will therefore be able to advertise that they have satisfied a certain level of "quality". In addition, other quality assurance schemes such as "ISO 9000" and "Investors in People" have similar sets of standards which aim at contracting the profession into compliance.

Contracting systems can be useful because firms will usually feel a greater sense of control over the way in which they carry out their obligations. The Law Society's Practice Management Standards, for example, currently allow for three levels of compliance. In contrast with full regulation, firms usually value the ability to enter into the contract of their own free will in the first place. Where there is some sense of coercion involved (as is suggested that at some point it will be necessary to have a Legal Aid Franchise in order to do legal aid work) there may be a tendency for contractors to cut their performance to the absolute minimum standard required by the contract. This would certainly be a form of behaviour expected within a quality system in manufacturing industry and elsewhere. But a "minimum" standard will also be true of a regulative system. Both can have the effect of encouraging conformity to a minimal standard.

In summary then, both direct regulation and indirect guidance and contract have advantages and some problems. The text now turns from the form of such regulation to consider more closely its content.

Rule 15 and Complaints Handling

Rule 15 of the Solicitor's Code of Conduct divides its regulation between elements which are applicable only to "principals" in firms, *i.e.* partners (rule 15(1)), and elements which are appropriate to every solicitor in private practice (rule 15(2)). Partners have an obligation to set up an internal complaints handling system within their firms. Such a system would handle all complaints including those from clients which are likely to be specifically about poor communication or poor service. It is clearly sensible that the bulk of complaints be handled at the firm level and in the context of the firm in which they arise; and clients should feel able to raise complaints directly and be assured of an appropriate response. Rule 15 became part of the Code of Conduct at about the same time the Solicitor's Complaints Bureau (the precursor to the Office for the Supervision of Solicitors) began. If the profession were to have to pay for the handling of complaints by the SCB, it would be much more sensible for the bulk of complaints to be handled in-house by solicitors' firms. The cost of complaint handling also should fall mainly on the firms who are the subject of the complaints rather than on the whole profession.

The regulation does not specify exactly how complaints should be handled except that there should be two tiers of complaint. Probably the first level should be the person who is handling the case and the upper level should be a more senior person, perhaps the senior, or managing, partner or head of a large department in a larger firm.

Register

Although the rule does not seem to clearly state this, there almost certainly needs to be a Complaints Register which records the date of the complaint, the source of the complaint, the person complained against and action taken. If the complaint goes further than the firm's internal procedures and moves on to the Office for the Supervision of Solicitors, they will ask to see the record of the original complaint at the firm and it will be useful to have such a record for this purpose. A Register of Complaints will also allow the firm to analyse its complaints over a period and to consider whether any policies need to be changed in order to avoid such problems in the future. Such policy changes could involve "management" type solutions such as different supervision or review procedures, or "training" type solutions, involving a regimen of training for those subject to complaint or new staff on induction (see Chapter Eight).

There is, however, no definition of a "complaint". If a client telephones to state that they have tried to contact their lawyer three times in one afternoon and the lawyer has not returned their calls, some might classify this as a "complaint". If a client telephones to complain about the bill, some might classify this as a complaint. Firms need a rule of thumb which will help them to decide which complaints to record and which "comments", "discussions", etc., to resolve without registering the problem centrally. Perhaps a good rule of thumb might be that any "complaint" which is made to the second level of complainee should be recorded as a complaint. The system of internal complaints handling presupposed by the Rule 15 regime therefore provides a useful way for firms to monitor client complaints and client reaction. Where such complaints are of a trivial nature the firm can clearly consider how to enhance their performance. Where they are more serious, a more active management reaction will be necessary. It would probably be better for a firm to do rather more than just relying on complaints in order to gain proper feedback on how well they handle clients. How to approach this task will depend largely on the nature of the clientele. If the firm is a "high street" practice and deals with walk-in clients and off-the-cuff advice and assistance, then a questionnaire after the first interview may well be a useful way to pick up information on a client's reactions. If the firm has long established clients for whom it carries out a range of work, then an annual "service review" meeting between two or three representatives of the firm and the clients can be helpful in gaining an understanding of how each could be more helpful to the other. It is probably wiser to obtain such comment within the context of a review than wait for a more serious reaction in the form of a complaint (see Chapter Eight above).

Information on name and status

The other elements of Rule 15 are aimed at every solicitor in private practice and not just at partners. They are therefore the obligation of every solicitor, and by implication, of every trainee solicitor operating in private practice. These elements relate to the information which must be given to clients. Clients must be told the name and status of the person handling their case, and of the other people involved as "supervisor" or client partner or matter partner. It is in the form of a regulation. There is now a conduct obligation to be clear and open to clients about the name and status of those involved in carrying out their work. Secondly clients must be given an understanding of who to complain to if there is any problem with the work or service they receive. This should include the two tiers of information mentioned above. In other words clients should be told that in the first instance, if there is a problem they should approach Mr X, probably the person handling the matter, and if not satisfied with the answer they should approach Ms Y, probably a senior partner in the firm.

It is difficult for someone to explain their status, say as trainee solicitor, at an initial interview, and it will also probably be difficult for lawyers to give information about "complaints handling". Many lawyers feel that this is tantamount to *asking* clients to complain. As a result, since firms started taking note of Rule 15 they have often tended to provide this information in written form by way of a letter following the first interview. The letter tends to be based on a precedent letter which may be partly modified for the purpose on each occasion. Such precedents tend to be rather formal in nature, making it very clear that they are written simply to comply with a set of Law Society rules, but that the essence of the real legal work will appear in other documents. One possible effect of regulation then is an unwilling compliance, "working to rule" according to the letter, but not the spirit of the client care regulations. This is an unnecessary effect. It is quite possible for the information required to be given under Rule 15 to be stated in a positive way both in oral and written form which will not disturb the client, cause a set of immediate complaints or appear unnatural. Each firm will want to word its letters and documents in its own style appropriate to its culture, its clientele and the areas of work in which it specialises. A purely formal letter accompanied by the "real" letter will hardly cause great admiration among clients. They would much rather see a meaningful approach to the issue of who is dealing with their case and how any complaints might be handled.

Information on the case

In addition to information on names and status, all solicitors in private practice:

> "shall, unless it is inappropriate in the circumstances, ensure that clients are at all relevant times given any appropriate information as to the issues raised and the progress of the matter"

> *Solicitors' Practice Rules 1990*, Rule 15 2C

It may be thought strange that solicitors be put under a specific conduct obligation to tell their clients about their case. Indeed, when such obvious issues need to be set down in black and white as regulations the rulebook may be seen to be quite detailed and specific in its approach. The previous edition of the Code of Conduct ran to 845 pages, the longest version yet. It is clear that this rule of conduct needed to be stated because it was felt that solicitors were not providing clients with information at appropriate times either as to the issues raised by the case or the progress of work on it.

Commentary 5 to this rule suggests that solicitors consider when it will be appropriate to confirm both instructions received and advice given in writing. It is suggested that it will always be appropriate to give such confirmation in writing. There may well be occasions when it should not be sent out to a client since it might be read by someone other than the client who may even be the defendant or respondent to proceedings or potential proceedings. But the record should always be in writing and should be available to the client at some stage. It is also important that this record can be read by any subsequent lawyer handling the case. Delay is mentioned specifically in commentary 3 to the rule as an occasion for keeping clients informed of progress or lack of progress. The commentary also discusses appropriate language, providing explanatory leaflets, sending copies of letters, answering requests for information promptly, advising on advocates, explaining the effect of any important documents, writing to clients concerning everything at the end of the case and noting future action to be taken by the client or the solicitor. All of this now provides in regulation form many of the approaches suggested in Chapter Six above.

In order to ensure compliance with the code and the enforcement of good practice it is sensible for firms to develop a simple list of occasions on which clients should be kept informed (say) every six weeks, unless another communication has occurred. Form letters can then be made available for each of these events, which would explain the particular circumstances and solicitors would be able to choose these forms and amend them for each client case. In addition, a file summary sheet at the beginning of the file (perhaps in a separate plastic folder) could note key dates, key information and special issues such as undertakings clearly so that any new lawyer could pick up the file easily and see what has happened, what is happening and what the client has been informed. A version of such a file summary sheet for the litigation context is included in the Appendices at the back of this book.

Written Standards and Costs

The original draft of Rule 15 which was put before the Law Society Council is said to have included a clause mandating the giving of information on costs. But the Law Society Council refused to turn that element into a conduct obligation. Instead the Written Professional Standards were redrafted to provide important guidance on costs that fell short of regulation. And the Law Society Council said that if solicitors still continued not to give full information on costs, this element would be turned into regulation within a year. Since then, each of the annual reports of the Lay Observer and, after the Courts and Legal Services Act, of the Legal Services Ombudsman have reported problems with information given by solicitors on costs. Since complaints which go to the Legal Services Ombudsman have to go through the Solicitors Complaints Bureau first the Law Society must be well aware of an even higher number of such complaints. However, no such regulation was made. Then a newspaper report of the Law Society Council's deliberations on this in early 1996 suggested that regulation was imminent. The proposed regulation was finally published in May 1997 in the Law Society Gazette. Although it has been agreed by the Lord Chancellor's Advisory Committee on Legal Education and Conduct, the Law Society appear to be still holding back on the promulgation of the new rule.

The written professional standards asked that information on costs be given to the client on taking instructions, on confirming instructions and on the happening of significant events in a case. Particular issues should be covered for privately paying clients both generally and specifically for contentious matters. Particular information also needs to be given to legally aided clients, and specifically about the effect of the statutory charge. In view of the generally poor response to Rule 15 at its inception, it may be considered that further regulation on costs could fare similarly. On the other hand, such regulation will make a clear statement about the Law Society's views in this area and might make a few more solicitors take notice if complaints to the Office for the Supervision of Solicitors on this issue were given more publicity or prominence in reports of professional misconduct.

Each element of the written standards on costs is already given a specific section and its own commentary in Chapter 13 of the Solicitor's Guide to Professional Conduct. For the sake of completeness these are included in Appendix 1. These sections deal in detail with initial information on costs, the basis of charging, method of payment, confirmation of what is included, confirmation of estimates, limits on costs, and the extra information for the special cases of privately paying clients and legally aided clients. A final short section looks at "discussing the risk" and states that this sort of information should be put in writing.

This detailed guidance provides the profession with useful standards on which to base their approach to giving costs information. The content of these is clearly not at fault. But policing is very lax. This would seem to be a good area to engender some detailed consumerism and if clients were made aware of what they ought to expect they might well demand more of such information (see Sherr and Domberger, *Competition on Conveyancing: An Analysis of Solicitors' Charges* (1997) 8 Fiscal Studies No. 3, pages 17–28).

Whilst waiting for regulation the Law Society and the Legal Aid Board have gone down the route of contracting for this information to be given. The Practice Management Standards basically repeat the written standards on costs in the section on handling clients and giving clients information. As appropriate to legal aid, the Legal Aid Franchising Specification sets out a similarly detailed guidance. Within franchising this is already monitored by auditors and may soon be monitored by asking clients what information they have received. When Practice Management Standards become an auditable accreditation the same will be true there. Regulation will now bring costs information in line with other information which must be given to clients.

Client Interviewing/Client Counselling Competition

Another method of promoting conceptions of good client handling is the International Client Counselling Competition and the English National Client Interviewing Competition.

The Client Counselling Competition began in the United States as the "Mock Law Office Competition". It was started by Professor Louis Brown of the University of Southern California Law Faculty in Los Angeles, as a reaction to the court and advocacy based competitions which were much more prevalent for law students, but not reflective of the life of practical lawyers. Professor Brown went on to pioneer "preventive law", another approach related more to the work of solicitors than barristers. The Client Counselling Competition took root in the United States at a time when the Ford Foundation had set up the Council for Legal Education in Professional Responsibility and funded clinical programmes in many law schools there. The idea was imported into the United Kingdom in the academic year 1985–1986 when Geoffrey Bindman and the author organised the first national competition at the University of Warwick.

The winning team from the United Kingdom final each year travelled to the International Competition final which was initially held in the United States but is beginning to be held alternately in other countries. The competition makes quite a fuss about client interviewing and counselling. This draws a good deal of attention among law students, and among the practitioners and academics who are involved in judging the competitions. It has been an important form of promotion of interest in client interviewing in all the places that the competition has taken hold.

The competition is judged on a clear basis. Working through the judging criteria with those who have not judged before is always an interesting experience. Sitting on judging panels with new judges is also fascinating. Many more experienced practitioners may be excellent client interviewers but rarely have the time to watch others carrying out a full interview or to think about the elements of their skills. The learning experience which the competition provides at this high level for those judging should not be underestimated. It is also an effective promotion of good interviewing conduct to the competitors themselves. They have to prepare carefully, learn about such issues, practice the skills involved and then take part in the competition.

Although there is much to be said in favour of the Client Interviewing Competition and its international equivalent it also has some problems. Good as it is with promotion of interest, it is poor in identifying for competitors what is the reality of interviewing clients, at least in an English context. Its principal difficulty is that, unlike representative advocacy or mooting, client interviewing is not naturally a "competitive" event. Empathising, understanding, advising and counselling are often about subordinating one's own ego to the interests and needs of a client. The act of competition just does not sit easily with this approach, even though the competitive element is to carry out those behaviours or skills in a better way.

Perhaps even more importantly the style of competitive judging promotes the need for acting out the lawyer role for the sake of the "audience" of judges rather than reacting to the client's approach, presentation, needs and desires. Although good judges can take these issues into account, it is hard to remember that a judge is not a client and that a client interviewed in this way will also feel differently about their behaviour. Perhaps, ideally, the best form of staging the competition would be for the judges to be in another room on a videolink or watching through a one way mirror (a style of performance assessment which is now more common in both the helping and teaching professions). This rarely occurs in the author's experience of the competition. In order to allow other students to learn from the performance and criticism of the judges an audience of other students sits in. At the first United Kingdom competition held at Warwick University in 1986 separate rooms were used with videolinks and one way mirrors. Strange though this system may feel, it has a much closer atmosphere to a real client interview room than the staged setting that has become more usual. If at all possible, it is strongly suggested that the video link system be used and relayed to students as well as judges. This would certainly assist in some of the recreation of reality and bolster the verisimilitude of the occasion.

The rules of the international competition, and hence national finals, seem to include that the lawyers interview in pairs. This has certain merits, but in general does not reflect the normal practice of "personal plight" type cases in England and Wales. Although in larger commercial firms clients, who may also come in some numbers, may well be met by more than one lawyer, this would not be usual for other cases.

One of the good effects of the pairing system is that the lawyer interviewers also have to devise a system for working together and the judges listen to their post interview discussion before deciding how well they performed. In this post interview reflective discussion the two lawyers can comment on anything that happened in the interview, or should have happened in the interview and on what steps they now intend to take. This allows a great deal of useful reflective discussion and comment on what was understood from the client—which may not have been capable of expression during the interview in front of the client but may be useful to demonstrate to the judges and the other lawyer competitor in the team after the interview.

This reflects good interviewing practice in which a lawyer may well be paying full attention to listening closely to the client and watching all behaviours during the interview. They might then continue developing their understanding, legal theories and practical solutions beyond the time spent with the client. In practice, often lawyers move from one task to another without allowing such "reflective" space to capitalise on what they have seen and understood. This means they are forced subsequently to repeat areas of information or try to recreate facts for files from memory. This aspect of the client interviewing competition then can be a very useful lesson for those involved. The only difficulty with this element at present is the more general problem of being "on stage". A real post reflective discussion would also be in the privacy of a client interviewing room or someone's office and the only person to impress would be the other lawyer. If the competition is carried out "on stage" then this element also has to be something of an act played out in the full glare of judge and audience spotlights, worrying about making any errors rather than taking each other through a useful checking process which might appear a little imperfect from the outside. Here again it is suggested the use of a video link or two way mirror provides a major advantage for the learning power of the competition on competitors.

The competition then is a useful form of promotion and an effective means of alerting undergraduates or others involved in the competition, those watching it and those judging it to many of the issues which are dealt with in this book. Its problems as a competitive acting "sport" can be alleviated through imaginative use of the competition venue and the now ubiquitous technology of video.

Conclusion

This chapter has considered how the advice presented in the first edition of this book is slowly being formalised in part into sets of regulations and guidance for lawyer communications. The chapter considered both conduct rules and contracted systems and ended with considering how the client interviewing or counselling competition has promoted many of the same ideas and issues.

THE GUIDE TO THE PROFESSIONAL CONDUCT
OF SOLICITORS 1996

Extract

Chapter 13
Client Care

13.01 Practice rule 15 (client care)
13.02 Complaints procedure–rule 15(1) and 15(2)(b)
13.03 Responsibility for client's matter–rule 15(2)(a)
13.04 General information for clients–15(2)(c)
13.05 Written professional standards–information on costs for clients
13.06 Standard (a)–initial information on costs
13.07 Standard (b)–confirmation of costs estimate or agreement
13.08 Standard (c)–further information for privately paying clients
13.09 Standard (d)—further information for privately paying clients–contentious matters
13.10 Standard (e)–further information for legally aided clients
13.11 Standard (f)—discussing the risk

13.01 Practice rule 15 (client care)

'(1) Every principal in private practice shall operate a complaints handling procedure which shall, *inter alia*, ensure that clients are informed whom to approach in the event of any problem with the service provided.

(2) Every solicitor in private practice shall, unless it is inappropriate in the circumstances:

   (a) ensure that clients know the name and status of the person responsible for the day to day conduct of the matter and the principal responsible for its overall supervision;

   (b) ensure that clients know whom to approach in the event of any problem with the service provided; and

   (c) ensure that clients are at all relevant times given any appropriate information as to the issues raised and the progress of the matter.

(3) Notwithstanding Rule 19(2) of these rules, this rule shall come into force on 1st May 1991.'

13.02 Complaints procedure—rule 15(1) and 15(2)(b)

1. Rule 15(1) applies to firms; rule 15(2) applies to all solicitors in private practice. The firm's complaints handling procedure should be in writing, and all staff should be aware of the procedure. If a complaint is made to the Solicitors Complaints Bureau a firm will have to explain its procedure and whether it had been followed. A booklet *Client care, a guide for solicitors* published by the Society contains a good practice advice on rule 15, including specimen terms of business letters. Information on avoiding complaints and on complaints procedures is available from the SCB.

2. The following are the basic elements of a complaints handling procedure:

   (a) Clients should be told that if they have any problem with the service provided, they should make it known.

   (b) Clients should be told whom to inform in the event of such a problem. This may be the fee-earner handling the case. It may be the senior partner, sole practitioner, principal with overall responsibility for the matter or another person within the practice nominated for the purpose. It could be someone outside the firm altogether.

   (c) The procedure should ensure that any complaint is investigated promptly and thoroughly, that an explanation of the investigation is given to the client and any appropriate action taken. It is advisable to keep a record of all stages.

   (d) Clients should be given details in writing of the firm's response to the complaint. If the client is not satisfied (or if there is any doubt) the client should be given information about the SCB. (The SCB can supply leaflets for this purpose.)

3. The client may be informed about the whole complaints procedure at the start of the matter, *e.g.* in any general information about the firm given to new clients. The rule requires that the client must be told at the outset at least the name of the person with whom any problems should be raised and this should preferably be confirmed in writing. If a problem does arise which cannot be resolved almost immediately the full procedure should be explained, preferably in writing.

4. Rule 15(2) provides that the duty in rule 15(2)(b) does not apply where it is 'inappropriate in the circumstances'. For example, it is not necessary to tell established clients each time they confirm new instructions, provided that they know whom to contact. If a complaint is subsequently investigated by the SCB, the firm will have to show that the client has been informed or why it was inappropriate to give the information. See also **13.03** note 3, p. 225.

13.03 Responsibility for client's matter—rule 15(2)(a)

1. The rule requires that the client be informed of both the name and status of the person responsible for conduct of the matter. Status refers to qualification as well as partnership status, *e.g.* whether the person is a solicitor or a legal executive. (For restriction of the term 'legal executive' to Fellows of the Institute of Legal Executives see paragraph 7(a)(ii) of the Publicity Code, Annex 11A at p. 200.)

2. If the conduct or the overall supervision of the whole or part of the client's matter is transferred to another person in the firm the client should be informed and the reasons must be explained.

3. Rule 15(2) provides that the duty to give information does not apply where it is 'inappropriate in the circumstances'. Solicitors must judge what is appropriate, and will have to justify the decision should the client feel aggrieved. The following are examples of instances where solicitors may consider it inappropriate to provide the full information required by the rule:

   (a) for the regular client for whom repetitive work is done—but it will be appropriate to inform such a client if there is a change to the way in which the work is handled, *e.g.* if a new member of staff becomes involved;
   (b) for major commercial clients sufficiently familiar with the conduct of their business and in a position to require the provision of further information if they want it;
   (c) where particular sensitivity is required in handling the matter, for example when preparing a death-bed will, in a domestic violence emergency, or when seeing a person very recently bereaved, although in the latter case it will be possible to give the information at a more appropriate time;

    (d) in case of urgency where it is not practical to provide full information, *e.g.* where emergency injunctive or similar relief is sought.

13.04 General information for clients—rule 15(2)(c)

1. One of the objects of this rule is to help clients who are unfamiliar with the law to understand what is happening. This will reduce areas of potential conflict and complaint. Different levels of information may be agreed or may be appropriate for different clients.

2. The client should normally be told in appropriate language at the outset of a matter or as soon as possible thereafter the issues in the case and how they will be dealt with. In particular, the immediate steps to be taken must be clearly explained. It may be helpful to give an explanatory leaflet to the client.

3. Solicitors should keep clients informed of the progress of matters. This may often be assisted by sending to clients copies of letters. In particular it is important to tell clients of the reason for any serious delay. Requests for information should be answered promptly.

4. The solicitor should advise the client when it is appropriate to instruct counsel. Whenever clients are to attend hearings at which they are to be represented, they must be told the name of the advocate whom it is intended will represent them.

5. Solicitors should normally explain to clients the effect of important and relevant documents. Information to be given also includes recent changes in law where those changes affect the subject matter of the retainer. At the end of the matter solicitors should normally write to clients confirming that it has been completed and summarising any future action to be taken by the client or the solicitor.

6. Solicitors should consider whether it is appropriate to confirm in writing the advice given and instructions received. Confirmation in writing of key points will both reduce the risk of misunderstanding by clients and assist colleagues who may have to deal with the matter.

7. Rule 15(2) provides that the duty to give information does not apply where it is 'inappropriate in the circumstances'. For examples see **13.03** note 3, p. 225.

13.05   Written professional standards—information on costs for clients

1. The standards which follow are of general application although one of their particular objects is to ensure that clients who are unfamiliar with the law and lawyers receive the information they need to make what is happening more comprehensible, and thus to reduce areas of potential conflict and complaint. Failure to give adequate information on costs is the most common complaint about solicitors.

2. Some of the standards may not be appropriate in every case—*e.g.* for regular clients for whom repetitive work is done. Where a solicitor decides in a particular case that a given standard is inapplicable, it will be for the solicitor to justify the decision should a client make a complaint.

3. A material breach of the standards will be treated by the SCB as establishing, prima facie, an inadequate professional service. Serious or persistent breaches can lead to a finding of professional misconduct. Unreasonable failure to advise a client properly on some matters, particularly on the risks as to costs in litigation or the availability of legal aid, may well give rise to a claim in negligence.

4. While the standards do not apply in their entirety to in-house solicitors, such solicitors will be expected to have regard to the standards where appropriate, *e.g.* when acting for clients other than their employer, where those clients may be responsible for the costs.

13.06   Standard (a)—initial information on costs

'On taking instructions the solicitor should:

(i)   **give clients the best information possible about the likely cost of the matter. If no fee has been agreed or estimate given, the solicitor should tell clients how the fee will be calculated, *e.g.* whether on the basis of an hourly rate plus mark-up, a percentage of the value of the transaction, or a combination of both, or any other proposed basis;**

(ii) **discuss with clients how the legal charges and disbursements are to be met and must consider whether they may be eligible and should apply for legal aid (including legal advice and assistance); and**

(iii) consider whether the client's liability for the costs may be covered by insurance.'

Written professional standards, standard (a)

1. It is an implied term in law that solicitors will be paid reasonable remuneration for their services (see section 15 of the Supply of Goods and Services Act 1982). Solicitors should not, however, rely solely upon this implied term but should explain to the client, so far as is possible, the work which is likely to be involved in carrying out the instructions and the time which may be taken, both of which will have direct relevance to the likely amount of fees.

2. Wherever possible, a solicitor should give an estimate of the likely cost of acting in a particular matter. If, because of the nature of the work, a solicitor cannot give even an approximate estimate of the fees and disbursements, the client should be informed accordingly and in that case should be given as good a general forecast as possible, and be kept informed about the costs as the matter proceeds. When giving such an estimate or forecast, regard should be had to Part III of the Consumer Protection Act 1987 which deals with misleading price indications.

3. When giving estimates, solicitors should take care to ensure that they are not binding themselves to an agreed fee unless this is their intention. Clear and appropriate words should be used to indicate the nature of the estimate. To give an estimate which has been pitched at an unrealistically low level solely to attract the work and subsequently to charge a higher fee for that work is improper because it misleads the client as to the true or likely cost. See also **13.07**, p. 229.

4. It may not be appropriate to give the same information on costs to all clients, or at the same stage: e.g. in the case of an emergency injunction application, where time may not allow for a full discussion; or in the case of a brief interview not leading to further work, where a fee is simply agreed and paid. It is appropriate to comply with the general standards where a client is legally aided and is interested in the costs because of contributions payable or the operation of the statutory charge.

5. Clients should be informed of the charging rate of the person doing the work, or alternatively, if charges are based on an expense rate, the expense rate of the person

doing the work and the range of the possible mark-up. Clients should also be informed if such rates to to be subject to periodic review. Clients should be told if factors other than time will be taken into account when setting the actual fee. The Conditional Fee Agreement Regulations 1995 prescribe both information to be given to the client and matters to be contained in a written agreement in conditional fee cases (see **14.06,** p. 236 and Annex 14B, p. 251).

6. In non-contentious matters, regard must be had to the Solicitors' (Non-Contentious Business) Remuneration Order 1994 (see Annex 14C, p. 253).

7. With regard to a solicitor's duty to a client where the client is legally aided, either in civil or criminal proceedings, see also **13.10,** p. 231. For the duty to advise a client on the availability of legal aid, see **5.01,** p. 128.

8. Where a client may be eligible for legal aid, the availability of an emergency certificate or the 'green form' scheme should be considered. A solicitor who commences or continues work without legal aid cover runs the risk of being unable to recover pre-certificate costs.

9. The duty to advise as to legal aid applies throughout the retainer and solicitors should ensure that any material change in a client's means of which they become aware is at once taken into consideration in the context of eligibility for legal aid.

10. For the position where a solicitor requires a client to make a payment on account of costs see **14.01,** p. 234.

11. There is no objection to solicitors accepting payment for their fees by the use of a credit card facility. See **14.03** note 2, p. 235.

12. Compliance with the standards may be important if the client's right to recover costs from a losing party is questioned. In *BWB v. Norman, The Times,* 11th November 1993, the Divisional Court suggested that if the standards on advance costs information are followed, so that it is clear that the client is liable for costs irrespective of the outcome of the proceedings, then there can be no objection to the solicitor agreeing that such liability need not be discharged until the outcome of those proceedings, if any, is known.

13.07 Standard (b)—confirmation of costs estimate or agreement

'When confirming clients' instructions in writing the solicitor should:

(i) **record whether a fee has been agreed and, if so, what it is and what it covers and whether it includes VAT and disbursements;**

(ii) **tell clients what other reasonably foreseeable payments they may have to make either to the solicitor or to a third party and the stages at which they are likely to be required; and**

(iii) **confirm oral estimates—the final amount payable should not vary substantially from the estimate unless clients have been informed of the changed circumstances in writing.'**

Written professional standards, standard (b)

1. If the agreement is for the solicitor to be remunerated by an agreed fee, the solicitor is bound to do the work covered by the agreement for that fee, even though circumstances arise which make the work unremunerative for the solicitor.

2. Section 57(3) of the Solicitors Act 1974 (see Annex 14A, p. 242) requires a non-contentious business agreement to be in writing and signed by the person to be bound by it. Under section 59(1) a contentious business agreement must also be in writing. (See Annex 14A at p. 243.)

3. A solicitor providing property selling services must, when accepting instructions to act in the sale of a property, give the client a written statement setting out certain details of their agreement. See **26.08,** p. 441, for further detail.

4. Under rule 9 of the Solicitors' Accounts Rules 1991, money received for or on account of an agreed fee which is paid by the client to the solicitor must not be paid into the client account (see **28.15,** p. 591).

5. Oral estimates should be confirmed in writing and clients should be informed immediately it appears that the estimate will be or is likely to be exceeded. In most cases this should happen before undertaking work that exceeds the estimate. Solicitors should not wait until submitting the bill of costs.

13.08 Standard (c)—further information for privately paying clients

'Where clients are personally liable for the costs, in appropriate cases the solicitor should:

(i) **inform them that they may set a limit on the costs which may be incurred without further reference;**

(ii) **explain that it is often not possible to estimate the costs in advance;**

(iii) **inform them every six months of the approximate amount of the costs to date, whether or not they have set a limit—in appropriate cases an interim bill should be delviered.'**

Written professional standards, standard (c)

1. Where clients want to set a limit on costs solicitors should warn of the consequences before accepting instructions. Any limit cannot be exceeded without the authority of the client. Further, where the limit imposed on the expenditure is insufficient the solicitor must, as soon as possible, obtain the client's instructions as to whether to continue with the matter.

2. Where a solicitor continues to act in such circumstances regardless of the limit and then presents a bill for a sum which exceeds that limit, he or she may be guilty of professional misconduct as well as having the excess disallowed on an application for a remuneration certificate and/or taxation.

3. The solicitor should monitor the position regularly regarding costs which have accrued to date. The keeping of adequate time records will assist.

4. Failure to keep the client informed, so far as possible, regarding the costs incurred, could prejudice a solicitor's ability to recover a fair and reasonable fee for the work done.

5. In non-contentious matters, a solicitor may render an interim bill if the client has agreed or acquiesced.

6. In contentious matters, the question of an interim bill in respect of costs incurred is dealt with by reference to section 65(2) of the Solicitors Act 1974.

7. The same ongoing information should be given in legal aid cases where the costs position is significant to the client because of contributions or the effect of the statutory charge.

13.09 Standard (d)—further information for privately paying clients—contentious matters

'Where clients are not legally aided but the matter is contentious they should be informed at the outset of a case and at appropriate stages thereafter:

(i) that in any event they will be personally responsible for payment of their own solicitor's bill of costs in full regardless of any order for costs made against opponents;

(ii) of the probability that if they lose they will have to pay their opponent's costs as well as their own;

(iii) that even if they win their opponent may not be ordered to pay the full amount of the clients' own costs and may not be capable of paying what they have been ordered to pay; and

(iv) that if their opponent is legally aided they may not recover their costs even if successful in civil proceedings.'

Written professional standards, standard (d)

In contentious matters solicitors must explain clearly both the liability to pay the client's own solicitor's bill as well as the possibility of having to pay the opponent's bill. All possibilities should be explained. Compliance with this standard will protect solicitors in the event that a losing opponent attempts to avoid payment of costs by alleging a breach of the indemnity principle. See *BWB v. Norman, The Times*, 11th November 1993.

13.10   Standard (e)—further information for legally aided clients

'Where clients are legally aided they should be informed at the outset of any case and at appropriate stages thereafter:

(i) of the effect of the statutory charge on the case;

(ii) that if they lose the case they may still be ordered by the court to contribute to their opponent's costs even though their own costs are covered by legal aid;

(iii) that even if they win their opponent may not be ordered to pay the full amount of their costs and may not be capable of paying what they have been ordered to pay;

(iv) of their obligations to pay any contribution assessed and of the consequences of any failure to do so.'

Written professional standards, standard (e)

It is important to correct any misapprehension that legal aid is free by clearly explaining the effect of the statutory charge. It may be helpful to confirm in writing the client's obligation to pay contributions, and the possible exposure to pay the costs of the other side should also be explained.

13.11 Standard (f)—discussing the risk

'In all matters a solicitor should consider with clients whether the likely outcome will justify the expense or risk involved.'

Written professional standards, standard (f)

1. It is in the interests of both the solicitor and the client that advice on the risks should be in writing, and that the advice is repeated at appropriate times throughout the transaction.

2. Breach of this standard will amount prima facie to inadequate professional services, giving the SCB power, *inter alia*, to reduce the solicitor's bill

THE LAW SOCIETY PRACTICE
MANAGEMENT STANDARDS

A Management Structure

A.1 Practices will have a written description of their management structure. There will be a named supervisor for each area of work (a supervisor may be responsible for more than one area).

A.1.1 The management structure should be appropriate for the partners, principals and staff, the size of the practice, its location, and the type of work it does.

A.1.2 Practices should be able to explain their management structure, for example to incoming partners, principals or staff, and the written description may for example:

    a. list the designated responsibilities of individuals in the practice (including responsibility for adherence to these standards);

    b. name committees (if any) and summarise their terms of reference;

    c. describe reporting structures in the practice, for example by including a 'family tree'.

B Services and Forward Planning

B.1 Practices will document:

    a. an outline strategy to provide a background against which the practice may review its performance and may take decisions about its future;

    b. what services it wishes to offer, the client groups to be served and how services are to be provided;

    c. their approach to marketing;

and practices may choose the format and level of detail of documentation that suits them best.

B.1.1 This documentation need not be disclosed to third parties.

Strategy

B.1.2 The strategy should be sufficient to provide a framework for decisions about, for example, purchase of computers, office location, staffing and targeting new business, but need not be written in considerable detail.

B.1.3 Most practices will already have agreed annual budgets, financial targets, etc. (as well as views about how the practice ought to develop) and these provide a useful starting-point for strategy planning.

B.1.4 Practice may wish to consider the following:

   a. setting goals for the practice for the coming three to five years;
   b. adopting a 'practice purpose statement' describing the long-term aims of the practice;
   c. identifying specific objectives that the practice would like to achieve.

Services

B.1.5 How the practice provides services will depend upon its clients and services. Issues may include location of offices, physical access to the premises, languages spoken, facilities for clients, electronic communication, etc.

Marketing

B.1.6 For practices satisfied with their current quality and level of business, a marketing plan will need to be less detailed than for a practice wishing to expand, develop a new specialism, or which is uncertain about its future client base. For some areas of work, the plan may need to describe how to contain demand to an acceptable level (rather than how to encourage additional business), taking account of that work's profitability and the resources of the practice.

B.1.7 A marketing plan may:

   a. describe the services to be provided and client groups to be served, how services will be delivered, and the practice's client care policy;
   b. describe the practice's resources including skills and knowledge;
   c. set out objectives for the clients or business to be developed, which should be measurable and in a time frame;
   d. explain how the structure or personnel or organisation of the practice will need to develop if those objectives are to be attained;

e. provide a timetable for marketing activities and a budget;
f. allocate and describe appropriate individual responsibility for the marketing activities;
g. describe arrangements for monitoring response to the marketing effort (for example, recording sources of referrals, etc.).

Non-discrimination

B.3 **Practices will have regard to guidance on non-discrimination in the provision of services issued by the Law Society from time to time.**

C   Financial Management

Responsibility

C.1 **Practices will be able to demonstrate** (for example, to providers of finance or to major clients) **who exercises responsibility for financial affairs.**

Financial information

C.2 **Practices will be able to demonstrate that they have the management and financial information necessary for monitoring income, expenditure, and cost, and for forward planning; and this will include the following:**

a. **annual budget (including, where appropriate, any capital expenditure proposed);**
b. **quarterly variance analysis of income and expenditure against budget;**
c. **annual profit and loss account;**
d. **annual balance sheet.**

C.2.1. In addition, practices may find it helpful to maintain the following management information (but note that it will not be practicable to produce much of this in the absence of full computerisation):

a. monthly or quarterly cashflow forecast for the coming 12 months;
b. separate capital expenditure budget;
c. weekly or monthly aged list of debtors;
d. analysis of the cost of services (including apportioned overheads);

     e. analysis of cases by category;
     f. analysis of cases by client name;
     g. analysis of fees by fee-earner;
     h. analysis of fees by category;
     i. analysis of working capital.

C.2.2 Note that practices will not normally disclose financial information to third parties; but, for example, they may in appropriate cases instead make available an accountant's certificate that systems to provide the relevant information within the practice itself are in place.

Computerisation

C.2.3 Implementation of a computerised accounting system will assist cost-effectiveness. It is unlikely that most practices could comply with these Standards in the absence of computerisation.

C.2.4 Computerised accounting systems can maintain financial records as required by the Solicitors' Accounts Rules and provide other reports and information as well. Details are given in the Society's annual directory publication [*Information Technology Directory*].

C.2.5 There is a significant cost in money and time attaching to planning for computerisation, purchase of a system, and to training and support following implementation. But, if properly planned, this investment will be worthwhile.

Time-recording

C.3 **Practices will have a system that ensures that time spent on casework can be properly recorded and attributed.**

C.3.1 The system may provide that some matters of types of matter need not be subject to time-recording (for example, where a fixed fee has been agreed) and, in that case, time-recording should be carried out on a sample basis.

D Managing People

Job descriptions

D.1 **Practices will document the skills, knowledge, and experience required of fee-earners and other staff and the tasks they are required to perform, usually in the form of a written job description; but employmet contracts may reserve job flexibility.**

D.1.1 Practices may prepare a personnel plan to help ensure that skills, knowledge and experience within the practice are developed to meet needs indicated in the forward planning documents (s.B).

Recuitment

D.2   Practices will have arrangements which evaluate the skills, knowledge and experience possessed by applicants for posts in the practice, and their integrity and suitability.

D.2.1. For example, applicants may be sent a copy of the job description and a form to complete. The contents of completed applications may then be checked against the requirements in the job description and questions at interviews may be related to the completed application and to the job description.

New postholders

D.3   Practices will have arrangements to provide an induction process for new postholders.

Objectives and performances appraisal

D.4   Practices will have arrangements to:

a. document the responsibilities and objectives of each partner, principal and member of staff in the practice;

b. evaluate performance of staff at least annually against those responsibilities and objectives.

c. record in writing the performance appraisal, the records to be kept confidential to the practice and to the postholder.

Training

D.5   Practices will have arrangements to ensure that:

a. all partners, principals and staff are trained to a level of competence appropriate to their work;

b. training and development needs are assessed for each person against the objectives of the practice and are reviewed at least annually;

c. skills and knowledge required for the management and organisation of the practice (as well as for legal

practice) are provided for in training and
development;

d. appropriate written training records are maintained.

D.5.1. Practices should also ensure that for cost-effectiveness and
to maximise development of the practice's own resources,
skills and knowledge acquired by fee-earners and other
staff are commonciated within the practice through training in-house.

Communications

**D.6   Practices will have arrangements (informal or otherwise)
which foster communication within the practice.**

Supervision

**D.7   Practices will ensure that there are appropriate arrange-
ments for supervision (supervision of casework is the
subject of F.10.**

Equal opportunity

**D.8   Practices will have regard to guidance on equality of
opportunity issued by the Law Society from time to time.**

E   Office Administration

Responsibilities

**E.1   Practices will designate administrative responsibilities as
part of the description of management structure (see part
A).**

Forms and procedures

**E.2   Practices will maintain an office manual collating infor-
mation on office practice which should be available to all
members of the practice.**

E.2.1 Precedents for office forms and procedures are offered in
the Society's *Solicitors' Office Manual.*

Legal reference material

E.3   Practices will institute arrangements to ensure that:

a. **fee-earners have ready access to up-to-date legal references material for the areas in which the practice offers a service;**
b. **fee-earners receive timely information about changes in the law relevant to their work** (for example, by circulation of journals and law reports; practices will need to ensure that such arrangements comply with copyright provisions).

F Case Management

Systems

F.1 **Practices will have arrangements to:**

a. **maintain an index of matters (for example, listing and numbering each matter);**
b. **facilitate identifying any conflict of interest;**
c. **monitor the number and type of matters undertaken by each fee-earner to ensure that they are within his or her capacity;**
d. **maintain a back-up record of key dates in matters** (for example, expiry of a limitation period; time limits for a review or an application under part II of the Landlord and Tenant Act 1954) so as to ensure action is taken by the fee-earner at the appropriate time (options include a record kept by a secretary or colleague, or office or departmental diaries);
e. **ensure proper authorisation and monitoring of undertakings given on behalf of the practice** (which may, for example, provide for forms in which an undertaking may be given; designation of fee-earners authorised to give undertakings; procedures for approval of undertakings; and for central records).

F.2 **Where required to do so by a third party funding the legal costs of a matter, or by a client instructing the practice in a number of matters, the practice will have a system which enables all relevant matters to be identified.**

Client care

F.3 **Practices will have procedures to ensure compliance with Practic Rule 15 and the Written Professional Standard on costs information and to provide for clear and regular communication with clients.**

F.3.1 Practices may use standardised checklists to ensure appropriate information is obtained and given at each stage of a matter.

At the outset of a case

F.4   Practices will establish a procedure for taking instruc-
        tions which will ensure that fee-earners (except where it
        would be inappropriate to do so; for example: in the case
        of the regular client for whom repetitive work is done; in
        cases of urgency where it is not practical to provide full
        information; or where particular sensitivity is required in
        handling the matter):

        a. agree and record:
             (i)   the client's instructions;
             (ii) advice given;
             (iii) action to be taken by the practice;
             (iv) terms of business;
             (v)   the basis of charging and the likely cost (or, if
                   this cannot be estimated, such information
                   about cost as can be given) or, in legally aided
                   cases, information on the effect of the statutory
                   charge (if appropriate);
             (vi) who will be responsible for the conduct of the
                   case;
        b. confirm these with the client (ordinarily in writing);
        c. provide written information to the client about com-
           plaints procedures;
        d. identify key dates in the matter and record these in
           the file and in the back-up system.

Progress of the matter

F.5   Practices will have policies designed to ensure that:
        a. information on progress of the matter is given to the
           client at appropriate intervals:
        b. information about changes in the action planned to
           be taken in the matter, its handling, or cost, is given
           to the client promptly;
        c. a timely response is made to correspondence and
           telephone calls;
        d. information on cost (or, in legally aided cases, the
           effect of the statutory charge, if any) is given to the
           client at least every six months and timely reference
           is made to the client when an agreed limit on costs or
           stage in progress is approached;
        e. a case plan may also be prepared in a complex
           matter, agreed with the client, and periodically
           reviewed and updated.

Documents, etc.

F.6   Practices will have procedures to ensure that they are
        able to identify and trace all documents, correspondence

and other information relating to a matter and that these are properly stored and are readily accessible.

At the end of the case

F.7   Practices will have procedures to ensure that at the conclusion of the matter, the practice:

a. reports to the client on the outcome and explains any further action that the client is required to take in the matter and what (if anything) the practice will do;

b. accounts to the client for any outstanding money;

c. returns to the client original documents and other property belonging to the client if required (save for items which are by agreement to be stored by the practice);

d. if appropriate, advises the client about arrangements for storage and retrieval of papers and other items retained (in so far as this had not been dealt with already, for example in terms of business);

e. advises the client whether they should review the matter in future, and if so, when.

Services from others

F.8   Practices will establish a procedure for using barristers, expert witnesses, etc., in providing the practice's legal services which will include provisions for the following:

a. use of clear selection criteria (which may include, for example, availability, recommendation, experience, etc.);

b. where appropriate, consultation with the client in relation to selection, and proper advice to the client on choice of advocate;

c. maintenance of records (centrally, by dpartment, or by office) on barristers and experts used (practices may wish to record reasons for inclusion, and in doing so will need to ensure compliance with the law relating to defamation, discrimination and data protection: this need not function as an exclusive list of those approved);

d. giving of instructions which clearly describe what is required;

e. checking of opinions and reports received to ensure they adequately provide the informations sought;

f. payment of fees.

File management

F.9 **Practices will have arrangements to ensure that:**

    a. **the status of the matter and action taken can be easily checked by other members of the practice,** for example by means of attendance notes, action lists, or correspondence with the client;

    b. **documents are arranged in the file in an orderly way;**

    c. **key information is shown clearly on the file** (*e.g.* at the front of the file) **which will include details of any undertakings given on behalf of the practice,** and which may additionally include for example:

        (i) any case plan or synopsis;

        (ii) time records (unless readily accessible in a central system);

        (iii) financial transactions (unless readily accessible in a central system);

        (iv) any list of documents.

File review

F.10 **Practices will have arrangements to supervise the conduct of casework, and these will include arrangements of the management of case-files to the reviewed periodically and the review will (except where there is only one fee-earner in the practice) be carried out by a fee-earner who has not been involved in the day-to-day conduct of the matter.**

F.10.1 It will be a matter for each practice to determine the frequency of such reviews and whether all files are reviewed or a sample selected.

F.10.2 Practices may also adopt other arrangements to ensure appropriate supervision of casework. Options include:

    a. checking incoming post;

    b. outgoing post signed by supervisor;

    c. regular review sessions with a supervisor, covering:

        (i) new cases taken on, and discussion of 'case plans' in complex cases;

        (ii) progress review for current cases;

        (iii) evaluation of outcomes of completed cases;

        (iv) consideration of training needs in relation to legal knowledge and skills.

Complaints

F.11 **Practices will have arrangements for:**

a. reporting and recording centrally every formal complaint made by a client;
b. responding appropriately to any complaint;
c. identifying the cause of any problem of which a client has complained, offering any appropriate redress, and correcting any unsatisfactory procedure.

Appendix 3

KEY FILE INFORMATION:
LITIGATION (GENERAL LITIGATION)

Client
File No: Client Partner: Matter Description:
Correspondence Files: Document Files   Matter Partner:
                                                        Deed Packets:

Brief Description:	Billing Procedure

File inception checklist completed (attached: Date .... Initials ....

Dramatis: Client Contact:
              Opponent
              Counsel
              Expert   Other

LIMITATION PERIOD/DATE

Rule 15 letter sent: Discovery letter sent:
Instructions to Counsel sent:

Pleadings served:

Summonses:	Orders:

Discovery: List .... Inspection ....
Directions: (Specify all procedural directions and relevant dates)

Latest Action Plan/ Note/ Letter

Witness Statements:

Hearing/ Trial Dates Set:

Setting Down:

Undertakings Given:	**OPEN?**

Most recent File Review:

File Closing Checklist Completed (attached):

N.B. This form is to be kept at all times at the top of the pocket on the current correspondence file and is to be updated: -on matter inception
-on happening of any recordable event
-on assistant's absence on holiday
-on permanent change of assistant

BIBLIOGRAPHY

Abercrombie, "The Anatomy of Judgment" [1960] M.L.J., Pt. 2

Bankowski, Z. and Mungham, G., *Images of Law* (Routledge & Kegan Paul, 1976)

Bellow, G. and Moulton, B., *The Lawyering Process—Materials for Clinical Instruction in Advocacy* (The Foundation Press, Inc., 1978)

Bergman, P., *It's not what you think but how you think it: A New Approach to Harmless Error* (Forthcoming, UCLA), 1985

Berlin, Sir Isaiah "The Concepts of Liberty" in *Four Essays on Liberty* (Oxford University Press, 1969)

Binder, D. A. and Price, S. C., *Legal Interviewing and Counselling: a Client Centred Approach* (West Publishing Co., 1979)

Byrne, P. S. and Long, B. E., *Doctors Talking to Patients* (DHSS, HMSO, 1976)

Cain, M., "Towards a Theory of General Practice Lawyers—A radical Approach" [1979] *International Journal of the Sociology of Law* 331

Cartwright, T. A., Hockey, L., Anderson, L. and Anderson, J.L., *Life Before Death* (Routledge & Kegan Paul, 1973)

Coltheart, Max, *Readings in Cognitive Psychology* (Holt, Rineheart and Winston of Canada, 1972)

De Bono, E., *De Bono's Thinking Course* (BBC, 1982)

Dent, Helen R., "Interviewing Child Witnesses" in *Practical Aspects of Memory* (M. M. Gruneberg, P. E. Morris and R. N. Sykes, eds.) (Academic Press, London, 1978)

Durkheim, E., *Suicide* (Alcan, 1897)

Fisher, R. and Ury, W., *Getting to Yes* (Hutchinson, 1982)

Flesch, R., "A new readability yardstick" [1948] *Journal of Applied Psychology* 32 at 221

Frank, J., *Courts on Trial—Myth and Reality in American Justice* (Princeton University Press, 1949)

Freeman, H. and Weihofen, H., *Cases and Text on Clinical Law Training—Interviewing and Counselling* (West Publishing Co., 1972)

Gawalt, G. W., *The New High Priests* (Greenwood Press, 1984)

Goodpaster, G. S., "The Human Arts of Lawyering" (1975) 27 *Journal of Legal Education* 33

Greenebaum, E., Understanding Clinical Experience (Unpublished, 1986)

Janis, I. L., *Stress and Frustration* (Harcourt, Brace and Jovanovich, 1971)

Janis, I. L. and Mann, L., *Decision Making: a Psychological Analysis of Conflict, Choice and Commitment* (Collier-MacMillan, 1977)

Johnson, T. J., *Professions and Power* (MacMillan, 1972)

Kahneman, D., Slovic, P, and Tversky, A. (eds.) *Judgment Under Uncertainty: Heuristics and Biases* (Cambridge University Press, 1982)

Kennedy, I., *The Unmasking of Medicine* (Allen & Unwin, 1981)

Klatzky, Roberta, *Human Memory: Structures and Processes* (2nd ed.) (Freeman, 1980).

Korsch, B. M., Gozzi, E. K. and Francis, V., "Gaps in doctor-patient communication: 1. Doctor-patient interaction and patient satisfaction" [1968] *Pediatrics* 42 at 855

Korsch, B., Freeman, B, and Negrete V., "Practical implications of doctor-patient interactions: analysis for pediatric practice" 1971 *American Journal of Diseases of Children* 121 at 110

Korsch, B. M. and Negrete V. F., "Doctor-patient Communication" [1972] *Scientific American* August; 66

Kuhn, T. S., *The Structure of Scientific Revolutions* (University of Chicago Press, 1970)

Law Society, *The Expense of Time* (3rd edn. 1981)

Ley, P., "Psychological Studies of Doctor-Patient Communication" in *Contributions to Medical Psychology* (Rachman, S. J., ed.) (Pergamon Press, 1977)

Llewellyn, K., *The Bramble Bush: on our Law and its Study* (Oceana, 1951)

Loftus, E., *Eyewitness Testimony* (Harvard University Press, 1979)

Miller, G. A., "The magical number seven, plus or minus two." (1956) 63 Psychological Review 81–97

Morley, I. E. and Hosking, D. M., "Decision-making and Negotiation: Leadership and Social Skills" in *Social Psychology and Organizational Behaviour* (Gruneberg, M. and Wall, T., ed.) (John Wiley & Sons, 1984)

National Consumer Council, *Plain English for Lawyers* (1984)

Nizer, J., *The Implosion Conspiracy* (Doubleday & Company, Inc., 1973)

Pennington, Donald C., *Social Cognition: Effects of Outcome Knowledge and Order of Information on Judgment Under Uncertainty.* (Ph.D. Thesis, University of Warwick, 1981)

Piaget, J., *The Origin of Intelligence in the Child* (Routledge & Kegan Paul, 1973)

Piaget, J., *The Construction of Reality in the Child* (Basic Books, 1954)

Pittinger, Hackett and Danehy, *The First Five Minutes* (1960)

Potok, C., *Wanderings: a History of the Jewish People* (Fawcett, Cres, 1980)

Rachman, S. J. (ed.), Contributions to Medical Psychology (Pergamon Press, 1977), Vol. 1

Raiffa, H., *The Art and Science of Negotiation* (Harvard University Press, 1982)

Redmount, R. S., "An Inquiry Into Legal Counselling" *The Journal of The Legal Profession* 181

Rodell, F., *Woe Unto You Lawyers* (Pageant Press, 1957)

Rosenthal, D. E., *Lawyer and Client: Who's In Charge?* (Russell Sage Foundation, 1974)

Royal Commission on the Provision of Legal Services, Cmnd. 7648 (1979), 7648–1

Shaffer, T. L., *Legal Interviewing and Counselling* (West Publishing Co., 1976)

Shaffer, T. L. and Redmount, R. S., *Legal Interviewing and Counselling* (Matthew Bender, 1980)

Sherr, A., "Lip Service Under Articles, or Chances Missed" [1982] *New Law Journal* 395

Sherr, A., "Lawyers and Clients: The First Meeting" (1986) 49 M.L.R. 323

Sherr, A., "Lawyer-Client Interviewing: An Analysis of Different Teaching Approaches" (Forthcoming, 1987)

Sim, Myre, *Psychiatry* (3rd ed.) (Churchill Livingston, 1974)

Spiegel, M., "Lawyering and Client Decision-Making: Informed Consent and the Legal Profession" [1979] University of Pennsylvania Law Review 41–140

Szasz, T., *The Myth of Mental Illness: Foundations of a Theory of Personal Conduct* (Hoeber, 1961)

Watson, A. S., *The Lawyer in the Interviewing and Counselling Process* (The Bobbs-Merrill Company, Inc., 1976)

INDEX

ABA Code of Professional
    Responsibility, 112
Abercrombie, 130
Active listening,
    encouragement to continue talking,
        17–18
    examples, 18–19
    meaning, 12, 17–18
    purpose, 19
Advance organisers, 59, 74
Advising, 50–79
    achieving compliance, 60
    advance organisers, 59, 74
    agreement of client, 71–73
    alternatives for action, 55–56
    amendment of, 71–73
    "any other business", 76–78
    application of law to client's
        circumstances, 53–55
    balance in, 62
    bearers of bad tidings, 66–67
    Benson report, 61–62
    "business person", lawyer as, 50
    categorisation, 59
    chunking, 60
    compliance, achieving, 60
    conclusions on, 78–79
    contact, stating next, 75–76
    content of advice, 60–71
        bearers of bad tidings, 66–67
        counselling, 64
        degrees of chance, 63–64
        dissatisfaction with, 61
        full story, 61–62
        game theory, 63
        generally, 60–61
        Jeremiahs, 66–67
        likelihood of success, 62–64
        lottery, litigation as, 62–64
        numbering systems, 63
        plan of action, 67
        predictions, 62–64
        preparing client, 65–66
        problems with, 61
        reaction of client, 64–65
        stress, easing, 65
        unpleasant, 65–66
        Which report, 61
        withholding information, 65–66

Advising—cont.
    costs 67–71. See also Costs
    counselling,
        client, 56
        distinguished, 105–106
    decisions for client, 56
    delays, 75
    Flesch Formula Readability Score,
        58
    follow-up work to be done,
        recounting,
            client , by, 73–74
            lawyer, by, 74–75
    form of advice, 52–56
    freezing, 57
    function of lawyer, 50–51
    funds, dealing with questions of, 51
    general statement of relevant law,
        52–53
    generally, 50
    "high priest", lawyer as, 50
    informed consent, 62
    jargon, 56–57
    Jeremiahs, 66–67
    learning by understanding, 59
    letter confirming advice, 74
    meaning, 8
    missing out stage, 9
    money 67–71. See also Costs
    next contact, stating, 75–76
    non-vigilant strategies, 72–73
    patronising clients, 58
    plan of action, 67
    practical approach, 55–56
    preliminary thoughts on function of
        lawyer, 50–51
    preparing client, 65–66
    problem solving approach, 51
    problems in giving, 56–60
        freezing, 57
        generally, 56
        jargon, 56–57
        readability scores, 58
        receiving advice, 57–58
        rehearsal, 58
        remembering, 58–60
        understanding advice, 57–58
    professional, lawyer as, 50–51
    purpose, 8
    reaction of client, 64–65

Advising—*cont.*
    readability scores, 58
    relevant law, statement of, 52–53
    repeat advice, 71–73
    research, 60
    role of lawyer, 50–51
    stating advice, 51–71
    "sunshine termination", 78
    Task 7, 51–71
    Task 12, 76–78
    Task 13, 78
    tasks, 10, 51–71, 76–78
    terminate, help out and goodbye, 78
    third stage of interview, 8
    understanding advice, 57–58
    vigilant strategies, 72
    Which report, 61
    "whole client", helping, 51
    withholding information, 65–66
Advisory Committee on Legal
        Education and Conduct, 154
Antioch School of Law in Washington,
        5
Appendix 1,
    Guide to the Professional Conduct
        of Solicitors,
        Chapter 13, 158–168
Appendix 2,
    The Law Society Practice
        Management Standards,
        Part 5, 169–179
Appendix 3,
    Key File Information, 180
Audio tape, 48

Bearers of bad tidings, 66–67
Behavioural change, 117–118
Bellow and Moulton, 113–114
Benson Report,
    advice, content of, 61–62
    dissatisfaction with solicitor, reasons
        for, 1, 61–62, 75
    listening, 12
    satisfaction with solicitor, reasons
        for, 1
Bergman, 58, 75
Bias,
    outcome, 26–27
Binder and Price, 9, 63, 104
Brain storming, 107
Byrne and Long's monitoring system, 9,
        120–124

Cartwright, 61
Case management. *See* Management
        techniques
Central Litigation Unit, 138–139

Chesterton, 4
Children, 89–91
    approaches to interviewing, 89–90
    Piaget, 90
    reception area provisions, 5
Chunking, 60
Client,
    advising. *See* Advising
    collection procedure, 7–8
    counselling. *See* Counselling client
    follow-up work, 73–74
    guilt, 23
    ideas, using client, 39
    involvement in case, 74
    management. *See* Management
        techniques
    needs, 36–39
        categorisation by lawyer, 4
        discovering, 36–39
        education, legal, 4
        explanation, 38–39
        framework, working within, 38
        importance of, 36
        reluctance, 37
    personal problems,
        generally, 22
        guilt, 23
        outcome bias, 26–27
        perception and memory, 26
        privacy, 23–24
        professionalism, 24
        questioning bias, 26
        suffering, 24
        uncertainty of relevance of
            information, 22–23
    preparation for 7. *See also*
        Preparation for interview
    privacy, 23–24
    professionalism when dealing with,
        24
    questioning. *See* Questioning
    questionnaires, 146–147
    reaction to advice, 64–65
    reviews, 146–147
    suffering, 24
    terminology, 21
    withholding information from, 65–66
Cognitive change, 117–118
Cognitive Theory, 90
Collection procedure, client, 7–8
Coltheart, 22
Commercial Firm Model, 139–142
Communication,
    complaints about poor, 2
    dissatisfaction with, 1
    expectations of client, 1–2
    importance of, 1

Communication—*cont.*
  poor, meaning of, 2
  research on, 1
Competition, Client Counselling, 155–
    157
Complaints,
  consumerism, 1–2
  definition, 150
  handling, 149–150
  information on name and status of
      solicitor, 151–152
  register, 150–151
Conduct regulation, 148–149
Confidentiality, 80–81
  atmosphere of, 80
  difficulties with, 80
  important issues, 80–81
  interruptions, 980–981
  Law Society's Professional Standards,
      80
  relationship between lawyer and
      client, 80
Consumerism, 1–2
Contact, stating next, 75–76
Continuing relationship,
  choice in, 114
  conclusions on, 114–116
  counselling. *See* Counselling client
    interview notes 92–99. *See also*
      Interview notes
Contracted systems,
  regulation of communications, 149
Costs, 67–71
  "bad news", 69
  clarity of advice on, 70
  difficulties with discussing, 69
  estimations, 70
  Green Form Scheme, 69
  hourly rate, 71
  Law Society's Professional Standards,
      67–69
  legal aid, 69
  prediction, 69–70
  timing discussion, 70
Counselling client, 104–114
  advising distinguished, 56, 105
  alternative courses of action, 106
  brain storming, 107
Counselling, client,
  Client Counselling Competition,
      155–157
Counselling client,
  decision making, 106
  definition, 104
  example, 107–112
  first interview, in, 104–105
  generally, 104

Counselling client—*cont.*
  interview distinguished, 104
  meaning, 104
  reflections on role, 112–113
  research, 104–105
  role, 112–113
  subsequent interview, in, 105
  suggestions, 106
  traditional lawyer model, 105
  vigilant approach, 107

De Bono, Edward, 106, 113
Dent, 90
Desks, 6
DGG, 138–139
Dirks, J., 138
Doctors. *See* Medical profession
Documents, 81–82
Dr. Seuss, 36
Durkheim, 88

Education, legal,
  Antioch School of Law in
      Washington, 5
  barriers, overcoming, 5
  categorisation of clients, 4
  experiencing client needs, 4–5
  function, 4
  needs of client, 4
  preparation for interview, 4
  reported cases, use of, 4
  role, 4
Examination question syndrome, 16–17
Experience, 126–137
  learning from, 126–137
  monitoring, 129
  planning, 126–129
  "practice makes perfect", 126
  pre-construction role play, 128–129
  preparatory readings, 127
  range, planning, 129
  repetition, 126
  reviewing, 129–131
  skills training, 127–128
  understanding, 131–132

Facts,
  generalisation levels, 25–26
  listening to, 25–26
  realist view of, 25
Files,
  review, 144–145
  supervision, 144–145
First five minutes, importance of, 14
First stage of interview 8. *See also*
      Listening
Fisher and Ury, 25

Flesch Formula Readability Score, 58, 124–126
Follow-up work to be done by client, recounting, 73–74
Framework,
thirteen tasks 10. *See also* Thirteen tasks
three stages of interview 9. *See also* Three stages of interview
Frank, J., 25
Freeman and Weihoffen, 104
Freezing, 57
Funnel sequence, 31–33

Game theory, 63
Gawalt, 50
Goodpaster, 9, 44, 127, 128, 131
Grahame Dunford Ford, 139
Green Form Scheme, 69, 82
Greenebaum, 117, 131
Greet, seat and introduce, 12–14
anxieties, client, 13
difficulties with, 13
Law Society's Professional Standards, 13
names, 13–14
responsibility for case, 14
Task 1, 12–14
Guilt, client, 23

Ideas, using client, 39
Identification, 21
Inexperienced practitioners, 71
Information processing, listening, 22
Informed consent, 62
Insurance, 145–146
Interruptions, 980–981
Interview,
advising. *See* Advising
centrality in legal work, 1–2
communication, importance of, 1
first five minutes, importance of, 14
functions, 1
legal, 1–2
listening. *See* Listening
meaning, 1
medical profession, analogy of interviews by, 2–3
notes. *See* Interview notes
physical preparation for. *See* Preparation for interview
preparation for. *See* Preparation for interview
purpose, 1
questioning. *See* Questioning
room, 6

Interview—*cont.*
stages. *See* Advising; Listening; Questioning; Three stages of interview
tasks. *See* Thirteen tasks
thirteen tasks 9–10. *See also* Thirteen tasks
three stages. *See* Advising; Listening; Questioning; Three stages of interview
Interview notes, 92–99
checklist, 93–95
factual information, 92–93
format, 92
forms, 92
impressions of lawyer, 95–97
lawyer's impressions, 95–97
legible, 92
reminders, 92
seeing file, client, 95
typed, 92
Introductions. *See* Greet, seat and introduce
ISO 9004 Standard, 145, 149

Janis, 65
Janis and Mann, 72
Jargon, use of, 56–57
Jeremiahs, 66–67

Klatzky, 21
Korsch and Negrete, 60, 77
Kuhn, 25

Language,
perception, 21
Law Society Council, 153
Law Society's Practice Management Standards, 142, 147
Law Society's Professional Standards, confidentiality, 80
costs, 67–69
greet, seat and introduce, 13
listening, 13
Learning process 117–118, 126–137. *See also* Experience
Legal aid, 69
Legal Aid Board's Franchising Specification, 142, 147
Legal education. *See* Education, legal
Legal Services Ombudsman, 15
Letters,
confirming advice, 74, 99–104
interview, confirming, 99–104
Lexcel, 149
Ley, 65

Listening, 12–28
  active,
    encouragement to continue
      talking, 17–18
    examples, 18–19
    meaning, 12, 17–18
    purpose, 19
  anxiety, reasons for client, 13
  approaches to, 17–18
  atmosphere for, creating, 19
  Benson Report, 12
  categorising problem, 16–17
  characteristics of stage, 8
  closed questions, 14–15
  conclusions on, 27–28
  construction of story by client,
    importance of, 17
  contact, maintaining, 17–18
  encouragement to continue talking,
    17–18
  events v. scenario, 25
  examination question syndrome, 16–
    17
  facts, 25–26
  filling in, 20–21
  first five minutes, importance of, 14
  first stage of interview, 8
  flow of client, 17
  generally, 12
  greet, seat and introduce, 12–14
  guilt, client, 23
  identification, 21
  information gatherer, problems of,
    20–22
  information processing, 22
  introductions, 12–14
  Law Society's Professional Standards,
    13
  meaning, 8
  names, 13–14
  note-taking, 17–18
  open questioning, 14–17
  open questions, 14–15
  outline story, 17
  perception, 21–22, 26
  personal problems of client, 22–25
    events v. scenario, 25
    facts, 25–26
    generally, 22
    guilt, 23
    perception, 26
    privacy, 23–24
    professionalism and lay client, 24
    suffering, 24
    uncertainty of relevance, 22–23
    unitary view, 25
  presenting problem, 15

Listening—*cont.*
  problems of, 17–27
  questioning,
    See also Questioning
    closed questions, 14–15
    eliciting story with open questions,
      14–17
    open questions, 14–15
    types, 14–15
  questioning bias, 26
  research, 12, 19
  responsibility for case, 14
  selective attention, 22
  short note taking, 17
  silence, 16
  skill, acquisition of, 17
  social pleasantries, 13
  stereotyping, 21
  suffering, client, 24
  tasks, 10, 12–19
  understanding, problems in, 12, 19–
    27
    filling in, 20–21
    generally, 19–20
    identification, 21
    information gatherer, problems of,
      20–22
    information processing, 22
    perception, 21–22
    personal problems of client, 22–25
    selective attention, 22
    sterotyping, 21
  unitary view, 25
  Warwick University research, 12, 27
Litigation,
  lottery, as, 62–64
Llewellyn, K., 25
Loftus, E., 26
Lottery, litigation as, 62–64

Management techniques,
  Commercial Firm Model, 139–142
  Deacon Goldrein Green Model,
    138–139
  DGG, 138–139
  Family Law Bureau, 139
  GDF, 139
  generally, 138
  Grahame Dunford Ford, 139
  insurance, 145–146
  ISO 9004 Standard, 145
  Law Society's Practice Management
    Standards, 142, 147
  Legal Aid Board's Franchising
    Specification, 142, 147
  prevention, 142–144

Management techniques—*cont.*
 questionnaires, client, 146–147
 review,
  client, 146–147
  files, 144–145
 risk management, 145–146
 Solicitors Indemnity Fund, 145
 standards, 145
 supervision of files, 144–145
 teaching, 142
 training, 142–144
Market economy, influence of, 2
Meaning, 8
 participation in, 8
Medical profession,
 communication, poor, 2–3
 consultation with doctor, 2–3
 criticism of, 1–2
 lawyers—analogy with, 2–3
 terminology used by, 1–2
 training, 3
Memory,
 fallibility, 26
 filling in, 26
 perception and, 26
Mentally disturbed people, 84–87
 apparent during interview, becoming,
  86–87
 awareness of needs, 85
 inexperienced lawyers, 86
 mental handicap, 85
 mental illness, 85
 neuroses, 85
 paranoid schizophrenia, 86
 psychoses, 85
 special skills needed, 84–85
Miller, 20, 22, 59
Money 67–71. *See also* Costs
Monitoring performance, 118–126
 Byrne and Long's monitoring system,
  120–124
 Flesch Formula Readability Score,
  124–126
 generally, 118
 stages, 118–120
 style descriptions for advice giving
  behaviours, 124
 tasks monitoring, 118–120
Moorhead, R. and Paterson, A., 138
Morely and Hosking, 72
"Musical tables", 6–7
Myre and Sim, 85

Names,
 greet, seat and introduce, 13–14
Negligent advice, 112
Next contact, stating, 75–76

Nizer, 113
Non-vigilant strategies, 72–73
Note-taking, 45–49
 after interview, 46
 audio tape, 48
 beginning, 45
 command, 47
 disadvantages, 46–47
 discussing with client, 48–49
 during interview, 46
 effect of, 46–49
 eye contact, losing, 46–47
 false importance, 47
 listening, 17–18
 occurrence, 45–46
 pace, 47
 positive effects, 46
 practice, 48
 reading aloud, 47–48
 suggestions for, 47–49
 tape, audio, 48
 Task 6, 45–49
 threat, 47

Objective opinions in, 96
 examples, 97
 parts, 99
 proposals for work to be done, 97–99
 suggested work, 97–99
Office, lawyer's, 6
Office for the Supervision of Solicitors,
  148, 150
Outcome bias, 26

Paranoid schizonphrenia, 86
Patronising clients, 58
Pennington, 26
Perception, 21–22
 client, 26
 Klatzky, 21
 language, 21
 listening, 21–22, 26
 memory and, 26
 primacy effects, 21
 recency effects, 21
 research, 21
 terminology, 21
Performance monitoring. *See*
 Monitoring performance
Physical preparation for interview. *See*
 Preparation for interview
Piaget, 90
Pittinger, Hackett and Danehy, 14
Plan of action, 51–71
Potok, 82
Practice management standards, 148,
  154

Pre-construction role play, 128–129
Preparation for interview, 4–8
　Chesterton, 4
　collection procedure, client, 7–8
　desks, 6
　education, legal, 4
　interview room, 6
　"musical tables", 6–7
　office, lawyer's, 6
　particular client, preparation for the,
　　7
　physical, 5–8
　　arrangement of work in office, 6
　　"busy" desk, 6
　　collection procedure, client, 7–8
　　desks, 6
　　interview room, 6
　　meeting client, 7
　　"musical tables", 6–7
　　office, lawyer's, 6
　　particular client, preparation for
　　　the, 7
　　reception area 5–6. *See also*
　　　Reception area
　　room, interview, 6
　　seating arrangements, 6–7
　　tables, 6–7
　reception area 5–6. *See also*
　　Reception area
　room, interview, 6
　seating arrangements, 6–7
　starting place, 5
　tables, 6–7
Presenting problem,
　expectations of, 15
　listening, 15
　meaning, 15
Privacy,
　client, 23–24
Professions,
　criticism of, 1–2
　medical. *See* Medical profession
Psychiatry,
　interviewing in, 14

Questioning, 29–49
　amendment of view of facts after,
　　43–45
　closed,
　　meaning, 14–15
　conclusions on, 49
　eliciting story with open questioning,
　　14–17
　facts, on, 29–45
　funnel sequence, 31–33
　general questioning, 30–36
　ideas, using client, 39

Questioning—*cont.*
　information categorisation, 39–42
　issues for attention, list of, 30
　lawyer uncertainty, 34
　meaning, 29
　needs, client, 36–39
　note-taking. *See* Note-taking
　objectives, 30
　open,
　　eliciting story with, 14–17
　　meaning, 14–15
　perspective, facts and needs in, 42–
　　43
　practical problems of client,
　　understanding, 42–43
　premature diagnosis, 29
　purpose, 8
　recounting lawyer's view of facts, 43–
　　45
　remedies approach, 42–43
　second stage of interview, 8, 29
　skills, 29
　style, 33–34
　summary, 35–36
　summing up, 43–45
　tasks, 10, 29
　time constraints, 34–35
　types of question, 14–15
Questionnaires, client, 146–147

Raiffa, 63
Readability scores, 58, 124–126
Reading aloud,
　note-taking, 47–48
Realists,
　facts, view of, 25
Reception area,
　brochures, 5–6
　children, 5
　decoration, 5
　drinking facilities, 5
　preparation for interview, 5–6
　reading material, 5
　strategy for, 5
　tidy, 5
　toilets, 6
　waiting times, 6
"Red files", 139
Redmount, 9, 113
Regulation of communications, 148–
　157
　case information, 152–153
　case, on, 152–153
　complaints handling, 149–150
　conduct regulation, 148–149
　contracted systems, 149

Regulation of communications—*cont.*
  costs, 153–154
  generally, 148
  information,
    name, 151–152
    status, 151–152
  Lexcel, 149
  name of solicitor, 151–152
  Office for the Supervision of
    Solicitors, 148, 150
  practice management standards, 148,
    154
  register, 150–151
  status, information on, 151–152
  written standards, 153–154
Reith Lectures, 2, 36
Remedies approach,
  questioning, 42–43
Reported cases, use of, 4
Research,
  advising, 60
  client satisfaction, 1
  counselling client, 104–105
  listening, 12, 19
  perception, 21
  suicide, 88
Responsibility for case, 14
Reviewing experience, 129–131
Reviews, client, 146–147
Risk management, 145–146
Rodell, F., 75
Role play, 128–129
Rosenthal, D., 19, 74, 105–106
Royal Commission on the Provision of
  Legal Services. *See* Benson
  Report

Seating arrangements, 6–7
Second stage of interview 8. *See also*
  Questioning
Selective attention,
  listening, 22
Shaffer, 78, 88, 89, 104, 113
Shakespeare, W., 36
Sherr, 9, 44, 75, 119, 130, 138
Sherr and Domberger, 154
Short note taking,
  listening, 17
Silence,
  listening, 16
  purpose, 16
Skills training, 127–128
Solicitors Code of Conduct, 148, 149–
  150
Solicitor's Complaints Bureau, 150, 153
Solicitors Indemnity Fund, 145
Spiegal, 62

Stages. *See* Advising; Listening;
    Questioning; Three stages of
  interview
Stereotyping, 21
Style,
  questioning, 33–34
Suffering, client, 24
Suicide, 87–89
Summing up,
  questioning, 43–45
  recounting lawyer's view of facts, 43–
    45
"Sunshine termination", 78
Supervision of files, 144–145
Szasz, Dr Thomas, 85

Tables, 6–7
Tape, audio,
  note-taking, 48
Tasks. *See* Thirteen tasks
Telephone systems, 1
Terminate, help out and goodbye, 78
Terminology,
  clients, 21
  medical, 1–2
  perception, 21
Third stage of interview 8. *See also*
  Advising
Thirteen tasks, 9–10
  advising 10. *See also* Advising
  agreement on facts with client, 43–45
  amendment of view of facts, 43–45
  "any other business", 76–78
  application to interviews, 10
  elicit story with opening question,
    14–17
  evolution, 10
  follow-up work to be done,
    recounting,
      client, by, 73–74
      lawyer, by, 74–75
  framework, 10
  greet, seat and introduce 12–14. *See*
    also Greet, seat and
  introduce
  listening, 10
  monitoring, 118–120
  next contact, stating, 75–76
  note-taking. *See* Note-taking
  outline story, listening to, 17
  purpose, 9, 10
  questioning 10,
    29. *See also* Questioning
  recounting lawyer's view of facts, 43–
    45
  repetition of advice, 72–73

Thirteen tasks—*cont.*
  summing up, 43–45
  Task 1, 12–14
  Task 3, 14–17
  Task 4, 29–43
  task 5, 43–45
  Task 6, 45–49
  Task 7, 51–71
  Task 8, 71–73
  Task 9, 73–74
  Task 10, 74–75
  Task 11, 75–76
  Task 12, 76–78
  Task 13, 78
  terminate, help out and goodbye, 78
  training schedule, 10
Three stages of interview, 8–9
  See also Thirteen tasks
  advising. *See* Advising
  blurring of demarcation between, 8
  doctor, analogy of visit to, 8, 9
  evolution, 9
  first 8. *See also* Listening
  framework, 9
  listening 8. *See also* Listening
  model, 9
  purpose of analysis, 8–9
  purpose of division into, 8
  questioning. *See* Questioning
  second. *See also* Questioning

Three stages of interview—*cont.*
  third 8. *See also* Advising
  understanding interview through, 8–9
  use by professionals, 9
  working within framework of, 9
Toilets, 6
Traditional lawyer model, 105
Training,
  management techniques, 142–144
  medical profession, 3
  methods, 131–137
  research into methods, 131–137
  schedule, thirteen tasks, 10
  skills, 127–128

Vigilant strategies, 72, 107

Waiting area. *See* Reception area
Waiting times, 6
Warwick University research,
  listening, 12, 27
Watson, 86, 96, 104
Welfare state, 2
Which report, 61
Witnesses,
  compulsion, 83–84
  interviewing, 82–84
  motivation of, 83
  rewards for, 83
Written word in interview, 81–82